Follow the Stars' Path to Gourmet Pleasure

Whether you're a Leo who loves good food and cooking for a few chosen friends . . . a Scorpio with a penchant for intimate romantic dinners . . . or a Gemini who's tempted to try many things . . . look no further than *Sydney Omarr's Cooking With Astrology* to plan the perfect meal!

Sydney Omarr, whose syndicated column is read by millions, teams up with the genius of Mike Roy, renowned culinary master, to produce more than 225 foolproof recipes specially selected for individual tastes and temperaments. You'll feast on these exquisite recipes:

Mars Tomatoes Florentine • Shrimp Maison • Aries Cucumber Soup • Uranian Olive Cheese Strata • Scampi Jupiter • Virgo Bran Muffins • Lemon Velvet Pie • Mercury Pears with Crème de Menthe Sauce • Moon Shrimp Curry • Neptune Lobster and Shrimp Vermouth • Scallops au Parmesan • Milky Way Key Lime Pie • Roquefort Chive French Bread • Chocolate Custard Cloud • Shrimp Salad Rolls • *and much more*

This extraordinary guide to zodiacal cookery will help you create perfect meals every time—be it a formal dinner for a special guest or a family affair with flair. Discover the fabulous way to personalized and perfect cooking!

About the Authors

Sydney Omarr, a Leo born in Philadelphia, is a published author, popular syndicated columnist, and leading authority on astrology. His daily column appears in some 300 newspapers, and his books have sold nearly 50 million copies worldwide. Dubbed "the celebrity's celebrity," he was Merv Griffin's "resident astrologer" and the confidant of literary greats and movie stars.

Mike Roy, a Cancer born in Hanaford, North Dakota, was a syndicated radio/television chef for over twenty years, having also written books on food preparation and supervising cuisines for Hollywood stars. Roy died in 1976.

To Write to the Author

SYDNEY OMARR'S

Cooking With

Astrology

Sydney Omarr
and
Mike Roy

1998
Llewellyn Publications
St. Paul, Minnesota 55164-0383, U.S.A.

SECOND EDITION
First Printing, 1998
(previously titled *Cooking With Astrology*)

Originally published by Signet Mystic Books © 1969

Cover design: Michael David Matheny
Cover art: Dave Matheny
Second edition editing and book design: Christine Snow

Library of Congress Cataloging In-Publication Data
Omarr, Sydney.
    Sydney Omarr's cooking with astrology / Sydney Omarr and Mike
    Roy. — 2nd ed.
        p.   cm.
    Includes index.
    ISBN 1-56718-506-1 (alk. paper)
      1. Cookery. 2. Astrology. I. Roy, Mike. II. Title.
TX652.0555 1998   98-39313
641.5—dc21   CIP

Note: These recipes have not been tested by the publisher and takes no position on their effectiveness. Personal sensitivities to ingredients should be researched before using.

Llewellyn Publications
A Division of Llewellyn Worldwide
P.O. Box 64383, Dept. K506-1
St. Paul, Minnesota 55164-0383

Printed in the United States of America

Forthcoming Llewellyn Books by Sydney Omarr

Sydney Omarr's Astrological Guide to Love and Romance
Astrological Revelations About You

Other Books by Sydney Omarr

Answer in the Sky, Almost
Astrological Revelations
Astrology and Its Role in Your Life
Astrology Guide for Teen-Agers
Henry Miller: His World of Urania
My World of Astrology
Sydney Omarr's Book of Winning Numbers
Thought Dial

Contents

Introduction

Cooking, Astrology, and Mike Roy

Foods, among other things, can bridge the generation gap. Entertaining with foods from the past as well as with pizzas and hamburgers can help two or more generations to understand each other. Not only does this apply to food but also to astrology. Blend the two and the combination represents understanding and unconditional love.

I instinctively felt this and when circumstances brought me together with famous Cancer chef Mike Roy, I could not resist asking, "Mike, do you realize that food, cooking, and astrology have much in common?" In a good-natured manner, the portly smiling chef responded, "Omarr, I don't know about astrology, but I know of your work and I believe in you, and if you say cooking and astrology go together, I am intrigued."

Following that "introduction," the subjects of our discussions varied from baseball to boxing and from "A" in alchemy to "Z" in zodiac. However, no matter what the subject, food was never left out—whether it be recipes or restaurants or chefs or history, food and cooking were not ignored.

It didn't take long for Mike to agree with me that a book on cooking with astrology would be both entertaining and informative in both areas, food and horoscopes. He said, "In doing this, please emphasize that I advocate low-heat cooking." He added, "I know that some chefs perhaps would not agree, but I want to reiterate low-heat cooking!"

Mike Roy is no longer with us, but he most certainly is not forgotten. It is my hope, in this new edition of our work, to keep his memory alive along with his fabulous zodiac recipes. It is an honor to be associated with both food and astrology and most certainly with the extraordinary Cancer-born Mike Roy.

—Sydney Omarr
October 1997

Sydney Omarr

and

Mike Roy

on the

Twelve Houses

Aries Menu One

pages 14–20

Aries Cucumber Soup
Rumaki *or* Trout Almondine
Green Garlic Noodles
Mars Tomatoes Florentine
Orange Cake au Rhum

Aries Menu Two

pages 21–26

Grapefruit Tossed Green Salad
First House Saucy Olive Beef Rolls
Vegetable Medley
Sour Cream Biscuits
Apple Pie with Cheese Crust

Aries Menu Three

pages 27–31

Shrimp Maison
Uranian Olive Cheese Strata
Asparagus with Onion Butter Sauce
Date Nut Meringue in Grapefruit Shells

First House
March 21–April 19

ARIES

Sydney Omarr on Aries

The First House is the beginning, the start—and the start is the first zodiacal sign, which is yours if you were born between March 21 and April 19. Your sign is associated with Mars, which symbolizes action, aggressiveness. You are willing to take the lead; this can be constructive when not carried to extremes. But when it is, others resent what they consider a domineering attitude.

You enjoy a dominant role in the part of chef. You are the director who coaches us, encourages us to try the new, to be daring; you cheer us on to spices, tantalizing flavors. The food you prepare has character and so does the setting.

Playboy publisher Hugh Hefner, born under your sign, displayed some of these characteristics when I joined him in a television replica of his fabulous Chicago penthouse. The wine flowed—red for Mars—and the "bunnies" were beauties. Although we were performing in a Hollywood studio, Hefner was intense in his role as host. He said my analysis of him, based on his horoscope, was extremely accurate. I naturally felt good; this was Aries in action—the host, the director, the performer. And the food was not merely to be consumed, but to be enjoyed as something different, special, and unique. When Mike Roy guides you through your House, the specifics will be there—the recipes, your astrological menus—designed and created for Aries. You would have it no other way: custom made, style, class.

In the kitchen, you take the lead

Gloria Swanson is another Aries, and, as I know from personal experience, a marvelous cook and a delightful hostess. Other celebrities born under your sign include Tennessee Williams, Omar Sharif, and Bette Davis.

In the kitchen, then, you take the lead. There is not apt to be any question about what ingredient goes into what pot or pan. You can be impulsive, yes, but with a definite sense of direction, enough so that others realize you know what you're about. That's the way it is with you, Aries, you get your way when it comes to dining or almost anything else.

It's wise to seat Aries at the head of the table

It isn't easy to tell you what to do; it seems that you have to learn from experience. You're the pioneer, willing to try, to experiment. The flavor of your temperament, quite naturally, makes itself known through your dining-cooking pattern; you are first the innovator. You experiment and, when host or hostess, the need is to present something unique.

It's wise to seat Aries at the head of the table, all the better to give directions, instructions, and lead the conversation. Aries is associated with Mars and the head; your sign belongs to the Fire element and friction creates a blaze here. The friction occurs when you prepare a culinary specialty and a guest is afraid to take a chance.

For you, Aries, food becomes security; dining in style transforms security into elegant luxury. You find "delicious" the freedom to choose, to dare in the kitchen. You, in charge of the menu, become a magnificent director. In order to lead us along new paths, the menu must be varied and different enough for us to question, to express doubt—all the better for you to reassure us, to explain, to take pride in the knowledge that you were there first, that you tested and tasted and that now, because of your pioneering attributes, it is our turn.

Sometimes you keep us waiting while you make sure your creations are "just right." However, it is foolhardy to keep you waiting. Aries wants us to be on time, just so long as we come in after Aries. Moreover, Aries, you desire a stimulating companion, but one who is also stimulated by what you serve and say.

You don't like the idea of lingering in the kitchen; what you do in the food area is likely to be fast, direct. You have a unique approach and, when you're in charge of dining, there is a spark, an air of expectation. Where specific dishes are concerned, which hold special appeal for you, the illustrious Mike Roy will go into details. What I am now interested in, Aries, is you: what makes you tick, what you are, how you impress others, and what you desire.

Where companions enter the picture, you often prefer the Aquarian type: the individual fascinated with far-out subjects, who can discuss the latest in electronic devices as well as an up-to-the-minute development in the field of unidentified flying objects.

The Leo type, however, is apt to strike you with one of Cupid's arrows. Leo, another Fire sign, affects that part of your solar horoscope associated with romance. For romantic dining, therefore, you are likely to choose one born under the sign of the Lion. For companionship, it is Aquarius. But where candlelight and quiet sighs are the order of the evening . . . it's Leo for you all the way.

Dining with Cancer or Capricorn individuals results, very often, in crossfire and crosscurrents; there is dissension and, when all is finished, you can be heard to complain, "They simply will not listen to reason!"

Libra subjects distract you with views that you find astounding: you feel, quite often, that Libra is simply too idealistic, living in a fool's paradise. Dinner conversation is likely to be involved with contracts,

You, in charge of the menu, become a magnificent director

Leos are apt to strike you with Cupid's arrow

business deals . . . even marriage. Your Mars and the Venus of Libra draw the two of you together, but the closer you come to each other the more likelihood there is for a good, old-fashioned quarrel.

You are a pacesetter; this being the case, you don't appreciate people who tell you what time to dine or when to finish. If such directives are to be issued, you would just as soon be the one to do the issuing.

Now, Aries, I do not want my remarks here to be misconstrued. Your motives are of the highest; you are protective, much in the manner that the Cancer-born would shelter us. The point I am trying to make is that your Martian qualities are not always understood by others. Where you are rushing to get something finished for the good of us all, we of little comprehension are sometimes apt to interpret this as "bossiness." To borrow the words of a popular song, "Try a little tenderness."

Red is an attractive color in food for you

Mars is the "red planet," and color and foods with eye appeal are meant for you. Tomatoes (though some Aries swear they have an aversion to them) attract . . . so do beets. The use of paprika is advisable, for it provides a reddish glow, which you find so attractive in food.

Pimiento-stuffed olives delight you, while the plain, green-alone variety would suit Pisces. You are not averse to the use of ketchup and the red tanginess of chile sauce is likely to satisfy your Aries taste. Sautéed trout could find a place on your table, too, and when Mike Roy takes the First House tour, this succulent fish dish will be on the menu.

Pimiento-stuffed olives delight you

Speaking of our master chef, do listen to his words carefully: harmonize my astrological information with his advice on what and how to prepare. Then, Aries, you will really be cooking with astrology.

Want to put across a money deal over lunch or dinner? Then you are likely to be discussing details with a Taurus. Check Mike's Taurus menus for foods, morsels, and special touches. It might make it easier to close the transaction in a manner favorable to you, and furthermore, you'll enjoy yourself while doing it.

Dining with Gemini seems invariably to bring up conversation about brothers, sisters, and other close relatives. Geminis do a lot of talking and gesticulating. This could frustrate you because, often, you prefer a good listener. But the two signs—Aries and Gemini—are harmonious.

And, Aries, if you like to laugh while you dine, then have a Gemini or two for company.

With a Cancer, you'll certainly obtain some valid hints about food and its preparation; a Cancer will appreciate. Cancer doesn't always agree, but you find natives of that sign a challenge. To you, they seem to have the secret of security—they will oversee and help in times of crisis in the kitchen. If unexpected guests arrive, they need not go hungry if you have a Cancer native by your side. He or she will pitch in and the menu will expand, with enough for all and the more the merrier.

Now, Aries, you're going to get some health hints and some talk about your digestive system if you dine with Virgo. The Virgo native, very likely, may pass you a few vitamins, too. A Virgo makes you aware of the necessity for moderation. Leo provides the flamboyance, the excitement; Libra is challenge and talks about contracts and stimulates thoughts of marriage. But a Virgo is bound and determined to keep you healthy!

Natives of the Cancer sign are a challenge to you

You are taken into confidence by Scorpio; secrets are featured in the dining conversation when you break bread with natives of this sign. Tension could build over the dining table if an Aries and Scorpio dominate. Thus, it is doubly important to take into account what Scorpio desires, wants, needs, and appreciates; that is, Aries, if you want to be a good host. And since you like to be first, this could be a first—the first time Scorpio became more interested in what was being eaten rather than in what was being confided.

A Sagittarius native likes the open road and the open mind; travel themes are apt to dominate when you dine with a native of this zodiacal sign. Your Mars significator combines with the Jupiter of Sagittarius to provide excitement, an air of exploration. You are the pioneer and a Sagittarius is the philosopher. Together, with good food as a tie, the combination could be exhilarating. Study Mike Roy's menu and food suggestions for Sagittarius, as well as for yourself. Then, Aries, you could turn what starts out to be an ordinary day into a crescendo of adventure, a sighting of faraway places. The conversation, enhanced by noble dining, could take its place beside any that ever swirled around the Algonquin round table during the heyday of Robert Benchley, Dorothy Parker, Alexander Woollcott, and other *bon vivants*. That's how the Sagittarius subject affects you; the epicurean delights you concoct, through the aid of astrology and Mike Roy, will be rivaled by the plans that arise through such a confrontation with Sagittarius.

Dining with Capricorn could arouse your ambitions, which is fine for planning your career advancement and enhancing your occupational income. If you want to talk business while eating, Capricorn is the sign for you. This is in direct contrast with Aquarius; here companionship is emphasized.

Dining with a Capricorn could enhance your ambitions

With Pisces, your attention centers on the theater, motion pictures, television. A theater dinner party is done to perfection when a Pisces is present. Pisces, a bit in the manner of Scorpio, lends an air of mystery and intrigue to the dining table, at least where you are concerned.

Your most harmonious dinner companions are those born under Aquarius, Gemini, Leo, and Sagittarius. With other Aries individuals, there could be conflict. It is a question of who takes the lead in explaining, diagnosing, even pointing out to others how each recipe should be tested and tasted.

In food preparation, as in other areas, you should strive to overcome impatience. The tendency is to act first, ask questions later. This could be considered adventurous; but too much or too little of a delicate ingredient could prove disastrous to a dish.

Harmonious dinner companions are Aquarius, Gemini, Leo, and Sagittarius

Food has to do with the Fourth House (Cancer), and Cancer is your Solar Fourth sector, indicating that the Moon (as well as your Mars significator) has a message where you and eating are concerned. You are quick and often impatient, because for you, food was at the start a means of survival. As you develop, as you become more sophisticated in this area (and you'll thank Mike Roy here), much of this tendency will be transformed into making dining an adventure, into realizing that with you the time-honored custom of breaking bread need not be a quick ceremony but could, instead, become one of life's great pleasures.

For you, the key to enjoyment at meals is receptivity. Listen as well as assert; know that you can gain by toning down a quality of aggressiveness. Your insights are sharp, your quick mind and intellectual curiosity add to the delights of fine dining. But you can gain even more plaudits by holding back on the sharp comment, the criticism. Enjoy others and, in turn, they will enjoy you. This creates a happy situation that immeasurably aids in the art of gastronomy.

Dare to listen, test, experiment; do not fear the results. Avoid aggravating yourself by doubting the outcome of your efforts in the kitchen. Have fun being a chef! This will assure you that others will respond; food, for you, is a way of preserving health, vitality. But it need not be something that is ultra-serious. You have a sense of humor when you want to utilize it. It is essential to overcome a tendency to brood; don't seek perfection. Instead, look for pleasure, a feeling of well-being. That comes when you know what you're doing, when your ultimate goal is outlined. That, of course, is what we are attempting to do for you with this effort.

Have fun being a chef

You are quick to become enthusiastic. But it isn't always easy for you to sustain your drive. Obviously, you need a goal, a challenge, a purpose. This applies to your role as chef. You excel when in charge of special occasions. You wane when the occasion is drab or lacks purpose. Point toward a goal. Create a theme for your culinary efforts. This applies whether you are serving three or thirty people.

Aries is synonymous with forceful ideas and themes. You excel in creating a dynamic atmosphere, but do so in a relaxed manner. This may appear contradictory. But, where you are concerned, it is essential. If you press on, without a break, others pick up your vibrations and then your efforts could go for naught.

You excel when in charge of special occasions

Take a Sagittarian into your confidence. An individual born under this sign can aid you in perceiving goals and themes. Then, a slight delay or mishap could become cause for humor rather than a frown. With a Sagittarius commenting, encouraging, cooperating, you'll find yourself delighting in culinary creations. There is a quality of optimism about Sagittarius that is an invaluable ingredient where you are concerned. You need humor while entertaining. Otherwise, you are too fast, too direct, and your guests could feel hurried.

Be a good listener; don't interrupt, even if you disagree. These hints, combined with Mike Roy's sage advice about what you can do best in the kitchen, should assure you that dining can become a pleasure rather than a burden.

I enjoy sharing cocktails and food with you, Aries, because I admire your forthrightness. There is purpose, adventure, a reason for what we do, as well as for how and on what we dine. But not everyone can "take" your directness. Your questions are pointed; and you seem to analyze our answers, often with a squint, a frown, a questioning expression. I don't mind; to me, this lends charm and challenge. But, then, being a Leo, I share your Fire sign qualities. However, Capricorn might find reason to be offended. Capricorn deals with time and takes plenty of it. You deal with action, and a show of impatience on your part could, for Capricorn, spoil your sincere effort to provide tantalizing dishes.

You and I, Aries, could fall in love over brandy and coffee; but some of the other signs claim that you too often want your own way. Know this, and avoid giving that impression, especially when dining.

Be less of a director; be more of a chef whose ingredients include a sympathetic ear, and one who is willing to take as well as give. Observe the Libra in this role; combine the Venusian qualities of that sign with your own most admirable Martian traits. Then, your efforts in cooking and other areas will be highly acclaimed.

Be a good listener and don't interrupt

You deal with action while Capricorn takes time

Mike Roy on Aries

And so Sydney Omarr has analyzed Aries. And when Omarr talks about astrology, I listen. This is not a newly formed habit with me. It seems as though I've been listening to him for ages, and with good reason. It began years ago when he was a senior news editor at a network radio station in Los Angeles and I was a feature reporter, food authority, *bon vivant*, and man about the world with the same organization.

I have always been interested in the curious, well-ordered mind that looked beyond the surface for the underlying reasons for human's behavior. I have never been interested in fables, other than for their entertainment value. And I might even go so far as to say I've enjoyed a lie or two, provided it was expertly told. But the person with the hard-nosed, perceptive intellect that searches for the basic philosophical needs of humans and, having found a reasonable, understandable premise, possesses the knowledge and integrity to pass it on—that is my kind of person. I have enjoyed these qualities in Sydney Omarr over the years we have known one another. What I've tried to capture here in the First House section is the idea that Omarr's head may be the stars but the discipline and honesty of his brilliant mind are firmly implanted on *terra firma*—and we all should be the better for it.

It is, perhaps, fortunate that we begin in the First House with Aries. I think there is a friendly connotation in the word "house." The dictionary tells us that the word means a building for common residence; a place of abode; a shelter or lodge (to make secure before a storm); and a one-twelfth part of the heavens.

I would like to take a moment here to digress a bit on the thoughts behind this marriage of the stars and the table. Since humans first etched their thoughts in time, they have lived with two appetites. One is inspired by the hunger of their mind. The other, of course, is the hunger of their stomachs. Only when their stomachs are filled can humans become philosophers. Show me a person with a full stomach, and I'll show you a person who can, only then, gaze upon the stars and contemplate humankind's place in the universe.

Only when their stomachs are filled can humans become philosophers

The kitchen of the house is indeed a friendly place where we can linger with our creative thoughts while we prepare the basic sustenance of our way of life. The chef in a restaurant finds complete payment for his or her efforts in the kitchen. The first gratuity comes from the expressions of joy of those who sup and sip on his or her fare. The second gratuity comes in the form of cold, hard cash. The expert chef, wise in the ways of the culinary world, has no trouble in commanding a high salary. So the payment is twofold, but the rewards are uncountable. Perhaps none is so great as the inner knowledge that he or she has made a contribution to the culture of the world.

As Omarr tells us of the order of the planets, so, too, is there order in the culinary way of doing things. Think for a moment of the magnificent feasts of history. And then realize that it wasn't until the era of Escoffier that we achieved order in cuisine. Until his time, course followed course, with no particular reason. Buckets of meats, tubs of birds, sweets by the bale followed one another in careless disarray—all of it washed down with copious quantities of whatever kind of wine was available.

And then the magic of Escoffier.

"We begin lightly," he said, perhaps some caviar, a simple pâté, possibly a Quiche Lorraine. His second course was soup. Then came the fish. At this point in the classic dinner we paused for an intermezzo—a sorbet (sherbet) to cleanse and rest our palate. Then we plunged into the main part of the meal, the meat entrée with suitable starch and vegetables. This was followed by salad, fruit, and cheeses. And finally the dessert and demitasse. Of course, appropriate wines followed along with each course, except with the salad and sorbet. For gala occasions and grand gourmet dining, this structure holds to this day.

But we Americans have changed it a bit. I suspect one reason is that it's just plain too much food. Another reason is that it's not practical. Also, some place the salad at the head of the meal (I disagree with this). But the simple facts are that you and I will accept an appetizer course, be it soup, salad, or something like a shrimp cocktail. We accept (and rightly so) a main course then, be it meat, fish, or seafood, trimmed with a starch and a vegetable. And we like to finish with a dessert and

Before Escoffier, course followed course with no particular reason

coffee. Rarely, as a practical matter, do we order more than one kind of wine with our meal, and it usually fits the main entrée. I find no fault with this, but I would plead for originality and creativity. And, if you haven't, just once—for me—try the salad after the main course. You'll feel better; Sydney Omarr and his stars will approve, too.

Before we enter the Aries kitchen, perhaps I should set forth a few ideas for the use of the menus and recipes you can find in these pages. Since the occupants of our various astrological Houses have certain characteristics and traits, it would be logical to assume that their kitchens would be stocked with culinary equipment and foodstuffs to satisfy these needs. Likewise, if you are inviting guests from other Houses, these items should provide satisfaction. I am setting forth a series of menus with the basic recipes for carrying them out. But this doesn't mean that each menu must be followed explicitly. Your moods might change and you might wish to select a first course from one menu and an entrée from another, a vegetable from another, and so on. Let your own creative thoughts govern your selection. And if you find a dish in another House that appeals, use it.

Omarr has pointed the way in his remarks about the characteristics of Aries in relation to the other signs. Aries are independent, daring, and inventive. In their food they love eye appeal. A dish about which they could say, "I've never seen this before," would be most satisfying to them. Try this first menu.

Just once, eat the salad after the main course

MENU ONE

Aries Cucumber Soup

Rumaki or
Trout Almondine

Green Garlic Noodles

Mars Tomatoes Florentine

Orange Cake au Rhum

This daring recipe was given to me by my good friend Ken Hansen, a Pisces, who owned and operated the famous Scandia Restaurant on Sunset Boulevard in Hollywood.

Aries Cucumber Soup
(serves 6)

3 medium cucumbers
2 tablespoons butter
½ cup chopped onion
2 bay leaves
1 tablespoon all-purpose flour
3 cups chicken broth

1 teaspoon salt
1 cup half-and-half
2 tablespoons lemon juice
½ teaspoon chopped dill weed
Sour cream

Pare cucumbers. Slice two of them and sauté in butter along with onions and bay leaves until tender, but not brown. Blend in flour. Add broth, stirring until smooth. Add salt and simmer (covered) about 25 minutes. Run mixture through a sieve. Chill well and skim off any fat. Scoop out seeds of remaining cucumber, grate, and add to chilled mixture. Add cream, lemon juice, and dill weed. Serve in chilled cups with a dollop of sour cream as a garnish. Sprinkle dill over top.

The very fact that this next dish is offered as an entrée makes it different. Of Polynesian origin, rumaki is often served as an appetizer, but along with the noodles and tomatoes it works nicely as a main course, especially for Aries.

Rumaki
(serves 6)

1½ pounds chicken livers
1 can water chestnuts
1 pound bacon strips
   Toothpicks
¼ cup chopped green onions
½ teaspoon salt
1 cup beef consommé
   (canned), undiluted

½ cup dry red wine *or* sherry
3 cups soy sauce
1 garlic clove, mashed
3 tablespoons lime or lemon
   juice
2 tablespoons brown sugar *or*
   honey

Slice chicken livers in half. Sandwich a water chestnut between two slices of chicken liver. Wrap with a half strip of bacon and secure with a toothpick. Combine the rest of the ingredients and let the rumaki marinate overnight in the refrigerator. Broil over fast coals or under oven broiler.

Following Omarr's suggestion, a trout, no doubt, would be to Aries' liking.

Trout Almondine
(serves 6)

6 (8-ounce) trout, cleaned,
   with heads left on
2 slightly beaten eggs
½ cup cream
½ cup flour

1 cup butter
½ cup sliced almonds
¼ cup lemon juice
3 tablespoons dry vermouth
   Salt and pepper to taste

continued

Season the trout with salt and pepper, inside and out, and dip them in combined cream and slightly beaten eggs. Dip in flour. Bring ½ cup of the butter to the bubbly stage and sauté the trout until golden on both sides. Remove trout to a hot serving platter. Add the other ½ cup of butter to the pan. Add the almonds and sauté until the butter is lightly browned. Remove from heat and blend in the lemon juice and wine. Pour sauce over trout and serve immediately.

The staff of life is present here in the form of the wheat and eggs in the noodles. The pungency of the cheese and garlic add aroma and taste to compliment the rumaki.

Green Garlic Noodles
(serves 6)

1 (8-ounce) package green (spinach) noodles	1 clove garlic, peeled and mashed
¼ cup butter or margarine	¼ cup Parmesan cheese

Add a teaspoon of salt and a tablespoon of salad oil to 2 quarts of boiling water and add noodles. Cook about 8 minutes or until tender. While noodles are boiling, bring the butter to a bubbly stage in a large skillet. Add the garlic and brown. Remove the garlic. Drain the noodles, and toss in the garlic butter and 1 tablespoon of the cheese. Serve topped with the remaining cheese.

A crowning touch of red to complete the eye appeal so necessary to Aries. The sizzling rumaki, the green noodles echoed in the soft spinach green in the tomatoes make this plate lovely to behold.

Mars Tomatoes Florentine
(serves 6)

6 medium tomatoes
Salt
½ cup half-and-half
1 egg yolk

2 packages frozen chopped spinach
3 tablespoons melted butter

Cut ¼-inch top off each tomato. Scoop out insides of juice and seeds, but not fruit. Sprinkle insides with salt. Combine cream and egg yolk; add chopped spinach and 1 tablespoon of the butter. Salt to taste. Heat and stir until just simmering. Fill tomatoes solid with creamed spinach. Place in a buttered baking dish. Top with melted butter. Bake at 375° for 20 minutes.

I heartily approve of the "convenience foods," and you'll find I make good use of them in these pages. But once in a while a great "scratch" recipe is downright satisfying. This magnificent dessert is one of them.

Orange Cake au Rhum

2¼ cups sifted cake flour
1½ cups sugar
 1 tablespoon baking powder
 1 teaspoon salt
 ½ cup salad oil
 6 eggs, separated
 2 tablespoons grated orange peel

¾ cup freshly squeezed
    orange juice
½ teaspoon cream of tartar
 Rum syrup (see page 20)
 Marmalade glaze
    (see page 20)

In large mixer bowl, sift together flour, sugar, baking powder, and salt. Add oil, egg yolks, orange peel, and juice; beat at medium speed until smooth, scraping sides of bowl. Remove beaters; scrape off any bits of clinging peel and stir into batter. Using large clean bowl and beaters, beat egg whites until frothy. Add cream of tartar and continue beating at high speed until stiff, but not dry. Carefully fold batter into beaten whites, blending thoroughly. Pour into an ungreased 10-inch tube pan. Bake at 325° for 1 hour, 10 minutes. Invert pan and let stand until cool. With long skewer or cake tester, pierce entire top of cake at 1-inch intervals. Slowly pour hot rum syrup over cake; refrigerate several hours. Remove cake from pan; spoon marmalade glaze over top. Let stand until cool.

continued

Rum Syrup

½ cup sugar   ½ cup water
1 tablespoon rum flavoring

In small saucepan, combine sugar and water; bring to a boil, stirring until sugar dissolves. Reduce heat and simmer for 15 minutes. Remove from heat and stir in rum flavoring.

Marmalade Glaze

1 jar (12 ounces) pure orange   1 teaspoon rum flavoring
      marmalade

Heat marmalade in small saucepan; stir in rum flavoring.

MENU TWO

Grapefruit Tossed Green Salad

First House Saucy Olive Beef Rolls

Vegetable Medley

Sour Cream Biscuits

Apple Pie with Cheese Crust

Grapefruit Tossed Green Salad
(6–8 servings)

2 medium (or large) California grapefruits, peeled and sectioned
2 quarts torn salad greens
2–3 green onions, sliced
5–6 radishes, sliced
½ cucumber, peeled and sliced

1 tablespoon fresh lemon juice
⅓–½ cup *French dressing* (see page 131)
Coarsely ground black pepper

Drain grapefruit sections. Reserve 5 or 6 sections for garnish; cut remaining sections into halves. In large bowl, combine cut grapefruit sections, salad greens, onions, radishes, and cucumber. Blend lemon juice with salad dressing; pour over salad ingredients. Sprinkle with ground pepper. Toss lightly until evenly coated with dressing. Arrange grapefruit sections on top. Serve at once.

There must be a jillion ground beef recipes. Here's one fancy enough for parties as well as family dining, especially appealing to Aries.

First House Saucy Olive Beef Rolls
(6–8 servings)

2 pounds ground beef (round or chuck)	Flour
2 eggs	2–3 tablespoons butter
2 teaspoons seasoned salt	½ cup milk
¼ teaspoon pepper	2 cups (1 pint) sour cream
1 tablespoon instant minced onion	1 cup (about ¼ pound) grated sharp Cheddar
1 jar (3 to 4 ounces) olives with pimiento	½ teaspoon salt, or to taste
	Dash of Tabasco

Combine ground beef with eggs, salt, pepper, and onion. Shape into 12 oblong rolls poking a whole stuffed olive in center of each. Coat rolls with flour. Melt 2 tablespoons butter in large skillet and brown rolls well on all sides over moderate heat, adding butter as needed. Remove beef rolls to heat-proof, shallow serving dish. Add milk to drippings in skillet and stir constantly over low heat about 1 minute. Remove from heat and stir in sour cream, cheese, and seasoning along with ⅓ cup sliced stuffed olives. Pour over beef rolls. Bake in 400° oven 10 to 12 minutes.

Vegetable Medley
(6–8 servings)

1 (10-ounce) package frozen cauliflower, cooked, *or* about 1¾ cups cooked cauliflower

2 packages frozen peas and carrots, cooled, *or* about 3 cups canned vegetables

1½ cups sour cream

1 tablespoon instant minced onion

1 teaspoon salt

3 tablespoons toasted bread crumbs

1 sliced tomato

Parsley

If using frozen vegetables, cook according to package directions, drain well, and combine. Fold sour cream, onion, and salt gently into the vegetables; place in 1½-quart casserole and with bread crumbs. Garnish baking dish with a circle of tomato slices. Bake 20 minutes in 350° oven. Place parsley sprig in center just before serving.

There's still a lot of good in what's "old." In these days of the "new" it's refreshing to find a couple of old-timers like sour cream biscuits and apple pie with cheese crust. Aries will appreciate the sentimentality.

Sour Cream Biscuits
(makes 12)

2 cups flour

1 tablespoon baking powder

¼ teaspoon baking soda

1 teaspoon salt

1 cup sour cream

¼ cup milk

Melted butter

continued

Sift together flour, baking powder, baking soda, and salt. Blend in sour cream. Stir in milk to make soft dough. Knead gently on lightly floured board. Roll or pat ½ inch thick. Cut with biscuit cutter; place on baking sheet. Bake 10 minutes in 450° oven. Brush tops with melted butter and serve immediately.

Apple Pie with Cheese Crust

8 tart apples	½ teaspoon salt
¾ cup sugar	*Cheese crust* (see page 26)
2 tablespoons flour	1 tablespoon lemon juice
½ teaspoon nutmeg	1 tablespoon butter or
1 teaspoon cinnamon	margarine

Peel and slice apples thin. Combine sugar, flour, nutmeg, cinnamon, and salt, blending well. Add sugar mixture to apples and mix well. Turn apples into pastry-lined 9-inch pie plate. Sprinkle with lemon juice and dot with butter. Flute the edges of lower pie crust. Lay pastry strips over top of filling to form latticed top. Bake at 425° for 45 to 50 minutes, or until apples are tender and crust is golden brown. Cool partially and serve warm, if wished.

continued

Cheese Crust

2½ cups sifted flour	¼ cup shredded Cheddar
1 teaspoon salt	cheese
¾ cup shortening	4–6 tablespoons ice water

Sift together flour and salt. Add shortening and cut in with pastry blender until mixture resembles coarse cornmeal. Add cheese and blend. Quickly sprinkle ice water, 1 tablespoon at a time, over pastry mixture, tossing lightly with fork. Shape pastry into a ball and chill. Roll out ⅔ of dough on lightly floured board to fit 9-inch pie plate. Roll remaining dough and cut into ½-inch wide strips for top.

MENU THREE

Shrimp Maison

Uranian Olive Cheese Strata

Asparagus with Onion Butter Sauce

*Date Nut Meringue in
Grapefruit Shells*

Shrimp dishes are definitely "in" on our menus. Sometimes we call them scampi, and I intend to feature that great dish, but here is a special Aries delight that's different and shows imagination and eye appeal.

Shrimp Maison
(serves 6)

24	large shrimp	1	teaspoon Ac'cent
2	tablespoons chives, chopped	½	teaspoon Tabasco sauce
3	tablespoons shallots, chopped	½	teaspoon Worcestershire
2	tablespoons white wine		Salt to taste
4	teaspoons whipping cream (no sugar)		Lemon juice
			Parmesan cheese

Peel the shrimp and split (not all the way). Dip in flour and sauté in butter. When the shrimp turn red, put chopped chives and shallots in and sauté for a few minutes. Add white wine, whipped cream, Ac'cent, Tabasco, lemon juice, and Worcestershire. Put in individual casseroles and sprinkle Parmesan cheese over all. Place under broiler just to glaze.

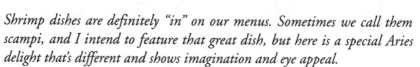

Casserole type dishes have become a way of life with us. This is fitting and proper. The casserole may be made ahead of time and popped in the oven. I don't know where the word "strata" came from in labeling this dish, but this one is truly different.

Uranian Olive Cheese Strata

(serves 6)

12 slices white bread	¼ cup chopped onion
1½ ounce package sliced American processed cheese	4 eggs
	2½ cups milk
½ cup finely chopped cooked ham	1 teaspoon salt
	½ teaspoon paprika
½ cup sliced stuffed olives	6 tomato slices

Trim crust from bread. Arrange half of bread in bottom of shallow 2-quart casserole. Cover with half the cheese slices. Combine ham, olives, and onion and spread over cheese. Top with remaining bread. Combine eggs, milk, salt, and paprika, beating slightly. Pour carefully over bread slices. Bake at 325° for 55 minutes or until egg mixture sets. Place remaining cheese on bread slices and top with sliced tomato. Bake five minutes longer. Let stand 10 minutes before serving. Garnish with additional olive slices.

Note: Better to let stand in refrigerator for a couple of hours after adding eggs and before baking.

Asparagus with Onion Butter Sauce
(serves 6)

¼ cup (½ stick) butter
1 (3½-ounce) jar cocktail
    onions
2 pounds fresh asparagus *or*
    2 (9-ounce) packages
    frozen asparagus

3 tablespoons chopped
    walnuts
Salt to taste

In a large covered skillet melt butter. Drain cocktail onions, reserving 2 tablespoons onion liquid; add liquid to melted butter. Place asparagus in skillet. Cover and bring to a steam over high heat. Turn heat to simmer; steam over low heat about 15 minutes or until asparagus is almost tender. Add cocktail onions and walnuts. Cover and steam an additional 5 minutes. Salt to taste.

Again—as with all the menus and recipes in this section—the Aries trend to the new and different is apparent. The need to be different, the daring nature, and the inventive tendency is manifested in this dish. I find the idea of using grapefruit shells as a cup for a meringue enchanting. I like the texture: the egg whites with brown sugar, the crunchiness of the nuts, and the natural sweetness of the dates. Omarr tells me Aries should be delighted.

Date Nut Meringue in Grapefruit Shells
(serves 6)

3 medium or large grapefruits	10 pitted dates, sliced
3 egg whites	¼ cup broken-up walnuts,
⅜ teaspoon cream of tartar	pecans, or almonds
¼ cup plus 2 tablespoons firmly	
packed brown sugar	

Cut in half each grapefruit; remove any seeds. With sharp knife, cut around each section to loosen fruit from membrane. Carefully scoop out sections with a spoon; drain well. Scrape any remaining membrane from shells, leaving them "clean" and intact. Beat egg whites until frothy; add cream of tartar and beat to soft peak stage. Gradually add brown sugar and continue beating until whites hold firm peaks. Fold in well-drained grapefruit pieces, dates, and nuts; spoon into grapefruit shells. Place on cookie sheet and bake at 325° for 20 minutes, or until lightly browned. Serve warm.

When you master these dynamic, pioneering, but basically simple dishes, any guest will feel like a king or queen, and your reputation, Aries, for being different, unique, and daring will be enhanced. I, for one, would welcome an invitation.

Taurus Menu One

pages 43–47

Mushroom Antipasto Salad
Bragole
Herb Bread
Venus Goodie

Taurus Menu Two

pages 48–53

Tangy Cauliflower Salad
Pineapple Acorn Squash
Taurus Spoon Bread
Veal Florentine
Cherry Glazed Ice Cream Cake

Taurus Menu Three

pages 54–59

Ensalada Verde
Second House Chicken
Buttered Brussels Sprouts and Filberts
Cottage Cheese-Potato Scallop
Banana Coconut Rolls of the Heavens

Second House

April 20–May 20

TAURUS

Sydney Omarr on Taurus

The Second House is Taurus—or, rather, Taurus is the natural Second Solar House—the second sign of the zodiac. Taurus is associated with Venus, and is an Earth sign. Taurus is associated with the throat, and the neck. Taurus can appear relaxed but, in actuality, Taurus is "heavy," in the sense of being solid, of being of substance as opposed to being feathery, light, or nondescript. When you deal with a Taurus, you have something to handle, someone to contend with—Taurus can be calm-looking, as is Joe Louis; but the steam can build if a red flag is waved in front of Taurus the Bull—and the response is predictable . . . .

I once met two famous Taureans: Carol Burnett and Perry Como. Of course, their horoscopes are different because a horoscope is based on the year, month, day, hour, and place of birth. But the birth signs, from Aries to Pisces, do reflect certain basic, identifiable characteristics. Perry Como, for example, is a Taurus, but has the Moon in Scorpio. This told me that he is quiet on the outside but is capable of seething on the inside. Carol Burnett has her Moon in Virgo, so although she gives the appearance of relaxed carelessness, the Virgo Moon tells us that she is meticulous, can be self-critical, is precise, quite earthy, determined, and willing and able to overcome numerous obstacles. Como and Burnett are both Taurus-born, but with variations, because the Moon signs are different; so, too, would be their rising signs and positions of the other planets in their charts. But both possess basic Taurus characteristics, just as you do if born from April 20 to May 20.

Taurus is practical, earthy, wants to know that everything is in its place

Taurus is, perhaps above all else, practical; that applies in the kitchen, too. Taurus wants to be practical about utensils, about what to serve. He or she wants a reason for this or that culinary creation. Taurus wants to know that everything is in its place.

Taurus could be called a meat-and-potatoes type: square, earthy, practical. Yet, Taurus, man or woman, the planet associated with your sign is romantic Venus. You love luxury and thick, heavy creams appeal. Mike Roy will help along these lines.

You want to "feel" what you eat, serve, and see. There must be substance to what is served. You are proud of your possessions, too. Taurus is a collector. You might have special dishes, mugs, or unique utensils. Just as an Aries wants to be first and the pioneer, you want others to know that what you give or serve is uniquely your own. You want people, guests to express their appreciation.

You love luxury and thick, heavy creams

Listen, Taurus: food, for you, should have a definite taste. Some, like Libra, desire the subtle, but you desire the definite. If something is on your mind—especially money, possessions, or income potential—you like nothing better than to discuss it over the dinner table. Along this line, your most appreciative audience is Aries because you can show Aries how to enhance his or her earning capacity. For your own benefit in this area, however, choose Gemini. People born under Gemini brighten your money sector; if you have a financial question, a Gemini (while dining) could come up with the right answer.

If you enjoy something, Taurus, you express yourself. And if you find the opposite is true, the odds are that your feelings (taste) will be made known. An Aries is sharply direct; you are bluntly direct. You don't pussyfoot; you are a gentle soul, but, for instance, when your taste buds are offended, you let the world know about it. Pity the waiter who attempts to bully the bull!

You are bluntly direct

You are four-square and practical. Where food is concerned, you desire purpose. Sustenance is important, while with other zodiacal signs this could be secondary. For you, food sustains life. Although you are not averse to beauty, you disdain frills. There usually is a reason for what you do, collect, eat, and serve. There must be desire.

The most companionable individuals for you to break bread with are likely to be those born under Pisces. You seem able to relax with these people, and relaxation is a necessity for you when dining. With Pisces, you get down to the business of eating. You feel free; you relax and enjoy pleasantries without losing sight of the goal, which is the consuming of morsels on your plate.

Pisces is your best dining companion

With another Taurus, there is laughter, a certain amount of gaiety; but you feel uneasy, as if the meat and potatoes of the meeting, the conversation, has slipped away. However, when dining with a Cancer, you enjoy discussing relatives, and there is a feeling of camaraderie. Dining with a Cancer results in a pleasant glow; topics of mutual interest rise like yeast. You are a wonderful guest or host with the Cancer-born, and, very likely, both Taurus and Cancer enjoy the same basic foods.

There are apt to be disagreements, on the other hand, with Leo. The meal begins on a pleasant note, but both you and Leo are of fixed signs—stubborn. Sooner or later there is a bone of contention. Leo seeks professional guidance, but you find Leo immovable. You give the advice sought, only to find that Leo has definite ideas. Leo wants to dawdle, perhaps over coffee and brandy, while you want to "bull" your way through to completion. Unless prepared for a debate, don't set up a two-person dinner with Leo. Both you and Leo can learn from each other; the relationship can be stimulating. However, when it comes to dining, there is likely to be disagreement. Leo is the showperson while you prefer the practical. You are also apt to be more cost-conscious than extravagant Leo. With Mike Roy's help, you won't have to worry about cost: the dishes are luscious, sophisticated, but practical and well within economic reach.

Aries individuals mystify you, too, especially when in the confinement of a dining room. You are ready to relax, to dig in, to enjoy yourself. But an Aries interrupts, asks about money, investments, possessions; just when you are about to answer the questions, Aries offers an explanation, an exposition of what you are about to enjoy. To you, Aries is fascinating to watch; you want to have them present, but don't try to keep up with his or her conversation. To Aries, you seem to represent stability, especially in the financial area. You appreciate each other, but you are not ideal dining companions. For easy, relaxed companionship, it is Pisces for you.

Leo causes debate; Aries mystifies you

You enjoy a hearty salad; it keeps your appetite alive. During Mike Roy's journey through the Second House, there will be specific information on how to prepare dishes especially suitable for the Taurus palate. For you, variations with bread are appealing. You like cauliflower. You want to see as well as taste and you want your food to be substantial. An Aries insists on a certain amount of decorative eye appeal. But you want to "see" in the sense of knowing that something solid exists. Taste, for you, tends to be more important than sight where food is concerned.

For you, taste tends to be more important than eye appeal

You are fond of the heavy or substantial creams; you want to taste and feel what you eat. You leave the delicacy for others, and with Leo, you often are forced to defend your tastes. Leo prefers the drama, the festival of food. To you, this is often a waste of time, to say nothing of money. Leo makes you security conscious. Dining with a Leo is, in a sense, like attending a stage performance. That's the way it strikes you. The Leo Sun and your Venus significator don't exactly blend.

Virgo is more to your liking and taste; he or she strikes a creative chord. Virgo is practical in the sense that food represents health, vitamins, a source of nourishment. That you can understand! You are aware of personal magnetism when sharing food with a Virgo. You admire the quick retort, the explanations that Virgo persons offer, and you feel gratified that Virgo seeks your opinion on philosophical matters. You enjoy discussing basic philosophies while dining; Virgo satisfies your basic needs. Even though a Virgo may disapprove of some of your tastes in food, you are charmed. Leo makes you want to defend; Virgo causes you to acquiesce. For a romantic evening, choose a Virgo.

A Libra shares your Venus planetary significator, but Libra is delicate while you are basic. You often comment that your Libra dining companions are not eating enough to sustain a bird. Libra, on the other hand, is intrigued by your earthiness. For you, Libra represents a chance to discuss work, health, or employment potential. You can enjoy yourself with a Libra, but real understanding does not always result. You experience a bit of apprehension about really digging in, Taurus-style, while partaking of food with the Libra-born. While you are practical, Libra seems more concerned with balance, design, and appearance, but certainly does appreciate your collection of dishes, silverware, and accessories.

If you want to enjoy talk about marriage, partnerships, or intricate legal maneuvers, then break bread with a Scorpio. You're stimulated by natives of this sign, although the views expressed are apt to be foreign to your own. Scorpio reveals secrets about food. A Scorpio tells you just how many oysters to serve in order to achieve the desired results; Mike Roy, in his Eighth House section, will explain more fully about the Scorpio tendency toward aphrodisiac-type delicacies. Scorpio amuses you because his or her ideas about why people eat what they do are apt to be startling. You won't be bored when dining with persons born under this Pluto-dominated sign. Your Venus aspect intrigues a Scorpio; there is mutual attraction, but much in the manner that opposites attract each other.

If you are seeking a perfectly harmonious dinner gathering, invite Pisces, Cancer, Virgo, and Capricorn subjects. Include Scorpio for

For a romantic evening, choose a Virgo

Dine with a Scorpio for talk about marriage, partnerships, food secrets

added spice. A Leo could disrupt the proceedings by wanting the center of attention.

A Sagittarius offers advice, say, on how to rid yourself of a legal burden. Natives of this sign love to eat with you. They admire your basic qualities. To you, Sagittarius is a puzzle here: seemingly more concerned with the history of food, its origin, and ingredients than in the actual consumption of it. When entertaining Sagittarius, be sure to include at least one foreign or exotic dish. In turn, Sagittarius is likely to fill you in on the lore, the subtle nuances of special preparation. Sagittarius, in the course of the meal, may also give you a hint about something close to your heart: the handling of special possessions, values, and how much such-and-such is worth.

For harmonious dinner gatherings, invite Pisces, Cancer, Virgo and Capricorn

Invite a Capricorn to dine when you want to talk travel. You affect natives of this sign in a favorable manner; discussion seems to turn to the possibility of taking a trip together. This is especially encouraged over fine food and wine. Study menus for Capricorns. You are both Earth signs; when you get together there is a greater degree of flexibility for both. There is also attraction here. Capricorn appreciates Taurus food, so you can prepare from Mike Roy's special Second House creations. Capricorn touches that part of your Solar horoscope related to long journeys. The Saturn significator of Capricorn combines with your Venus ruler very often to bring about a permanent relationship. You would especially enjoy shipboard dining with Capricorn. Your imagination is stirred by natives of this sign; often, they encourage you to write, publish, advertise. Naturally, you are flattered; for you, like Leo, flattery is welcome—a great addition to any feast. Capricorn finds you physically attractive; knowing this, you certainly enjoy this dining company.

Sagittarius loves to eat with you and admires you

An Aquarius is another story. If you want ideas on how to put across a business deal, invite an Aquarius to dinner. Now, Aquarius is not this way with everyone—this is the way Aquarius affects you, Taurus. Vary your menu with Aquarius: choose from Libra, Gemini, and Aquarius dishes, as detailed by chef Roy.

When preparing food, Taurus, you enjoy a feeling of luxury. You desire "plenty to go around." This being the case, don't skimp on ingredients. You may have a tendency to concentrate on quantity, but never forget quality. It's not that you don't know the difference, it is just that, often at the last minute, you get a panicky feeling that there won't be enough. Then you are, at these times, apt to settle for second best. Plan. Don't overstock. Try going away from the table not too satiated. Your guests won't starve and neither will you.

One of the world's most famous restaurant owners was born under your sign: Toots Shor. Because Taurus is basic and loyal, Toots attracted celebrated athletes and theatrical figures as well as journalists who kept his name in the spotlight. Because you are, at times, a meat-and-potatoes type, you should maintain a sensible balance, doing so with expert advice from a qualified dietician. Have fun, Taurus, but overcome the temptation to overeat. Otherwise, you add girth and become hefty. Kate Smith is a Taurus; so is Orson Welles and Raymond Burr, to say nothing of Joe Louis and Sonny Liston.

You desire plenty of food to go around

You are sensuous; you enjoy the feeling of being well fed, and who can blame you? You can be quite serious where meals enter the picture. You enjoy the planning; you know where everything is, where it will be of the most use. And you do enjoy seeing guests consume your creations. You may not be the pioneer Aries is, but none of us is likely to go hungry while you are in charge of the kitchen.

Plentiful, rich—that's the way you enjoy your food. The tea-and-crumpet set leaves you cold. But listen, Taurus: I would like to see you partake of a greater variety. Don't always insist on the old standby, try something different. Test the menus of other Houses as detailed by Mike Roy. Break up those habits.

Some claim that you overindulge or that you are self-indulgent. However, if the truth be known, you do burn up much energy. You require nourishment to a greater degree, perhaps, than do the other zodiacal types. I know one thing, Taurus. If I were hungry and thirsty, having finished a hard day's work, I would like nothing better than to dine at your table, to enjoy your fare. You wouldn't let me down. And with Mike Roy's menus for Taurus, you aren't likely to let yourself down either.

You are sensuous; you enjoy the feeling of being well fed

Mike Roy on Taurus

Don't always insist on the old standby; try something different

Welcome to the House of the hearty eaters. Omarr has given the word. Taurus people are meat-and-potato people, and this seems to fit with the fact that the Earth element is ever present. But let's be realistic about this "meat-and-potatoes" bit. The phrase can mean different things to residents of different parts of the country or world. Foreign elements in the background can bring varied appetite preferences into play.

In the great Midwestern farm lands, meat and potatoes may mean fried chicken, pork chops, mashed potatoes, gravy, and apple pie. Should we journey southward, we'd find the meat and potatoes taking the form of hog jowl, sow belly, mustard or collard greens, and black-eyed peas, not to mention hominy grits with red-eye gravy. Visit the rockbound coast of Maine and we'd find the Down-Easters supping on codfish cakes, baked beans, boiled vegetables, and meat. In the Southwest, refried beans, barbecues, salads, and fresh fruits might be the favorites.

Taurus, in any part of the country, is still Taurus. He or she is not so much concerned with a great variety as he or she is with good, solid fare.

We should be aware of a couple of points about this great variety of food as it pertains to the various regions: it is sound, balanced food. And whether the sons and daughters of the Second House come from the North, South, East, or West, they are solid physical specimens. The induction centers of the United States Armed Forces furnish proof that these menus provide ample dietary value.

Taurus, as Omarr states, is associated with the planet Venus. You, Taurus, like good eating places, and sometimes you own them. You like things uniquely yours. Your own possessions go hand in hand with the Second House, but these must be especially yours. This also applies to your menus.

Now again, let me point out that meat and potatoes may take many forms and it doesn't follow that they are literally meat and potatoes as such. In the Southwest, refried beans, Spanish rice, and so on would fit the pattern.

And let me suggest that, whatever our signs, we can always be creative in our culinary efforts. It should be a matter of pride to all of us to do well in the kitchen. Let's face it: we should all eat three meals a day. But many of us (and I'm the first to admit it) make a quick cup of coffee do for breakfast, even though it fights with our metabolism and we may be guilty of this lapse seven days a week. Inasmuch as the morning meal should be a "must," doesn't it follow that we should have it with as much grace and taste as possible?

There is a kind of evolution that occurs when someone who does not like to cook begins to be interested in food. The big challenge is to the creative instincts. Once aroused, the fun of doing something appealing and different becomes the name of the game. The payoff, of course, comes in personal satisfaction, knowing that we have accomplished something for our family, friends, and ourselves.

You like good eating places and things uniquely yours

And there is more to it than satisfaction. There is the rather complicated business of better understanding ourselves and our fellow humans. One of the early and brilliant writers on food was a distinguished French gourmet named Jean Anthelme Brillat-Savarin. It was he who first pointed out that "man is what he eats." (I'd also better tell you that this same man made the statement: "If Adam and Eve did what they did for an apple, think what they would have done for a truffle-stuffed turkey.")

If cuisine has variations here in America, look at what happens around the world. The hot, equatorial countries serve up a blaze of peppery, hot food. The dishes vary according to country—the chilies of Latin America, the curries of India, the couscous (an Algerian dish) of the Sahara. Journey to the far north and you'll find the heavy fats on the menu to cushion bodies against the rigors of the winter's cold. These are only a couple of instances to set forth the proposition that if we know what people eat, we know what they are. Two keys to the understanding of people are their diets and their birth dates.

Somewhere, within the foregoing lines, is part of a key to peace in the world. Across the conference table there is doubt and suspicion. Across the kitchen table there is joy and good will. The fact remains: people don't usually start actual wars in kitchens.

And so, Taurus, let us consider some menus and recipes to match the generous kitchens of the Second House.

MENU ONE

Mushroom Antipasto Salad

Bragole

Herb Bread

Venus Goodie

Taurus, you should really go for this hearty salad. It's got the substance to satisfy that hunger of yours for something solid to begin a meal.

Mushroom Antipasto Salad
(serves 6)

1 head Boston lettuce	2 zucchini, thinly sliced
6 ½-inch slices tomato	Salt
10 large mushrooms, thinly sliced	*Italian dressing*

Arrange cups from outer leaves of lettuce on 6 salad plates. Shred remaining lettuce and make a bed in lettuce cups. Place tomato slices in the center and top with mushroom slices. Arrange zucchini as a border to the tomatoes in overlapping rows. Sprinkle with salt and Italian dressing.

Italian Dressing

6 tablespoons olive oil	½ teaspoon ground pepper
2 tablespoons lemon juice	¼ teaspoon powdered oregano
1 tablespoon wine vinegar	

Note: When using this dressing with other salads, add salt to taste; garlic may also be added. Glorify the salad as you wish. You might want to add anchovies, capers, pimiento, cheeses, salami, scallions, pickled beets, or pickled garbanzos.

Taurus, the Bull, loves meat. And, regardless of background, this Italian-originated recipe should make Taureans happy.

Bragole
(serves 6)

1 large round steak about
  ½ inch thick

½ pound ground lean beef

4 slices bread

2 eggs

2 tablespoons grated Romano
  or Parmesan cheese

  Salt and pepper to taste

¼ teaspoon nutmeg

2 tablespoons chopped parsley

2 slices lean bacon

4 hard-cooked eggs

3 slices salami

3 slices Provolone cheese

2 tablespoons olive oil

1 onion

½ cup dry red wine

2 (8-ounce) cans tomato sauce

1 package frozen peas

Soak bread in water and wring out; add to chopped meat. Add the two eggs, grated cheese, salt, pepper, nutmeg, and parsley. Mix thoroughly until well blended. Cut bacon into pieces about 1 inch wide. Slice hard-cooked eggs, salami, and Provolone into julienne strips or slivers. Pound the round steak well. Coat it with the ground meat mixture leaving about a ½-inch rim. Place the julienne on top of the ground mixture. Roll the whole thing as you would a jelly roll and tie it well with a string. Heat the oil in a Dutch oven. Add the onions and the bragole and brown the meat well. Add the wine and let it reduce by about half. Add salt and pepper and the tomato sauce. Add enough water to cover the meat. Cover the kettle and let it simmer for an hour. Add the peas and cook 15 minutes more. When meat is done and peas are tender, remove the meat to a hot serving platter. Cut the strings and remove. Cut serving slices sidewise and dress with tomato sauce with peas.

Should you like, you may serve a pasta such as spaghetti or macaroni shells with this. If you do, cover them with sauce from the meat and sprinkle well with Parmesan cheese.

Wherever you find meat and potatoes, you're almost sure to find bread. Here's one of the tastiest loaves I've found and I don't think you'll find better any place on Earth—or in the heavens either for that matter. The recipe came to me from my old friends George and Alice Drake.

Herb Bread
(serves 6)

1 loaf unsliced white bread   *Herb butter*
    Brown wrapping paper

Trim off the ends, side, and top crusts of bread loaf, leaving the bottom crust. Slice bread in 1-inch slices down to the bottom crust. Spread slices thickly with herb butter. Wrap in a double thickness of plain wrapping paper and tie with string. If possible, let the wrapped loaf stand overnight in the refrigerator. Bake in a 350° oven for 30 minutes. Unwrap and serve.

Herb Butter

¼ pound soft butter
2 tablespoons chopped parsley
2 tablespoons chives or green
    onion tops
½ teaspoon lemon juice

1 tablespoon chopped celery
    leaves
1 teaspoon herbs: oregano,
    thyme, basil, rosemary,
    or combination

Blend ingredients well.

Sugar and spice and everything nice is a necessary closing of this sumptuous menu. This recipe is generous, so you'll probably have some left over for tomorrow.

Venus Goodie
(serves 6)

1 (12-ounce) package semisweet chocolate pieces	⅛ teaspoon salt
2 tablespoons confectioners' sugar	1 egg separated, plus 1 egg white
3 tablespoons dark rum *or* strong, cold coffee	1 cup whipping cream
	½ large angel food cake

Melt chocolate pieces with sugar, rum, and salt over hot water or very low heat, stirring to blend thoroughly. Remove from heat and beat in egg yolk. Beat egg whites until they form stiff peaks. Fold into chocolate mixture. Beat whipping cream until stiff and fold into the chocolate mixture. Tear angel food cake into chunks (about 1-inch pieces) and fold into chocolate. Spoon into a 9 x 13 x 2-inch pan. Refrigerate at least 12 hours before serving. If desired, this mixture may be frozen.

MENU TWO

Tangy Cauliflower Salad

Pineapple Acorn Squash

Taurus Spoon Bread

Veal Florentine

Cherry Glazed Ice Cream Cake

Sydney Omarr tells us that Taurus enjoys luxury as well as meat and potatoes. Of course he also tells us that Taurus loves love. Anybody who enjoys hearty food, luxury, and love can't be all bad. So, Taurus, try this menu on for size and see if it doesn't fulfill all three preferences.

Cauliflower is one of "those" vegetables. A lot of us would just as soon let it bloom and forget it. Yet it's delicious when properly prepared. Not enough of us realize how great it is raw, dressed with tasty garnishes and flavored with just the right dressing.

Tangy Cauliflower Salad
(serves 6)

1 medium cauliflower	1 small avocado
½ cup *French dressing* (see page 131)	½ cup sliced green stuffed olives
3 carrots, shredded	¼ cup Roquefort cheese, crumbled
6 lettuce cups	

Wash and separate cauliflower into flowerets. Cut them into crosswise slices. Cover with French dressing and let stand at least 1 hour. Just before serving, shred carrots and dice avocado. Add these along with olives and cheese. Toss lightly and serve in crisp lettuce cups.

Again we head to the meat department to satisfy that Taurus demand. And again the flavor of Italy beckons.

Veal Florentine
(serves 6)

1½ pounds fresh spinach,
    washed and trimmed
1 cup whipped cream
2 tablespoons prepared mustard
1 tablespoon fresh lemon juice
5 tablespoons sweet butter
2 (2-ounce) cans sliced button
    mushrooms, drained
    Finely chopped parsley

2 tablespoons dry sherry *or*
    dry white wine
6 (⅛-inch thick) slices top
    round of veal (about
    4–6 ounces each)
    Salt and pepper
½ cup flour
2 tablespoons oil

Steam spinach, adding no water, over low flame 3–5 minutes or until crisp and tender. Drain. In a small bowl, blend with a French whip the cream, mustard, and lemon juice. Allow the sauce to stand for about 5 minutes. Melt 2 tablespoons butter in saucepan. Add mushrooms and sauté until lightly browned. Turn flame off. Add wine. Add mustard-cream mixture and cook, stirring constantly, over a medium-high flame until sauce is reduced to a thick consistency. Keep warm over low flame.

Lightly season veal slices with salt and pepper, then dredge each side in flour. Heat remaining 3 tablespoons butter and oil over a full flame until butter just begins to brown. Immediately add veal and brown each side about 1 minute. Place veal on heated serving platter. Keep warm in low-temperature oven at 170°. Add 2–3 tablespoons water and ¼ teaspoon salt to skillet in which the veal was browned. Simmer for 2 or 3 minutes. Add drained spinach and heat quickly. To serve, arrange spinach in center of platter with slices of veal on each side. Pour mushroom sauce over veal slices *only*. Sprinkle sauce with parsley.

The need for eye appeal finds a colorful addition to this menu. The next dish gives us the balance we need, too.

Pineapple Acorn Squash
(serves 6)

3 medium acorn squash
    (about 4 pounds)
    Salt
⅓ cup butter or margarine

1½ cups pineapple chunks
1 apple, diced
2 tablespoons brown sugar

Wash squash; cut in half. Leave seeds in and stem on. Cook in small amount of salted water or steamer until almost tender, 30–40 minutes. Remove seeds. Sprinkle each cavity with salt and 1 tablespoon butter. Mix pineapple chunks and apple with brown sugar. Fill in cavity. Bake in 350° oven for 30 minutes, basting with pineapple juice.

Hold still for just a minute, Taurus. This time around let's forget the potatoes, again literally, and offer a starch that truly is different, yet just as filling as your favorite fruit.

Taurus Spoon Bread
(serves 6)

¾ cup milk
½ cup corn meal
1 teaspoon salt
1 tablespoon sugar
3 egg yolks, slightly beaten

3 tablespoons butter
1 cup small curd cottage cheese
3 egg whites
Melted butter

In a medium-size saucepan scald milk. Add corn meal and cook, stirring constantly until thickened. Mix in salt and sugar. Blend a small amount of hot corn meal mixture with egg yolks, then return to saucepan, mixing thoroughly. Stir in butter and cottage cheese. Beat egg whites until stiff but not dry; then gradually fold corn meal mixture into them. Pour into 1½-quart casserole and bake for 35 minutes in preheated 375° oven. Serve immediately with plenty of melted butter.

Luxury, I repeat, is one of the loves of Taurus, according to Sydney Omarr. I can't think of a more luxurious dessert than this one.

Cherry Glazed Ice Cream Cake
(serves 6)

1 *nut crumb crust*, baked in 9-inch pan, chilled
1 quart vanilla ice cream, softened
2 cups (1-pound can) red sour pitted cherries
½ cup sugar
3½ tablespoons cornstarch
¼ teaspoon salt
10–12 drops red food coloring
6 drops almond extract
1 tablespoon toasted sliced almonds
½ cup whipping cream, whipped and sweetened

Spread ice cream in crust; cover with foil and freeze. Drain cherries; reserve juice. In a saucepan thoroughly mix sugar, cornstarch, and salt. Gradually blend in juice from cherries. Cook, stirring constantly, until thick and clear. Stir in cherries, food coloring, and extract; chill. To serve, remove foil from crust, spread cherries over ice cream, and sprinkle with almonds. Serve immediately, topping each serving with spoonful of whipped cream.

Nut Crumb Crust

1 cup vanilla wafer crumbs
½ cup finely chopped nuts
⅓ cup butter, melted

Combine ingredients; mix well. Press firmly against bottom and sides of 9-inch pie plate (the easy way is to use an 8-inch pie plate inside the 9-inch plate to press crumbs into shape). Bake 8–10 minutes in 350° oven.

MENU THREE

Ensalada Verde

Second House Chicken

Buttered Brussels Sprouts and Filberts

Cottage Cheese-Potato Scallop

Banana Coconut Rolls of the Heavens

Down Mexico way, a Taurus would be delighted with this salad, dressed with the pungency of garlic and the sunshine softness of golden olive oil, with a dash of vinegar and lemon for tartness. This is an all-green salad, verdant and cool.

Ensalada Verde
(6–8 servings)

2 avocados, sliced
½ cup olive oil or salad oil
2 tablespoons vinegar
1 clove garlic, halved
1 teaspoon dry mustard
1 teaspoon salt
¼ teaspoon pepper
1 cup pimiento-stuffed olives
1 package frozen Italian green
   beans, cooked, drained

1 package frozen French-style
   green beans, cooked,
   drained
1 package frozen green peas,
   cooked, drained
1 package frozen asparagus
   spears, cooked,
   drained
1 large cucumber, thinly sliced
   Aioli dressing

Combine for marinade: oil, vinegar, and seasonings. Beat or shake well. Arrange avocados, olives, and vegetables in serving dish. Pour marinade over vegetables and chill several hours.

Aioli Dressing

6 cloves garlic, crushed
2 egg yolks
1 cup olive oil

Juice of 1 lemon
Salt and pepper to taste

Beat egg yolks and crushed garlic. With fork or wire whisk, slowly beat in the oil and lemon juice. Add salt and pepper to taste. Makes about 1 cup. (This is like making mayonnaise, and you may use any "beater" or "blender" method.)

Now, Taurus, let's turn our attention to chicken. You will want a dish that is your own creation and yours alone. Others will serve chicken in many ways, but you alone may do best with this recipe.

Second House Chicken
(6 servings)

2 cups sour cream	1½ cups corn flake crumbs
1 teaspoon tarragon	¼ cup butter
1 teaspoon thyme	1 cup (½ pound) cooked,
½ teaspoon garlic powder	cleaned prawns *or* 1 cup
1 teaspoon paprika	canned, tiny shrimp
2½ teaspoons salt	¼ cup diced ripe olives
6 chicken breasts *or* 2 pounds broiler-fryer chicken	

Combine sour cream with tarragon, thyme, garlic powder, paprika, and salt. Dip chicken pieces into sour cream mixture, then into corn flake crumbs, coating well. Melt butter in baking dish. Place chicken, skin side down, in dish and bake 45 minutes in a 350° oven, turn and bake approximately 20 minutes longer. Meanwhile, to the remaining sour cream mixture add shrimp/prawns and olives. Pour sauce over chicken during last 10 minutes of baking time, or heat sauce and serve separately. This chicken may be baked and then frozen.

Here's a delightfully different way with another difficult vegetable. The tarragon leaves, lemon juice, and filberts give a tart crunchiness that makes this dish a perfect companion for the chicken.

Buttered Brussels Sprouts and Filberts
(serves 6–8)

2   (10-ounce) packages frozen brussels sprouts
⅔   cup chopped filberts, toasted
½   cup sliced onions
½   cup butter or margarine

½   teaspoon tarragon leaves
½   teaspoon salt
¼   teaspoon pepper
2   tablespoons lemon juice
    Parsley for garnish

Sauté brussels sprouts, filberts, and onions with seasonings in butter or margarine on medium heat until lightly browned. Remove from heat and stir in lemon juice.

And now, Taurus, that long-awaited potato dish:

Cottage Cheese-Potato Scallop
(serves 6)

6 medium potatoes, cooked	2 cups cottage cheese
3 tablespoons grated onion	1 cup sour cream
1 teaspoon salt	1¼ cups shredded Cheddar
¼ teaspoon freshly ground	cheese
pepper	Paprika

Peel and slice potatoes; place in 1½-quart baking dish. Sprinkle onion, salt, and pepper over potatoes. Combine cottage cheese and sour cream; spoon over potatoes. Top with Cheddar cheese, sprinkle with paprika, and bake 20 minutes in a 300° oven.

✷ 🕊 ✷

Rich and bubbling with heated fruit juices, our dessert carries with it an aura of the tropics. When I first tested this recipe and tasted it, I thought it might just be too good for mere mortals.

Banana Coconut Rolls of the Heavens
(for each serving)

1 firm banana	2 tablespoons shredded
½ tablespoon melted butter	coconut
or margarine	Pineapple slices *or*
Orange sauce (see page 59)	orange slices *or*
½ tablespoon lemon or lime	cherries
juice	

continued

Peel banana and cut crosswise into halves. Place into a well-greased baking dish. Brush thoroughly with butter or margarine, then with lemon or lime juice. Sprinkle bananas with coconut. Bake in 375° oven for 15–20 minutes, or until coconut is browned and bananas are tender (easily pierced with a fork). Garnish with sliced pineapple, fluted orange slices, and cherries if desired. Serve hot with hot orange sauce.

Orange Sauce

½ cup sugar	2 tablespoons butter or
1 tablespoon cornstarch	margarine
Dash of salt	1 teaspoon grated orange rind
Dash of cinnamon	¼ cup orange juice
¾ cup boiling water	1 teaspoon lemon juice

Mix together sugar, cornstarch, salt, and cinnamon in sauce pan. Add water gradually. Bring to a boil and cook about 5 minutes or until sauce is thickened, stirring constantly. Add butter or margarine, orange rind, orange juice, and lemon juice. Reheat to boiling temperature. Makes about 1 cup of sauce.

And so, Taurus, wend your way through these menus secure in the knowledge that they were designed for you and you alone. I wish you a luxurious appetite!

Gemini Menu One

pages 71–75

Gemini Soup
Shrimp Fleur De Lys
Party Broccoli
Buttermilk Sky Bread
Upside-Down Peach Gingerbread

Gemini Menu Two

pages 76–81

Celestial Pear Salad
Parmesan Veal Chops
Corn Pone Cracklin' Bread
Old Country Rice Pudding

Gemini Menu Three

pages 82–87

Airy Coleslaw
Salmon and Green Olive Casserole
Eggplant Parmesan
Chive Swiss Bread
Mercury Pears with Crème de Menthe
        Sauce

Third House
May 21–June 20

GEMINI

Sydney Omarr on Gemini

Gemini is the natural third zodiacal sign, associated with Mercury, and related to the hands and arms. Born under this sign, you possess intellectual curiosity and are fond of talking, gesticulating. In the kitchen you are active and quick; you experiment, and you are conscious of what close relatives think of your culinary concoctions.

People like to be around you. Those who share your food creations remember more about your active way, your bright sayings than they do about the food or wine. This, of course, will change—with Mike Roy's help! You keynote the impromptu, the funny surprise; you take pleasure in explaining to guests how

61

you got the idea for this or that—ideas are food for you. Food for thought, where you are concerned, is more than a saying.

You love change, travel, variety; you are restless and anxious to explore. This applies to food as well as other areas. Your sign is of the Air element; you are fun to be with, but you burn up a great deal of energy, which means that those around your table are treated to numerous snacks—sometimes so much so that by the time the entrée is served, appetites have waned. It takes a bit of planning for the appetizers to serve their proper function. When around you, people love to chat over hors d'oeuvre.

Food must be interesting and have appeal

For you, food must be interesting and have appeal. Your own intuitive intellect and curiosity assures you that your excitement is contagious; it rubs off on others. You talk about a lot of things, and many can tell, from this and other traits, that indeed you were born under Gemini.

Talkative Gemini, you often back up your statements, too. New York Jets quarterback Joe Namath proved that when he boasted that the heavily favored Baltimore Colts would come out second-best in the now famous Super Bowl upset. Geminis grow on people. Ask Judy Garland's legion of fans. She was a Gemini, and her animated life and career typify many of your characteristics. The quick quip is Gemini-like, as exemplified by Bob Hope, born under your sign.

The quick quip is Gemini-like, as exemplified by Bob Hope

You are mercurial, possess a delightful sense of humor, and have a definite tendency to scatter your forces. You are here, there, and everywhere—and this also applies to your role as host or hostess. Thus, your creations in the culinary area should not be designed to keep you away too long from company.

Where Taurus is stolid, slow, and deliberate, you are quick, nimble, and talkative. Your brothers, sisters, and other close relatives are an important part of your personal scheme; you enjoy having them for dinner and the feeling is reciprocated.

Your mind changes quickly; meal planning often finds you indecisive because you want to try a bit of everything. You have a dual nature: first desiring to stay, then deciding to be on the move. Your likes, dislikes are sporadic. You are fond of nibbling; you want to taste everything. You imbue others with enthusiasm when entertaining with a meal. Where Aries is dynamic, a leader and director, you are willing to vacillate, to be persuaded. Dinner plans are subject to change, where this would be almost unthinkable for a Taurus.

You enjoy the company of Aries—and the most harmonious dinner group for you would include Aries, Leo, Libra, and Aquarius people. With another Gemini, it is a question of who takes the lead—who listens and who talks. Relating to another Gemini usually results in a new project, adventure, or creative endeavors. However, the conversation and ultimate result, especially in the kitchen, could be somewhat shallow. For a romantic evening, dine with a Libra; you tend to be physically attracted to natives of that zodiacal sign.

For a romantic evening, dine with a Libra

Taurus people make you feel as though you are partaking in a secret—the atmosphere is one of a clandestine meeting. With Taurus, you feel you are being let in on something mysterious and maybe even sacred. The Venus of Taurus combines with your Mercury significator to produce an elevation of ideas; you are able to articulate feelings, moods. But, when Gemini is dining with Taurus, the atmosphere is apt to be rather somber as compared to a liaison with Leo. Natives of Leo encourage you to talk, especially about relatives, and this you enjoy. Leo stimulates but also makes you more restless than usual, which is saying a lot. Alone at dinner with Leo, the two of you might not get past the before-meal snacks!

When breaking bread with Cancer, your interest is in security, personal possessions, and money. Cancer stimulates that part of your solar horoscope associated with income potential. Cancer people tend to be slightly in awe and a bit envious of you. Cancer seems to think you have some romantic secrets. In order to be your companion, a Cancer can reveal some financial information that could be quite advantageous. If you want to know how to increase your income, talk money with a Cancer, especially over the results of one of Mike Roy's special astrological menus. Cancer loves good food; prepare a Cancer menu, or one of your own. Cancer is appreciative and especially likes your vibrant manner. He or she is more conservative, steadier than you are. The Cancer

If you want to know how to increase your income, talk money with a Cancer over dinner

Moon and your ruling planet, Mercury, blend to create a confidential atmosphere. You are provided with information not yet made public. This makes for a fine setting. Complement it with a fine gourmet delight. Then you'll be cooking with astrology—for a profit!

Food for you is variety. Sameness, when dining, bores you. You have to be kept busy, measuring, taking notes, testing, and tasting. Your sense of touch is highly developed; you enjoy feeling what you eat. In this, you have much in common with Virgo. Because a Virgo is concerned about your general welfare and health, you gain a sense of security when dining with this individual. The Virgo person stimulates you, encourages you to come up with new ideas. Your confidence is built up, you feel you can lead, be an innovator. Dining with Virgo can result in building for the future via a new enterprise. You won't always agree with Virgo's ideas, but you may find yourself being swayed toward a more practical course of action. Check the Virgo menu—combine it with Gemini. Be resourceful because that's one quality a Virgo admires in you.

I have said about a Gemini woman that, if one is not careful, she is liable to grow on one; one acquires a taste for her. To a great extent, this applies also to the men of Gemini.

Geminis can make their guests like almost anything they prepare

Being a Gemini, you can make your guests like almost anything you prepare. This is because of your ebullience; you do your best and, thus, you are enthusiastic about your creations. The enthusiasm spreads, combines with talk, ideas—and the culinary delights are enhanced.

In truth, you usually are resourceful, versatile. You have an "affinity" with buttermilk, for instance. You successfully use it in your recipes, and during your tour of the Third House under Mike Roy's supervision, there will be a buttermilk dish that could become one of your favorites. Coleslaw is a specific Gemini dish; it's one that almost symbolizes your sign in the food area. You are attracted to beer, gingerbread, and, for you, soup cannot merely be soup. It must be blended, a concoction, a mixture. Your soups become conversation pieces, and conversation helps in your relations with all other zodiacal groups.

With Scorpio, you unburden yourself of work and health problems. Eating with a Scorpio enlarges your horizons. You are intrigued because natives of this sign are somewhat mysterious, and you are fond of puzzles. Incidentally, the Scorpio menus are among the more fascinating. You learn from a Scorpio; employment, health, how to promote your own interests—these factors are highlighted when you dine with natives of this sign.

Listen, Gemini, when having a meal, try to be a bit more relaxed. You are too concerned with business, the ways of the world. You also are busy analyzing the characters of guests, host, hostess, friends, associates. You may appear to be sitting still, but your mind is whirling. Restless Gemini, you think ahead and perceive motives. You're never satisfied to know how a dish is prepared—you want to know why it is made this way or that way. You are fond of garnishes, decorations—they give you something to nibble!

Rumor, gossip are your spices. Much of the time, leisurely dining is a stranger to you. Strive to finish, for your own good. This admonition means don't just peck.

You are dynamic and the life of the party—especially the dinner party. With a Sagittarius, your charms seem to be enhanced. You exude a kind of sex appeal when partaking of food with members of this zodiacal group. There is definite attraction here; often the talk turns to contracts, partnerships, and even marriage. There is a community of interests. But while you express quick ideas, Sagittarius is likely to philosophize, making for a nice balance. The two signs—Gemini and Sagittarius—are opposites, but there is innate mutual sympathy and magnetism.

Because Capricorn is apt to be withdrawn, you find these persons a challenge. You delight in preparing entertainment that may cause the Capricorn to doubt, to ask, to talk, to probe. With a Capricorn, you are tempted to kick over the traces, to tear down even in order to rebuild. Capricorn tends to be quiet while you talk, but before the dinner is finished, it is a good wager that you will have drawn the Capricorn individual out of his or her shell. Where talk is concerned, it may center on areas like psychic phenomena and legacies. Ask questions of Capricorn; your display of interest will make the meal more of a delight for him or her. A Capricorn feels that you have his or her best interest at heart.

Geminis are dynamic and the life of the party— especially the dinner party

There is definite attraction between you and Sagittarius

And if you can get Capricorn to relax and unwind, then dining becomes all the more festive.

You delight in having the classical Aquarius to dinner. Aquarius seems to understand your quickness, restlessness, your tendency to have a bit of this and some of that, with the emphasis on variety. Aquarius arouses your curiosity and, where you are concerned, curiosity is the name of the game. An Aquarius activates your interest in faraway places; you enjoy foreign food when dining with him or her. Discussion often centers on languages, writing, advertising, or publishing. The religions and philosophies of people also tend to dominate. An Aquarius harmonizes with a Gemini, and when the two dine together, pleasure abounds. The trouble, Gemini, is that you are apt to do more listening and talking than eating. Strive for greater balance, for the sake of your own nourishment.

Aquarius arouses your curiosity

You are such an excellent conversationalist that dining with you is a treat. That is, provided those with you do not regard eating as something that is a mere necessity. Realize this and choose your companions wisely. It's best to skip those guests for whom food represents nothing more than a means of survival. Being of an Air sign, you are intellectual and good talk is as necessary as a basic entrée to you.

You are happy when people ask questions

You are active, and you are capable of meeting and impressing the public. Where dining is concerned, you supply the ingredient of freshness. You want what you serve to be enchanting, almost a curiosity piece. You are happy when people ask questions or when you can query others. You are versatile—your menus should be varied.

With Pisces as a dining partner, talk turns often to career opportunity. The Neptune of Pisces and your Mercury combined act almost like a mind-expanding drug. There are differences, to be sure, but there is also a community of practical interests. Your desires coincide. It's wonderful if your boss is a Pisces and is coming to dinner.

A Pisces is intrigued by the way you use your hands; you're able to balance a dish, say, while preparing something else. Pisces shares some of your duality—he or she can sympathize with your curiosity and is intrigued by your vitality. You help Pisces overcome shyness, just as you are able to aid a Capricorn to discard reticence. By the time you are finished wining and dining, usually quiet Pisces and Capricorn guests can become absolutely verbose!

You use your hands; you don't hesitate to show your appreciation of good food by putting out finger bowls. You are intrigued by fancy napkins, too, and silverware provides inspiration for conversation and helps set the tone for your enjoyment of dining. Using your hands with cooking utensils is as necessary to you as a before-dinner cocktail is apt to be for the Water signs (Cancer, Scorpio, Pisces).

You could make others jealous through the use of your hands. Touching the arm of a guest could make his or her spouse or date come up with the wrong idea. You want to reach people around you—you get a feeling of warmth from this. This is security for a Gemini.

You make others jealous through the use of your hands

The odds are that you, above all of the other zodiacal signs, will be the first to test, to experiment with Mike Roy's menus. By this I do not mean only those created for your own sign; you'll try Aquarius, then Libra perhaps. You'll also test what I've said about the various signs in relation to you. That's how you are, Gemini: possessed of curiosity, with an insatiable desire to know more, to try more, to find out, to learn, to experiment with a variety of methods as well as foods. The Sagittarius menus, with foreign foods prominent in them, are bound to appeal to you. And, remember, dining with a Sagittarian could, with other things being equal, lead to marriage, or at least to a solid, permanent relationship.

You enjoy reading and studying recipes. You are intrigued with various ingredients, measurements. You like the sounds of food names. But you really should try to be more patient and less restless. Do justice to your creations.

Dining with a Sagittarian could lead to marriage or a permanent relationship

Your appetite is good, but you prefer to eat less more often than not. Taurus prefers the big, basic meal. You could learn from each other— you and Taurus—where dining habits are concerned.

Listen: dining with you is an adventure, because emotions run the gamut. We may not all think you're the world's greatest cook, but we are going to "think" if we eat with you. Furthermore, your sense of humor comes bubbling to the top, and we're soon laughing. And laughter is a marvelous ingredient in any meal.

Study your Gemini menus, and then begin experimenting. It will make you happy, Gemini.

Dining with a Gemini is an adventure

Mike Roy on Gemini

Sydney Omarr's interpretation of Gemini indicates to me that I'm face to face with one of the most difficult signs of the zodiac. It matters not so much to Gemini that the food be gourmet. Mercury is your planet, and you like people around you. A Gemini does like new things, variety—you are a versatile individual. But a Gemini doesn't want to be stuck in the kitchen. You like to chatter your way through a myriad choice of subjects. Yet, it is the chef's job to make sure everyone eats well. I hope you'll enjoy these recipes.

If you are entertaining a Gemini, you'd best be on the creative side to the nth degree. Try to come up with something that will dare the appetite—perhaps make the food a topic of conversation. When you stop to consider it, this should not be too difficult.

Perhaps a look at the future of food might intrigue Gemini. What we're about to experience is boldly set forth in a book by Henry Still (*Man: The Next Thirty Years*, Hawthorn Books, Inc., New York, 1968). Mr. Still tells us that former Agricultural Secretary Orville Freeman had predicted that soils throughout the world will have to be inventoried. Each crop, wherever it may be, will be grown either on the soil best suited for it or on soil chemically modified for the highest output. A running inventory will be kept by computer of all land under cultivation so that accurate predictions may be made from one day to the next to guide marketing and production. We all remember the Biblical stories of seven years of feast and seven years of famine. Drastic inequalities in food supply have been a problem source for untold centuries. A look ahead tells us that human's scientific mind is well on the way to controlling the maturity point in this area. The population explosion notwithstanding, human's ability to meet the problem is already well on

If you are entertaining a Gemini, you'd best be on the creative side

the way through an ever-growing knowledge explosion. The wonders of science and technology, applied to the complex problems of agriculture, could make an easier life for the farmer who would then enjoy an income and standard of living more commensurate with other economic sectors of society. The proper use of the oceans, the forests, and the deserts could someday provide a yield beyond our present dreams.

It probably won't happen fast enough to satisfy you, Gemini, for you like things to happen fast. You, Gemini, often contemplate the pantry of tomorrow. It will certainly contain square tomatoes, bred that way in the field for ease of handling and shipment. There will probably be a steak made of controlled bacteria. It will not only taste like meat, but its shape, consistency, and texture will be so much like a slice of beef that you won't be able to tell the difference.

I'd like to relieve your mind about one aspect of these futuristic changes. The authority for the information is Professor John Yudkin, nutrition specialist at Queen Elizabeth College of London, who pointed out in an international conference on nutrition (thank God):

You like things to happen fast

> In spite of the almost universal belief that we shall sooner or later be eating pills, we shall in fact have to eat the sorts of foods which need a plate, knife, fork, and spoon. The amount of protein, fat, and carbohydrate which our bodies need each day, with its mineral elements and vitamins, weighs something like one pound . . . . This would make up a hundred or so quite large pills, and I doubt whether this is quite what people have in mind when they imagine food in this form. On the contrary, what is becoming more and more clear is that people will eat only food which is palatable to them—food which is pleasant to look at, to smell, to taste and chew.

You would say "hurray" to that, Gemini!

The materials in our pantry may change. Years from now there may be sheets of freeze-dried ketchup, barbecue sauce, gravy, pickle relish, and syrup, ready to be reconstituted by the simple addition of water. A full year's supply will require relatively small space and be ready to be stored without refrigeration.

We've only begun to speculate about meals in years ahead, Gemini. Put your mind to work, and think about this food of the future as you prepare your menus. You could hasten these changes.

MENU ONE

Gemini Soup

Shrimp Fleur De Lys

Party Broccoli

Buttermilk Sky Bread

Upside-Down Peach Gingerbread

Since cold soups are more or less a new appetizer idea on our culinary horizon, Gemini soup should start the conversational ball rolling.

Gemini Soup
(serves 6–8)

3 avocados	3 tablespoons lemon juice
3 cups chicken broth or bouillon	1½ teaspoons salt
	Dash Tabasco
1½ cucumbers, peeled, sliced	3 large tomatoes, peeled, diced
¾ cup sour cream	

Puree avocados with all ingredients except tomatoes. Chill thoroughly, then garnish with the tomatoes.

The briny deep has always fascinated man. And we will be eating seafood more and more in the future. The daring cook will put his creative ability to a true test in coming up with a new twist to a seafood dish. Tall tales of men who go down to the sea in ships, in fact, usually furnish a favorite topic for Geminis, too.

Shrimp Fleur De Lys
(serves 6–8)

2 pounds shrimp (12 to the pound or larger)	1 teaspoon salt
	½ teaspoon white pepper
¼ cup butter	3 tablespoons cornstarch
1 tablespoon chopped garlic	½ cup water
2 cups dry white wine	Chopped chives
2 cups whipping cream	

Peel and devein shrimp and slice in half lengthwise. Melt butter in sauté pan until it bubbles. Add shrimp and garlic and sauté 3 minutes. Add wine and salt and pepper and simmer 5 minutes. Blend in whipping cream and simmer gently 30 minutes. Combine cornstarch and water and blend into pan, stirring constantly until mixture thickens. Transfer to a heated serving dish and garnish with chopped chives.

Here's a new way with an old favorite vegetable which should hasten any Gemini to the table.

Party Broccoli
(serves 6)

2 tablespoons butter	¼ teaspoon salt
2 tablespoons minced onion	Dash of cayenne pepper
1½ cups sour cream	2 packages frozen broccoli,
2 teaspoons sugar	cooked just until tender
1 teaspoon white vinegar	and drained
½ teaspoon poppy seed	⅓ cup chopped cashews
½ teaspoon paprika	

In a small saucepan melt butter; sauté onion. Remove from heat and stir in sour cream, sugar, vinegar, poppy seed, paprika, salt, and cayenne pepper. Arrange broccoli on heated platter and pour sour cream sauce over it. Sprinkle on cashews. If not to be served immediately, heat sour cream sauce just enough for serving temperature.

And this out-of-the-ordinary recipe yields a delicious result.

Buttermilk Sky Bread

1½ cups buttermilk
1   egg
3   cups biscuit mix
2   tablespoons sugar
1   cup (about ¼ pound)
    grated Swiss cheese

1   cup sliced pimiento-stuffed
    olives, drained
¾   cup chopped walnuts
    (optional)

Combine buttermilk, egg, biscuit mix, and sugar; beat 1 minute to blend thoroughly. Gently stir in Swiss cheese, olives, and walnuts. Spoon into well-buttered loaf pan (9 x 5 x 3-inch or comparable size). Bake in a moderate (350°) oven 50 to 55 minutes. A crack along the top of the loaf usually occurs. Cool 5 minutes before removing from pan. Continue cooling on wire rack.

And now, you're about to turn things around for a Gemini. Here's a dessert that will delight him to the point where he'll end up talking to himself. (This one is a little on the generous side for this menu, but you'll probably be glad to have a little extra.)

Upside-Down Peach Gingerbread
(8–10 servings)

2 cans (1 pound, 4 ounces) sliced cling peaches	2 cups flour
1 cup butter	1½ teaspoons ginger
1 cup brown sugar	1 teaspoon nutmeg
2 tablespoons light corn syrup	1 teaspoon baking soda
Maraschino cherry halves, drained	½ teaspoon salt
Pecan halves	½ cup molasses
½ cup chopped pecans	½ cup boiling water
1 cup sugar	2 eggs
	1 teaspoon grated lemon rind
	Whipped cream (optional)

Drain the peaches as dry as possible on paper toweling. Melt ½ cup butter in a heavy 10-inch skillet with an oven-proof handle. Add the brown sugar and corn syrup. Stir over medium heat until blended. Allow to cool. Now arrange the peach slices in a circular pattern on top, covering as much of the sugar as possible. Fill any spaces with maraschino cherry and pecan halves. Sprinkle with chopped nuts.

Cream ½ cup butter with 1 cup sugar until light and fluffy. Sift the flour, ginger, nutmeg, baking soda, and salt together twice. In a separate bowl, mix the molasses and boiling water. Add the eggs, one at a time, to the creamed butter and sugar, beating well after each addition. Flavor with grated lemon rind. Add the dry ingredients alternately with the molasses. Spread evenly in the skillet. Bake in a moderate oven (350°) for about 1½ hours. Cool slightly. Loosen the sides with a spatula and turn out onto a platter. Serve hot or cold with whipped cream.

MENU TWO

Celestial Pear Salad

Parmesan Veal Chops

Mushrooms Romanoff

Corn Pone Cracklin' Bread

Old Country Rice Pudding

When the pears are fresh and crispy it is the time to serve the following refreshing salad.

Celestial Pear Salad
(serves 6)

3 fresh Anjou, Bosc, or
   Comice pears
1 cup canned chunk-style
   pineapple

1 (10-ounce) package frozen
   raspberries
Crisp salad greens
Cottage cheese dressing

Chill ripe pears, then halve and core them. Drain pineapple and dip cut side of pears in pineapple syrup. Thaw raspberries and drain well. Reserve ½ cup raspberries for dressing. Arrange fruits on crisp greens. Serve with cottage cheese dressing.

Cottage Cheese Dressing

1 cup cream-style cottage
   cheese
½ cup drained raspberries
   (reserved from above)

¼ cup sour cream
¼ teaspoon salt
1 tablespoon lemon juice

Blend all ingredients and chill well. Yield: 1½ cups.

Sometimes a recipe simply flavored is the most successful. The combination of Parmesan cheese, chives, and wine provides a savory quality that's almost eloquent.

Parmesan Veal Chops
(serves 6)

6 veal chops	2½ tablespoons butter
Salt and pepper	¾ cup sauterne or other white
Flour	dinner wine
2 eggs, slightly beaten	1½ tablespoons chopped chives
½ cup plus 2 tablespoons grated Parmesan cheese	

Score fat on edges of chops; sprinkle with salt and pepper and dip in flour. Dip chops in egg then in cheese; brown slightly in butter. Add wine and chives; cover and simmer until meat is tender and wine is almost evaporated. Sprinkle with additional chives when served.

This is a deliciously different vegetable. We liked it so well at our house we often served it as an entrée for a simple supper. (With it we served a tossed green salad and hot sourdough French bread.)

Mushrooms Romanoff

(serves 6)

1⅓ pounds mushrooms	1 cup sour cream
½ cup (1 stick) butter	3 tablespoons chopped dill
½ teaspoon salt	Pinch of nutmeg
Pepper to taste	Toasted bread crumbs
1 tablespoon lemon juice	

Trim off stems of mushrooms and wash the buttons; drain well. Melt butter in a fry pan; add the mushrooms, salt, pepper, and lemon juice and sauté until the mushrooms are lightly browned. Remove pan from fire and fold in sour cream (that has been allowed to come to room temperature), dill weed, and nutmeg. Pour into a baking dish and top with bread crumbs and serve. (If not served immediately, baking dish may be kept warm in a low oven.)

As you've probably deduced by now, I like to go back into the years for some recipes. Try this one; it's been tried, and it's true.

Corn Pone Cracklin' Bread

¾ cup finely diced salt pork
 2 cups corn meal (water-
       ground if available)
1½ teaspoons baking powder
 ½ teaspoon baking soda

1 teaspoon salt
2 eggs, well beaten
1 cup buttermilk
2 tablespoons salt pork
      drippings

Fry salt pork over low heat until nicely browned. Drain fat, saving both the drippings and the cracklings. Sift together corn meal, baking powder, baking soda, and salt. Combine eggs, buttermilk, and drippings. Stir into corn meal mixture along with the cracklings. Spread dough in a greased 11 x 7 x 1½-inch baking pan and bake in a preheated 400° oven 25 to 30 minutes.

Once you've got a good thing, keep it going. This dessert has been around as long as I can remember. My mother, a Gemini, always said this was her favorite recipe. If she thought that highly of it, so should you.

Old Country Rice Pudding
(serves 6–8)

½ cup regular white rice
¼ teaspoon salt
½ cup honey
1 (13-ounce) can undiluted
    evaporated milk

3 cups milk
1 tablespoon vanilla
  Nutmeg
½ cup golden raisins *or* diced
    dates (optional)

In a 2-quart buttered baking dish, combine raw rice, salt, honey, milk, and vanilla. Sprinkle top with nutmeg. Bake uncovered at 300° (slow) 2½ hours, stirring occasionally with fork to prevent rice from settling. Do not stir during last ½ hour of baking.

Note: During the last hour of baking, ½ cup golden raisins or diced dates may be added to the pudding.

MENU THREE

Airy Coleslaw

Salmon and Green Olive Casserole

Eggplant Parmesan

Chive-Swiss Bread

Mercury Pears with Crème de Menthe Sauce

This is a smooth and tangy way with a coleslaw, just the right combination of ingredients to please a Gemini palate.

Airy Coleslaw
(serves 6–8)

3 pounds cabbage, shredded	½ cup crushed pineapple,
1 carrot, grated or shredded	drained
¼ teaspoon celery seed	1 tablespoon sugar
¼ teaspoon white pepper	*Dressing*

Cover the shredded cabbage and carrot with ice water and let stand 15 minutes. Drain well. Add the rest of the ingredients and toss well. Add the following dressing and toss again.

Dressing

1 cup sour cream	1 or more teaspoons sugar
1 tablespoon wine vinegar	½ teaspoon salt
2 tablespoons pineapple juice	

It's probably a fair assumption that casseroles are the backbone of American family cookery. You, Gemini, will want to keep this one handy for company as well as family.

Salmon and Green Olive Casserole
(serves 6)

2 tablespoons chopped shallot or green onion	1½ cups (approximately) light cream
¼ cup butter	½ cup green olives, pitted and diced
1 (16-ounce) can red salmon	2 teaspoons dill
¼ cup flour Freshly ground pepper and salt	3 tablespoons buttered crumbs

Sauté the shallot or green onion in the butter until wilted. Drain the salmon, leaving the juice. Add the flour and a couple of good grindings of pepper to the pan in which the shallot was cooked, and mix in the reserved salmon juice combined with enough light cream to make 2 cups of liquid. Cook, stirring constantly, until thick and smooth. Add the olives and dill weed and taste for seasoning, adding salt if necessary. Remove skin from the salmon, break it into large pieces, and place in a 1-quart casserole. Pour in the sauce, turn two or three times with a fork to mix, and sprinkle top with buttered crumbs. Cook in a 400° oven for 15 minutes, or until hot and brown.

This is a convenient vegetable dish that will bake in the oven along with the casserole. If you have any left, chill it and serve the next day as a salad, dressed with a little olive oil and wine vinegar.

Eggplant Parmesan
(serves 6)

1 large eggplant
 Salt and pepper
½ cup (1 stick) butter
1 cup (8-ounce can) pizza
  sauce

⅓ cup grated Parmesan cheese
2 cups small curd cottage
  cheese
¼ cup buttered bread crumbs

Peel eggplant and cut into ½-inch slices; sprinkle with salt and pepper. In a skillet melt butter; sauté eggplant on both sides until lightly browned. In 1½-quart casserole, layer half of eggplant slices, ½ cup pizza sauce and half of Parmesan cheese. Cover with 1 cup cottage cheese. Repeat layers, ending with cottage cheese and topping of bread crumbs. Bake for 30 minutes in a 325° oven.

For a starch, try this recipe.

Chive-Swiss Bread
(serves 6)

1 loaf sourdough French bread	⅓ cup mayonnaise
½ pound Swiss cheese, grated	1 tablespoon milk
½ cup chopped chives	

Combine all ingredients except bread. Spread onto bread slices. Place under broiler until cheese melts and bubbles.

Cold and crisp, dressed with a sauce that spells "refreshing," this dessert commands the attention of the most gregarious Gemini.

Mercury Pears
with Crème de Menthe Sauce
(serves 6)

6 pears, cored and halved   *Crème de Menthe sauce*
6 iceberg lettuce cups

Place two pear halves on each iceberg lettuce cup. Top each serving with ¼ cup crème de menthe sauce.

Crème de Menthe Sauce

1 egg   2 teaspoons crème de menthe
½ cup confectioners' sugar   *or* ¼ teaspoon pure
½ cup whipping cream   mint extract with 2 drops
                                        green food coloring

Beat egg until thick; add sugar gradually and continue beating until thoroughly blended. Whip cream very stiff and add crème de menthe or mint extract and food coloring. Combine cream mixture with egg. Beat thoroughly. The secret of the success of this recipe is thorough beating. Sauce will keep for hours in the refrigerator. Makes 1½ cups.

And so, Gemini, start cooking, with an eye to the future. There's enough here to keep you busy and happy for quite a spell.

 # Cancer Menu One

pages 99–103

Moon Shrimp Curry
Chicken in Cherries Jubilee
Butter Almond Peas
Potatoes Duchèsse
Cloud Cake

 # Cancer Menu Two

pages 104–109

Neptune Lobster and Shrimp Vermouth
Prime Rib Roast in Salt with Whipped Cream
    Horseradish Sauce
Sweet and Sour Green Beans
Stuffed Baked Potatoes
Milky Way Key Lime Pie

 # Cancer Menu Three

pages 110–115

Escargots in Red Wine
Shrimp-Stuffed Sole à la Saturn
Orange and Lemon Beets, Terra
Old Country Soda Bread
Lazy Rum Cake

Fourth House

CANCER

Sydney Omarr on Cancer

This is Mike Roy's sign. Of the Water element, the natural Fourth House, Cancer, has much to do with food and dining. Born under this sign, you are not likely to have a bare kitchen. You enjoy food. You can be inspired by a well-prepared meal and can detect subtle nuances in cooking. The planning of a menu can be a delight for you. With the Sun in this sign—and if you have other planets in favorable aspect in Cancer (especially in the second and eighth sectors), you could make money with food. Many great chefs boast your Sun sign. Cancer is impressionable, sensitive; he or she is aware of security and can accumulate wealth. Once this is accomplished, a

Cancer can also become a gourmet, a gourmand, an artist in the kitchen. You desire reliable utensils; the newfangled, the ultramodern belongs elsewhere. Listen: When you invite people to dine with you, it is an occasion. Nothing halfway—it's all the way or nothing.

Check newly married Cancer couples. Despite the size of the bankroll—even if there are scanty furnishings throughout the apartment or house—there will be plenty of equipment in the kitchen, and there will be a reverence for meal time. It brings the family together and keeps them that way—so says Cancer.

Food, for you, has balance. It involves justice and the settling of differences. It is beautiful and puts an end to doubt. Food is basic but lovely, fulsome but delicate, uniting home and hearth; it signifies the welding together of differences, the bringing together and cementing of relationships.

Cancers have plenty of equipment in the kitchen, and a reverence for meal time

Cancer, like Libra, is fond of the visual, the setting; thus, linens are important as are arrangements, patterns, and general eye appeal. Food is festive for you. It means the gathering of the clan, the breaking of bread in the best sense. Your sign is associated with the Moon; during New and Full Moon days you should prepare one of Mike Roy's special Cancer menus.

You are fond of the visual, the setting, such as arrangements and table linens

Aries enjoys being the director. You, Cancer, take a maternal or paternal view. You are protective about the family as well as dining. You take others under your wing. Virgo is concerned about vitamins, minerals, general health; you are more concerned, for instance, with people having enough to eat. The table, under your auspices, could groan with food. Plenty is your key word. Food planning and preparation adds to pleasure for you. Of all the zodiacal signs, your own is the one most related to food, dining, and pleasure as the result of a good meal shared with family and loved ones.

Obviously, you are an excellent host or hostess. You can identify restaurants and their specialties. But the real pleasure comes in creating your own atmosphere, and, in cuisine, your own unique dishes. You are romantic about dining. A feast is nothing you take for granted; it is special and relates to love.

Scorpio is the ideal companion for you when it comes to moonlight and roses; natives of that sign hit you in the romance area. There is a feeling of comfort with a Scorpio because you feel this individual responds. You are romantic and Scorpio is intense; dining together makes for a fascinating combination with great potential.

In your eating-cooking patterns, there is a need for moderation. You enjoy, but realize, Cancer, that too much of a good thing could spoil the broth.

You are fond of soups, foods that require boiling—liquid is important to you. You are not the kind of individual who wants to leave the table hungry. For you, food must provide a feeling of satisfaction. The connotation of well-being combined with prosperity goes with food, where you are concerned. You are the natural cook, chef, mother or father image; you are the protector, and providing a full larder is part of this pattern. Those who accept your dining invitations soon learn to arrive hungry; being your guest assures that appetites will be satisfied.

You are generous, but you like to feel that you protect, guide. Some tend, eventually, to resent this implication. Thus, it is not unusual that people close to you, especially family members, tend to rebel. You must learn to "let go," to loosen the reins; permit others to make suggestions.

Listen, Cancer, I know that you feel you know best, that you want to prepare a meal, for instance, that is wholesome and delicious. But you must not take for granted that others will always agree. An Aries, for example, may want to change some of your methods of preparation. A Virgo might want to dissect and correct. Pour the wine and fill the cup of joy in an amiable manner. Serve it with an attitude of receptivity. Then, almost as if by magic, the compliments will multiply.

You love to experiment, to vary; thus, you will enjoy trying Mike Roy's recipe creations for the other zodiacal signs. You also will vary Mike's directions for your own sign. Food is an adventure for you, an event, an occasion. You enjoy company, especially family members. But you are practical. If someone complains that the soup is too hot, you are likely to retort, "Well, it was cooked on fire."

You are romantic about dining and Scorpio is the ideal companion

You are the natural cook and you love to experiment

You have a good feeling when there are plenty of basics available; you are fond of the staples. Taurus desires the meat and potatoes, the steaks, the roast beefs; you want to be assured that there is flour, butter, salad dressing, wine—you want to be assured that essentials are present and not short.

You adore those who appreciate your efforts in the culinary area. You do not appreciate finicky eaters. A dish pushed aside, unless empty, is taken as an affront. You want to know, "What was wrong?" Perhaps you must learn to be more moderate in serving. Leave them wanting more, as the old show business saying goes. This applies to you, Cancer, especially where the serving of food is concerned.

Cancer does not appreciate finicky eaters

You find Taureans wonderful dinner companions. They share many of your views about food, although you prefer a greater variety and less of the solids. However, for good fun while dining, Taurus fits the bill for you.

With another of your sign, boredom could set in. There are so many areas of agreement that a kind of hypnotic rhythm begins.

You desire family members at your table. The friends are apt to be Taurus natives. The people who have much in common with you where possessions and the desire to build the proverbial nest egg are concerned are likely to be born under Leo. That's how members of that sign affect you; you feel Leo can help you add to what you own. You admire the Leo showmanship and there is mutual attraction. It makes for interesting dining.

Taureans are wonderful dinner companions

Gemini is restless while you are settled; a Gemini is a mystery to you—if you want to prepare one of Mike Roy's provocative dishes, try it with a Gemini.

With Aries, dining conversation often turns to career matters. Your ambitions and standing in the community come to fore with him. There could be some squabbles here. An Aries wants to tell you what should be done, while you reiterate, "Eat, eat, the food is on the table."

You may find that, with you and Virgo, the talk turns to brothers, sisters, and other relatives. The Mercury of Virgo combines with your

Moon significator to produce talk and plans that lack substance. You harmonize with Virgo. But you enjoy food for its own sake but a Virgo is apt to be health or diet conscious. A Virgo wants to discuss what's good for people while you want to discuss what's good.

Libra provides a balance for you and a feeling of security. You do not generally harmonize. But, when breaking bread, there is mutual understanding. You appreciate a Libra because members of this sign flatter, compliment, perceive what you have tried to do with your food creations. A Libra also can enjoy your meal for its own sake.

Jellies and jams appeal to you and you enjoy canning, preserving, and preparing food for the future. It is security that is your great concern; this carries over to the food area. You don't understand people who are flighty about food on the table. You love to dine out, but you usually compare what is served with what you are capable of doing. You might collect menus; it is almost a certainty that you will tell anecdotes about waiters and chefs. You want comfort with your meal, and, above all else, you want to be made to feel "at home."

A Scorpio is for you, again, when a romantic evening is prepared, or when children are included among the guests. A Sagittarian shares your work interests. Natives of Sagittarius also offer health tips, and you may find this more bearable than hints along this line from Virgo. Conversation is easy for you with a Sagittarian. People of this sign have a way of taking journeys of the mind, of perceiving future indications. For you, this relates to security. You enjoy speculating about the future and its needs. Thus, you appreciate being with and dining with Sagittarians. Also, Sagittarius tends to be optimistic and this lends an air of reassurance to the tempting morsels you prepare. Good food and reassurance, for you, represent an unbeatable combination.

Capricorn natives affect that part of your solar horoscope related to partnerships, marriage, legal agreements, public relations. The Saturn of Capricorn combines with your Moon to produce a kind of freshness, originality, independence. You learn about the "outside world" while dining with a Capricorn. Capricorns can teach you, and you admire

A Virgo wants to discuss what's good for people while you want to discuss what's good

these people for their appreciation of time. A well-prepared and well-planned meal is right up your alley, and a Capricorn compliments you for your patience. You have much in common with natives of this sign, and they make excellent dinner companions. The subject of marriage could also arise during meal time with Capricorn.

Other people's money may come up for discussion when you eat with an Aquarius. There is less talk than with Virgo, but the subject is apt to be more basic. You discuss secrets with Aquarius: how much so-and-so left his wife, what the inheritance taxes are apt to leave for the family. These are representative topics for discussion when you dine with an Aquarius.

With Pisces, you enjoy foreign food; natives of this sign inspire you to faraway thoughts, travel, and give you a taste for the exotic. You are likely to express a desire to leave a current situation, and you seek the advice of a Pisces, especially over the dinner table. You harmonize with this sign; Pisces strengthens your basic philosophy. When with Pisces, your dining habits are subject to change—from the basic to the imaginative. You also tend to procrastinate. When your dinner is late, the odds are that you are preparing to dine with a Pisces.

You are fond of reading food features and restaurant columns. You, above all other signs, should cherish Mike Roy's astrological menu creations. Where food is concerned, you are the first to stand up and be counted. If a friend wakes you up for coffee, you are likely to be grateful rather than grumpy. Incidentally your body tends to retain fluids, too.

You are not easily fooled, especially in the food area. You can detect substitutes. You don't take kindly to the host who serves from a famous brand bottle, but has actually poured a cheaper drink. You are not likely to enjoy something that is supposed to be butter when it is not; when it is coffee, you want it freshly brewed. You do not consider money spent for the finest cuts of meat to be an extravagance. Part of your style, your tradition, is the best in food. You find reprehensible the host who is short on food or drink. You expect kitchens to be clean, attractive, inviting.

Capricorn teaches you and Aquarius provides secrets

You are not easily fooled—you can detect substitutes

You tend to "mother" us but you also feed us well. Those who do not appreciate you have not learned the finer points of good living. You can organize for huge parties or groups. You know what you're doing and an extra person or two seldom affects your poise. You are, in plain words, at home in the kitchen. You could be adept at preparing vegetable specialties; you enjoy them, that's a certainty. You are of the "cook-with-butter" school. Chicken must be prepared in an unusual manner to live up to Cancer standards. Prime rib roasts stand high on your list of favorites. The baked potato becomes a gourmet's delight, enough so to please the palate of the most discriminating Idahoan, when you are the cook. For variety, you can delight with escargots. You utilize garnishes in your dishes. Your creations, although not the flaming productions of Leo, show the distinctive mark of a knowing chef. Almonds serve as one of your unusual garnishes.

You are at home in the kitchen

You are sensitive to the moods of others, especially in the dining room. You can make people open up. Seldom is a dinner guest able to contain a grudge, resentment, or frustration; you cause people to confide, confess—and eat.

Cancers are sensitive to the moods of others

You could have a weight problem—when unhappy, you turn to food. Control this tendency with the aid of competent, professional advice. When something in the food line appeals to you, you try it. It makes no difference that you might have eaten a short time ago. Food is a living adventure for you; if it looks good, it is apt to stimulate your appetite. Then you try it, you comment on it, you ask for the recipe. You invite others to join you at a later date when you will try your hand at its preparation. Capricorns love you for this; a Gemini is intrigued by the characteristic. Geminis enjoy having certain relatives for dinner; you want the whole kit and kaboodle—the entire family. You are gregarious when it comes to dining. Leo can talk and express and be the showperson, but Leo isn't as practical as you when it comes to food. Leo eats and makes a display while playing the role of chef. You also eat but are less of a showperson in the kitchen. But the food gets served—and, very likely, at a reasonable time.

Inviting guests for dinner is an occasion, a cause for inner joy

Mike Roy has Cancer rising in his natal chart; his Sun is in that sign. Thus, his creations for you should be a special delight. He knows whereof he speaks where the Cancer menu is concerned. There is anticipation when you or Mike invite guests for dinner; it is an occasion, a cause for inner joy. That's you and cooking: something special and substantial.

Mike Roy on Cancer

Welcome to my House. I've waited to bring you to this point. I've dwelled here a long time under the influence of the friendly Moon.

Cancer is truly a chef's House

If you want to know the truth, I have never really sat down to pen my own thoughts about myself and my relationship with food and wine. And, even as I start now, I wonder what I'll discover about me. Omarr has told me many things about myself, and I believe him. He has said that this is truly a chef's House, coupled with family tradition and the ease and contentment that go with it.

Perhaps you share some of my approach to life. I fully realize that knowledge of one's self is a necessary attribute of maturity. I've always known, pretty well, my position in the world—I've spent many years before the microphone: I was Danny Thomas' first announcer; I was the first announcer on the old soap opera "Road of Life"; I was Martin and Lewis' first announcer; I handled announcing on such shows as "Duffy's Tavern," "Abbott and Costello," "Screen Guild Players," "The Victory Parade of Spotlight Bands," the "Gracie Fields Show," "Club Matinee," and a host of others. I made the transition from radio to television through the medium of a cooking show, because I'd always been a food consultant.

I never knew I was a gourmet until I saw a trade paper television ad saying I was. (The station I was telecasting for took a large ad billing me as "Mike Roy—Every Woman's Gourmet.") Rather, I'd always considered myself a roving bumpkin from up North Dakota way who relished good food, good drink, and the good companionship that goes hand in hand with the two.

Since I was then an "advertised" gourmet, I thought I'd better find out indeed just what I was. After a bit of research I found I hadn't even known how to spell it—it came out "gormet."

The next thing was to discover what it meant. One confiding soul volunteered the information that Poppy Cannon had a gourmet cookbook in paperback form that might help me. Poppy headed up the *Ladies' Home Journal* food department at that time. Certainly, no one enjoyed a more exalted position in the world of cookery than Poppy. But she let me down. All she did was tell me what a gourmet isn't. All of which left me strictly on my own.

I suspect that a gourmet's definition of his or her own character is a deeply personal thing, that the old philosophical saw about "one man's meat being another man's poison" is, indeed, true. There is love involved, which has to do with all humankind, and a need to live on this planet in truth and understanding, and an awareness that our sphere of living is broadened through knowledge. If we are to understand our neighbors in a universe brought closer and closer together through modern communication and transportation, we must know others' intimate habits as we know our own, and give them the same right to their faults and foibles as we have to ours.

Most emphatically, I love the good food and drink that, actually, is found all too seldom in the life of the true gourmet. Oh, there are many fine meals, but the magnificence of perfection is a rare and beautiful thing. The search is the real goal, because I know that, along the way, I'll meet the people who are at ease with the world and I'll drink long and well from the fountains of their knowledge. I'll bask in the warm glow of their genuine good will, knowing all the while that my personal world is enriched by the experience.

Good food and good drink are signposts on the path of history. They join the diplomats at the conference tables of the nations; they brighten the tables where trade tycoons weave their financial tapestry of business; they are present in the peasant hut in a far-off land where shepherds sup; they are present in synagogue, temple, and church; they were present in

The magnificence of perfection is a rare and beautiful thing

the Garden of Eden long ago. These thoughts are with me often when I sip from a sparkling glass and sample a recipe from the kitchen.

So, Cancer, and friends of Cancer, enter "My House"—the Fourth House. Many of you belong here.

The menus I suggest are sometimes spectacular, sometimes historical, but always different and tasty, designed to win your plaudits and excite your palate. (Is it a predestined paradox that I haven't included one crab recipe under the sign of Cancer, the Crab?)

Let's begin.

MENU ONE

Moon Shrimp Curry

Chicken in Cherries Jubilee

Butter Almond Peas

Potatoes Duchèsse

Cloud Cake

I've often served this dish as an entrée for a luncheon. Moon people will love the compliments it brings.

Moon Shrimp Curry
(serves 6)

½ cup mayonnaise
½ cup yogurt
2 drops hot sauce
¼ teaspoon dill weed
½ teaspoon curry powder

1 teaspoon chives
1 teaspoon plain gelatin
2 teaspoons cold water
1½ cups cooked baby shrimp
2 medium heads iceberg lettuce

Remove core of lettuce. Fill center of head with heavy stream of cold water. Turn upside down to drain. Cut lengthwise. Remove heart of lettuce and make a cavity to hold dressing. Blend mayonnaise, yogurt, sauce, dill weed, curry, and chives together. (Let stand for a couple of hours if possible to blend flavors.) Add shrimp when ready to put in lettuce shells, but save several shrimp for garnish.

Note: When stuffing the head of lettuce, sprinkle gelatin on cold water and dissolve over hot water. Add gelatin to curry mixture. Hollow out head from the core end and make a cavity large enough to hold mixture. Stand upright in refrigerator until set. Cut slices crosswise.

Sometimes a recipe becomes noted for its uniquely different taste. Sometimes those to whom it's served gasp at the spectacular nature of the service. Here is a recipe that combines them all.

Chicken in Cherries Jubilee

(serves 6)

6–8	chicken breasts	1	cup chicken broth
½	cup flour	½	cup dry vermouth
1	teaspoon salt	2	cups pitted bing cherries, drained
½	teaspoon pepper		
1	teaspoon paprika	8	orange segments
2	tablespoons butter or margarine	½	cup brandy
		¼	cup cherry juice
2	tablespoons oil		

Dust the chicken breasts with the flour, salt, pepper, and paprika. Brown slowly in the oil and butter. When chicken is nicely browned, add the broth and vermouth. Cover and simmer in 350° oven until the chicken is done and tender, about 20 minutes. Remove cover and add the fruits. Add the brandy, allow to heat through and set aflame. When brandy stops burning, blend in the cherry juice and serve.

Color is a key word in cookery, especially to Cancer. This is a lovely vegetable dish to give eye appeal to the dinner plate of this menu. The deep red of the cherries is garnished with the bright green of the peas.

Butter Almond Peas
(serves 6)

2 (10-ounce) packages frozen
    peas
¼ cup water
1 teaspoon salt

¼ cup (½ stick) butter
⅓ cup slivered almonds

In 2-quart covered saucepan place peas, water, and salt; cover and bring to boil. Stir to break up peas. Bring to boil again, reduce heat to simmer, and cook until just tender, about 6 minutes. Meanwhile, in a small saucepan melt butter; add almonds and sauté until butter and nuts are golden. Stir butter-almond mixture into drained peas.

A different way with so mundane a vegetable as the potato adds the perfect starch to this meal.

Potatoes Duchèsse
(serves 6)

2 pounds potatoes, peeled and
    cut in pieces
2 tablespoons butter
1 teaspoon salt

Pepper to taste
Dash nutmeg
2 egg yolks
2 whole eggs

continued

Cook the potatoes in boiling salted water until soft but not mushy. Drain well and put the potatoes through a sieve or ricer. Work the mixture with a wooden spoon until very smooth. Add butter, salt, pepper, nutmeg, and the 2 whole eggs that have been slightly beaten with the 2 egg yolks. Beat mixture briskly until very fluffy.

Note: These potatoes may be served in alternate ways: dropped from a tablespoon onto a buttered cookie sheet, brushed with melted butter, and browned in a 400° oven about 15 minutes until crispy. Or they may be dropped from a tablespoon into hot, deep fat fryer.

This is another recipe I inherited from my mother and her Scandinavian heritage. You'll agree—it's like eating among the clouds.

Cloud Cake
(serves 8)

2 cups bread or cake crumbs	½ pint whipping cream
1 tablespoon sugar	2 tablespoons sugar
½ cup butter	Red jelly (optional)
2½ cups applesauce	

The crumbs may be from dried French bread, cake, or from a combination of these. Brown the crumbs well in a skillet with butter and sugar. Place the prepared crumbs in a serving dish in alternate layers with the cooled, tart applesauce. Allow to harden in the refrigerator or, if you prefer, place in a well-buttered spring-mold baking pan. Bake 1 hour at 350°. Remove from mold, serve cold with whipped cream sweetened with granulated or brown sugar. Decorate with dabs of red jelly.

MENU TWO

Neptune Lobster and Shrimp Vermouth

Prime Rib Roast in Salt
with Whipped Cream Horseradish Sauce

Sweet and Sour Green Beans

Stuffed Baked Potatoes

Milky Way Key Lime Pie

The constant Cancer urge to be creative lures me to present this menu, built around an ordinary standing rib roast of prime beef. It's hearty fare, and the accompanying dishes make this a delightful meal for Cancer and friends.

I don't know just how it came about, but we succumbed, as a nation, to the shrimp cocktail as an appetizer. It became a culinary status symbol and a sign of affluence when we began with it. I'm the first to admit that seafood does make a lovely first course. But, for heaven's sake (no pun intended), let's be different about it.

Neptune Lobster and Shrimp Vermouth
(serves 6)

3 tablespoons butter
2 tablespoons oil
¾ pound cooked shrimp, peeled and deveined
Juice of 2 lemons

¾ pound lobster tails, cut in bite-size pieces
½ cup vermouth
Salt and pepper

Combine butter and oil and heat in chafing dish. Add seafood and cook about 5 minutes; then add vermouth and salt and pepper and cook 5 minutes longer. Add lemon juice and allow guests to help themselves with toothpicks.

As I promised at the head of this menu, we will have a most different way with prime rib. If you like beef well done, this is the only way I know to keep it juicy. It's spectacular when you bring it to the table and crack the salt cover from it.

Prime Rib Roast in Salt
with Whipped Cream Horseradish Sauce
(Allow a full pound, bone in, per serving)

Prime rib roast
   (one pound per serving)
Several pounds of salt

Water
Freshly cracked pepper
Garlic (optional)

Use coarse or water softener salt, enough to form a 1½-inch layer of salt around the rib, roughly about 10 pounds of salt for a 5-pound roast. Place salt in a large bowl and for each 5 pounds of salt add about ¼ cup of water. Toss the salt so that a little water has touched each grain of salt. Rub the roast with fresh cracked pepper and a little garlic if you desire. To facilitate handling, use a large sheet of heavy-duty aluminum foil. Spread a good 1½-inch layer of salt on the foil and set the roast on the middle of it. Fold the sides of the foil up so there is a 1½-inch space between the foil and the roast. Fill this area with more salt. Insert a meat thermometer in the thickest part of the meat, being careful that the thermometer does not touch the bone. Cover the top with a 1½-inch layer of salt. Place in a 450° oven or place over a hot coals (barbecue) about an inch away. A 4- to 5-pound roast reaches medium rare in about an hour. A 6-pound roast in about 1 hour, 20 minutes. The salt will form a heavy crust, and you may need a hammer to crack it free. (No, it does not make the meat too salty.)

continued

Whipped Cream Horseradish Sauce

½ cup whipping cream
    (whipped)
½ teaspoon seasoned salt

¼ cup horseradish
    Few drops Tabasco

Let horseradish stand in a sieve or strainer and allow it to thoroughly drain. Fold the horseradish into the whipped cream along with other ingredients.

Our entrée of prime rib fairly cries out for a green vegetable and a baked potato. Here are the two recipes I've chosen, as a son of Cancer, to go with the delectable beef.

Sweet and Sour Green Beans
(serves 6–8)

2 packages frozen green beans:
    French-style, cut up,
    or whole
¾ teaspoon Ac'cent
4 slices bacon

1⁄16 teaspoon pepper
2 tablespoons finely chopped
    onion
1 tablespoon vinegar
¼ teaspoon sugar

Cook beans according to package directions. Drain; sprinkle with Ac'cent. While beans are cooking, fry bacon until crisp. Remove from skillet; crumble. Add onion to bacon drippings and cook until tender but not brown. Stir in vinegar, sugar, pepper, and crumbled bacon; pour over hot cooked beans.

Stuffed Baked Potatoes
(Allow 1 potato per serving)

Baking potatoes
Sour cream
Chopped chives
Chopped parsley

Celery salt or seasoned salt
Cheddar cheese in ½-inch
   wide strips

Bake the potatoes until done. Cut top quarter of potato off lengthwise. Scoop out the meat of the potato from the top. Break up until the potato meat is in small chunks rather than mashed. Add rest of ingredients, except the cheese, and blend well. Return mixture to potato jackets and garnish with a couple of strips of the cheese. Dust with paprika. Preparation may be done far in advance and kept in the refrigerator. To serve, place in a very hot oven until potato is thoroughly heated and cheese is melted.

To top off this rich and bountiful menu we need a light dessert.

Milky Way Key Lime Pie

1 (3-ounce) package lime gelatin	1 teaspoon aromatic bitters (Angostura)
1 cup boiling water	
½ cup lime juice	2 egg whites
1–2 teaspoons grated lime rind	Green food coloring (optional)
2 egg yolks, well beaten	
1⅓ cups (14-ounce can) sweetened condensed milk	1 (9-inch) pie shell, baked and cooled

Dissolve gelatin in boiling water. Add juice and rind; then slowly add to egg yolks, stirring constantly. Add milk and bitters. Beat egg whites until stiff peaks form. Fold into gelatin mixture with a few drops of food coloring. Pour into pie shell. Chill until firm. Garnish with prepared whipped topping, if desired.

MENU THREE

Escargots in Red Wine

Shrimp-Stuffed Sole à la Saturn

Orange and Lemon Beets, Terra

Old Country Soda Bread

Lazy Rum Cake

I'm enjoying this brief sojourn in the Fourth House. Perhaps it's because it's my House, and it seems so clear that the things Omarr has said about all of us under the sign of Cancer are true. He once told me that I was the kind of person who could live with apple crates for furniture so long as the larder was full. But he pointed out that this was not a selfish characteristic, that Cancer not only wants to be well fed—he or she wants everybody around them well fed. I'll drink to that, and come up with another Cancer menu.

Only the brave and the daring will venture into the realm of the lowly garden snail. But, having sampled them the first time, Cancer won't be able to get enough of them. You'll find this recipe that calls for a red wine broth interesting.

Escargots in Red Wine
(serves 6)

2 cans snails (18 snails per can)	½ teaspoon red pepper *or* ¼ teaspoon Tabasco
3½ cups dry red wine	2 cloves
2 onions, chopped fine	½ bay leaf
3 cloves garlic	¼ teaspoon thyme

Bring wine, onions, and garlic to a boil. Add the red pepper, chopped fine, the rest of the seasonings, and the snails. Cover and simmer for 30 minutes. Serve in a soup tureen or individual bowls with finger slices of sourdough French bread.

It's altogether fitting that this dish be named after Saturn. The rolled sole fillets surround the shrimp like the rings about the planet. The flavors blend to perfection, which will gladden Cancer's heart.

Shrimp-Stuffed Sole à la Saturn

(serves 6)

6 fillets of sole	½ cup fine, soft bread crumbs
10 shrimp, cooked, shelled, deveined, and chopped	1 egg, beaten
¼ pound mushrooms, chopped	¼ teaspoon salt
½ cup chopped onion	Pepper to taste
¼ cup olive oil	1 lemon, thinly sliced
½ cup chopped celery	1 cup white wine

Cook mushrooms and onion slowly in oil until onion is transparent. Add to shrimp with minced celery, bread crumbs, and egg. Season with salt and pepper. Divide into six parts; place in center of fillets, roll up, and secure with toothpicks. Cut 6 large squares of aluminum foil; brush inside of each with oil. Place rolled-up fillets in center. Lay lemon slice on each; spoon wine over each and fold foil over to seal. Bake in 350° oven 35 minutes. Serve fish in foil, folding back edges.

The tangy acid nature of the citrus, combined with beets, makes this a perfect vegetable to go along with the sole.

Orange and Lemon Beets, Terra
(serves 6)

3 pounds fresh beets or 2 cans (about 1 pound)	1½ tablespoons cornstarch Salt and pepper to taste
¼ cup lemon juice	¼ cup butter
½ cup orange juice	½ teaspoon grated orange peel
2 tablespoons wine vinegar	½ teaspoon grated lemon peel
2 tablespoons honey	

Prepare, cook, drain, and slice fresh beets in ¼-inch slices. If canned sliced beets are used, drain well. In a saucepan, combine fruit juices, vinegar, honey, cornstarch, and seasonings. Stir until smooth. Bring to boil, stirring; continue cooking until sauce is thick and clear. Add beets, butter, and fruit peel. Heat to serving temperature.

I have always liked this old recipe for soda bread as the starch item in a menu. It's probably better now than it was ages ago because of the refinements in our flours. Its tartness makes it an ideal companion for the fish.

Old Country Soda Bread

3 cups white flour	1 teaspoon baking soda
2 cups wheat flour	4 ounces butter
1 teaspoon salt	2 tablespoons honey
2 heaping teaspoons baking powder	½ cup buttermilk
	2 eggs, beaten

Melt butter and honey together over fire. When hot, combine with buttermilk. Mix all dry ingredients together. Add to beaten buttermilk and egg mixture and knead. Cut dough in quarters and place on floured cookie sheet or pizza pan. Bake in 325° oven for 55 minutes.

The piquant flavor of rum in this cake will cleanse Cancer's palate of the last seafood vestige.

Lazy Rum Cake

1 package yellow or chocolate
   cake mix, already prepared
   and baked *or* any
   leftover cake
   Rum

Apricot jam
Cherry jam
Whipped cream *or*
   buttercream frosting
Chopped nuts

Ideally this is a recipe for using leftover cake, but if you should just want to make a rum cake, use one package each of yellow and chocolate cake mixes. Prepare according to directions on box, adding a tablespoon of rum to each of the batters.

When cake layers are done, remove from pans and chill (if you desire, you can cut layers in half horizontally). Place a chocolate layer on a cake plate and sprinkle with rum. Spread thinly with a layer of apricot jam. Place a yellow (or white) layer on top of the apricot jam, sprinkle with rum, and then spread thinly with cherry jam (whipped cream may be used for one of these layers). Repeat procedure until you have a 4-layer (or 8-layer) cake. Sprinkle whole cake with more rum. Frost with whipped cream or your favorite buttercream icing. Sprinkle with chopped nuts and refrigerate at least 8 hours.

When using leftover cake, just improvise with the above recipe . . . it's great fun.

So, Cancer, eat, drink, and be merry. Regretfully I leave this House. But I look forward to Leo. It's Omarr's sign.

Leo Menu One

pages 125–128

Neptune's Delight Seafood
Steak Beaujolais
Spinach and Bacon Salad
*Crusty Bread and Camembert Cheese
*Fresh Pears and Apples

Leo Menu Two

pages 129–137

Caesar Salad
Sunny Fondue
Stuffed Zucchini
*French Bread
Pale Moon Lemon Pie

Leo Menu Three

pages 138–141

Bean Sprout Salad
Moon Tide Cioppino
*Sourdough French Bread
Sour Cream Raisin Pie

Recipe not included

Fifth House

July 23–August 22

LEO

Sydney Omarr on Leo

Colorful Leo is the natural Fifth House of the zodiac, a Fire sign associated with the back and heart, and perhaps the most creative of the zodiacal group. Leo can be flamboyant in the kitchen. If born under this sign, you prefer flaming dishes, flambés; you cook, not only with fire, but with showmanship. You have an individual touch and cook with a flourish.

For you, food and sex can be closely associated. Where Scorpio prefers secrets, aphrodisiacs, the hidden, and the mysterious, you light the lights and bring on a "production." It is open and blaring romance for you. You associate fine dinners with fine relationships. Food is allied with conversation. Dining, for you, is an evening of light and stars and music—it is the glow of the creative urge.

For you, the food must be good, the best—the service, too—and you are an excellent host or hostess. The term "fit for a king" applies to you and the way you treat your guests. If you are a king, then indeed your guests are royalty.

You are the life of any gathering, and you like your food hot

Leo is associated with the Sun, the Sun with heat and the giving of life. You are the life of any gathering, and you like your food hot. The impromptu sandwich has its place in the scheme of things, but your style runs more to champagne and a flaming centerpiece. Your presence, your efforts and creations accent youth and vigor. What you serve, you serve with pride: a creation, something unique, specially prepared for an occasion.

Some consider you extravagant, but where the good things in life are concerned, including food, the sky is the limit. You do, at times, have a tendency to take the play away from guests. On a more mature level, you bring out the interests, talents of others.

You make wonderful use of herbs and spices. One of your favorites is likely to be dill. Your desserts are on the showy, sensational side. Your appetizers are substantial, but still hors d'oeuvres compared to the rather quick snacks emphasized by Gemini. Your main course is a production, and Mike Roy in his Fifth House tour will be of immeasurable aid to you along all of these Leo lines.

You are exuberant when guests are happy

A festival, a feast—that's your trademark, and this applies whether the gathering be a large or a small one. You are exuberant when guests are happy. Just as Cancer is sensitive to moods, you are aware of them and wish to mold and direct them. Although you appear forward, open, giving, fun-loving, your happiness actually depends on how happy and relaxed your guests are. In this sense, you are extremely idealistic. Every meal a banquet—that's your style. And every guest a member of the royal court. That's your aim.

Food, for you, is sensuous, related to the creative; a life force. For you, food is also entertainment. It is fun, something you look forward to, so much so that you'll have a workout prior to eating so that your appetite is sharp and perceptive. You are prone to flattery—flattery and food. You can fall in love with an individual who flatters and feeds you well.

The flaming dish, the hot sauce, the glamour, the appearance, the show—all are part of dinner for you, a microcosm of life itself. Of all people, you will pay the closest attention to Mike Roy's menus, especially those created specifically for you. You are intrigued by acts of creation, especially those connected with the life force, which food can represent for you.

You can become almost as passionate about your favorite dishes as you can about a man or a woman. You are intense where service and preparation are concerned: nothing careless, nothing halfway. All the way for Leo and in a grand style.

You are intense where service and preparation are concerned

To love someone, you also have to enjoy dining with that person. Although Leo is a fixed sign, you crave variety. Not so with Taurus, a fixed sign that can become set in ways of eating and serving and in the choosing of menus. Taurus is basically fixed, while you are fixed in the sense that your patterns are ever-changing in the food area. It is predictable that you will choose "something different." Variety is the spice of life for you—and variety in food choice is an essential.

Nothing gives you greater pleasure than having celebrities as guests—or people with special, unique talents, even eccentricities. You like the gathering of the clan—but for you the "clan" is this person who sings, that one who writes poems, the other one who is capable of brilliance with sleight of hand. You are fond of children and pets—you delight in preparing something special for a child, and a pet is always invited to partake of the repast.

Variety is the spice of life for Leos

You can put across a business deal over dinner. This is because you are at your best then—you exude a kind of personal magnetism that inspires confidence. It is not the food per se, but the idea of companionship. You don't like to eat alone and, quite often, you will skip a meal for lack of company. One of my favorite Leos was the late Aldous Huxley. Dining with him was a pleasure; he was articulate with the spoken as well as the written word. And that's the way it is with Leo—a pleasure when it comes to food—cooking, eating, the savoring of ideas along with dishes. Leo has a zest for living. Famous Leo personalities exemplifying this include Leo Durocher, Mae West, and Arlene Dahl.

You are gregarious, generous, and idealistic. Most of all, you appreciate. That's why people like to cook for you. You enjoy. You respond. You are willing to try, to experiment, to be different, to be as formal or informal as the occasion demands. You want food to be either spicy or subtle. You want it to be definite, to have a style and an identity. It is almost as if you expected each dish to stand up and take a bow!

Gemini makes a fine companion at the table for you. Gemini is responsive and witty; he or she talks, gestures, and is animated. This, so to speak, is your cup of tea. Sagittarians affect that part of your chart having to do with romance; dining with a Sagittarian could be a prelude to an affair of the heart. With another Leo, your tendency is to back off—each wants to let the other have center stage. With a Scorpio, you get a feeling of security, but the talk is apt to be of basic matters, and the food could become of secondary importance.

You particularly enjoy foreign dishes when with Aries. You affect Aries in a physical manner. While your responses may be idealistic, Aries has more amorous notions when breaking bread with you. You have fun with an Aquarius and the discussion could turn to partnerships and marriage.

Listen, Leo: You enjoy a break between courses, a breather, a stroll. Anticipation is important to you, and you delight in surprise. "What's next?" is your favorite question. "Surprise me" is apt to be your answer to the query of what you might want for an appetizer, entrée, or dessert.

You are not always at ease when dining with Taurus. You want to appear pleased, but the Taurus taste is apt to be a bit mundane to you. With a Cancer, it's always a good evening for you. You look forward to a tête-à-tête over special dishes with natives of this sign. A Cancer gains money-making ideas from you. And you are intrigued by the numerous subjects Cancer seems to have become expert at discussing. That, at least, is your view of this sign. Cancer affects that part of your chart associated with organizations, groups, the mysterious, the inner sanctum. A

You enjoy foreign dishes when with Aries

Dining with a Sagittarian could be a prelude to an affair of the heart

Cancer is the companion for you at a public banquet. Your horizons expand. You trade recipes; you compare notes on chefs, restaurants, waiters, and other matters.

A Virgo is an ideal dining companion when you are in the mood to discuss possessions and how to increase income potential. But Virgo could displease you with a tendency to lecture about how much to drink—or not to drink. Virgo, being health conscious, could curb your desire for rich foods. A Virgo expresses pleasure at your knowledge of food, but may draw the line at trying something that could be a threat to digestion. As for you, all stops are out; try it, enjoy it, savor it, live today—that's your motto, especially at the table.

A Libra stimulates your ideas, as well as your appetite. You talk a great deal about relatives when dining with a Libra. You enjoy Libra company—you revere the Libra delicacy and strive to create dishes that will meet with Libra approval. The Libra taste is actually a bit too delicate to suit you, but the enjoyment gained from being with a Libra more than makes up for lack of spice and wine.

With a Capricorn, your differences of opinion seem to be aired while dining. Oddly, when dining out with Capricorn you change your mind often at the last minute when it comes to ordering. Capricorn tends to become argumentative when sharing food with you. You find pleasure in discussing your work with a Capricorn over dinner, however. You find a Capricorn a challenge because natives of that sign seem to be "holding back." You may ply Capricorn with food and spirits in an effort to make him or her "open up."

Dining with Pisces often causes the conversation to turn to inheritance, legacies, and longevity and how to attain it. Pisces exhibits a tendency to be psychic, ultra sensitive, and you find this charming. The Neptune of Pisces with your Sun significator makes for intriguing dinner talk. It may involve extrasensory perception, sex, the occult, or how to handle big money transactions. Just as you find Libra tastes delicate, you may feel a Pisces is too sensitive about experimenting in the food and beverage department. But you love a mystery and Pisceans tend to awe you with their secretive natures.

Virgo is an ideal dining companion when in the mood to discuss increasing your income potential

One of your great pleasures is serving guests for a special occasion, a purpose. Perhaps a television program of unique appeal is to be aired later in the evening. Maybe a special new record will be played. Perhaps it's someone's birthday. Food, for you, provides incentive and brings together people who care about art and love and life. That's Leo, the party giver, the marvelous host, the creative spark.

Leo: the party giver, the marvelous host, the creative spark

Some claim you are overly dramatic. Some disagree with your views on food and how you prepare and serve it. But few, if any, ever forget your efforts as a chef. This will be doubly certain when you begin utilizing Mike Roy's Leo creations. And, being a Leo, you will want to partake of other zodiacal menus, from Aries to Pisces, around the circle, with variations and added specialties for fun on Full, New, and Quarter Moon nights.

You are a noble chef. You charm your guests, and your utensils seem to have a "ring" to them. You have a special touch: the egg becomes an omelet; a slice of bacon is transformed into a unique, appetizing garnish. Shrimp, crab, and oysters are magically turned into Neptune's Delight (see page 126). Steak is a delicacy, and potatoes become not a staple, but a piquant vision of color, with the yellow of butter, the brown of the skin, the white of the meat, the green of parsley—all is a blend, a veritable symphony aimed at stimulating the music of the appetite. Ah! That, indeed, is the Fifth House: creation, life, eating not to live, but eating because one is alive.

You enjoy the basics as well as the specialties

Lest there be a misunderstanding, let me make it clear that you are no "Fancy Dan." You enjoy the basics as well as the specialties. Bread and cheese and a bottle of beer can give pleasure just as caviar and champagne can. It is the mood, the atmosphere that count with you. You are expert at creating moods: you are the actor, the writer, the painter. You are able to bring others to your height. Seldom does one dining with you fail to respond to a challenge of elegance.

Change, travel, variety, and romance—these are your special ingredients. And this atmosphere is reflected at your table in your menus. Sagittarians appear to bring these qualities out in you in the food area. To a lesser extent, this is also true of Gemini. Both signs possess an abundance of intellectual curiosity, and it is this quality that inspires you to create special dishes, provoke questions, assertions, and opinions.

Listen, Leo: I don't want to make you appear too grand. You are, above all else, very human. Your moods can be up and down, similar to the Cancer native. You are generous, but you can make others feel uncomfortable when generosity turns to extravagance. You can serve too much of a good thing. Domestic wines or beers can be excellent, but, for you, the imports seem to dominate. A dessert doesn't have to be "on fire" to be good, but you seem to think there must always be heat and light. You can also be stubborn, and, at those times, there is more heat than light thrown on subjects under discussion.

Your appetite tends to increase as you consume food. Everything is large as life: the way you serve and eat, the way you make people comfortable or otherwise. Maybe what I'm trying to say, Leo, is that you could do with the ingredient of moderation. Some get an inferiority complex around you; others secretly feel you are ostentatious.

You are attractive to the opposite sex and this arouses envy. Your attentions, given in the spirit of being the fine host or hostess, can be misconstrued. That's the way of life, Leo. Better you learn it here and now than the hard way.

Because people accept your dinner invitations does not mean they must accept your views. I know your intentions are good, but you must tread lightly. Not all are equipped to accept your rich tastes. That's why I have urged Mike Roy to create some "simple" Leo dishes along with the more typical. You could do with a change of pace.

The Leo chef, the Leo menu—grand and gorgeous—those are but two adjectives that apply to your efforts in the field of gastronomy. The blinding light of the Sun becomes the flaming climax to a dinner fit for a king, which is where it's at with Leo at the head of the table, under the chef's hat.

Salud!

For you Leo, everything is large as life

You are attractive to the opposite sex and this arouses envy

Mike Roy on Leo

The fare here literally flames with heat. Even as it is difficult to deny the rays of the Sun, so is it almost impossible to avoid the contagious personality "rays" of your flamboyant personality. Sydney Omarr is a Leo.

I have been Omarr's guest at dinner. I think you'll be interested in his menu and the recipes for the dishes he served.

It is almost impossible to avoid your contagious personality

He served the same menu to Poppy Cannon. Poppy wrote about it later in her column in *Ladies' Home Journal*. She thought Omarr had some interesting theories about cooks and cooking, as well as the stars. She also pointed out that Omarr is true to his horoscope; he loves good food, loves to cook for a few chosen friends, and does it with flair, drama, and more than a touch of impatience. He gets, said Poppy, fine effects—and fast. The following menus are what Omarr served.

MENU ONE

Neptune's Delight Seafood

Steak Beaujolais

Spinach and Bacon Salad

Camembert Cheese

Crusty Bread

Fresh Pears and Apples

To begin, Omarr served Neptune's Delight in a large silver moon of a dish, set on a copper stand blazoned with the signs of the zodiac, naturally.

Neptune's Delight Seafood
(serves 6)

1 pound shrimp, cleaned, deveined, and cut in bite-size pieces
1 (6-ounce) package frozen crab meat
2 dozen oysters *or* 1 large can oysters, drained
4 tablespoons butter

Juice of a lemon (about 3 tablespoons)
½ cup dry white table wine *or* dry vermouth
Salt and pepper to taste
Dash of Tabasco
Dill seed

In a chafing dish or a large skillet, melt the butter, add shrimp and crab meat, and sauté about 3 minutes. Add the oysters and cook 2 minutes longer. Add the lemon juice, the wine, salt and pepper, and Tabasco. Sprinkle liberally with dill seed.

I once knew a man who didn't like steak. Nothing ever happened to him.... Omarr's recipe is one to tempt the palate of every Leo and their guests. (Omarr says he likes to use a shell steak. The name for this varies in different parts of the country. In the West it is called a New York steak with the flat side of the "T" bone left on. In the East it is known as a sirloin stripper. In the Midwest, South, and Southwest it is probably called a Kansas City sirloin.)

Steak Beaujolais
(allow about 12 ounces per serving)

	Large steak about 2 inches thick	2	teaspoons dijon mustard
3–4	tablespoons butter	1	tablespoon brandy or bourbon
½	cup beaujolais		*Marinade*

Marinade

2	tablespoons olive oil	½	teaspoon garlic salt
1	tablespoon wine vinegar	1	teaspoon fresh cracked pepper

Cover steak with marinade and let stand a couple of hours at room temperature. Broil "blue," as the French say—meaning very rare. Slice ¾ inch thick on the bias. At the table, place butter in blazer pan of chafing dish and, when it is hot, sauté the sliced steak about 30 seconds on a side. Remove the steak to a hot platter and keep warm. Add to the drippings in the pan the remaining ingredients. Allow to sizzle a couple of minutes and pour blazing hot over steak.

Salads seem to run in cycles. At the close of World War II we were Caesar salad mad. This was followed in turn by Roquefort or blue cheese salad and green goddess salad. Finally everyone began serving spinach and bacon salad. I enjoyed Omarr's version, and I think you will, too.

Spinach and Bacon Salad
(serves 6)

2 bunches fresh spinach, washed and cut in bite-size pieces

4 strips bacon

4 tablespoons white vinegar

½ teaspoon sugar

½ teaspoon mustard

½ teaspoon pepper

Place spinach in a well-chilled bowl. Cut the bacon into bits and fry until clear but not overdone. Pour off all but 4 tablespoons of the bacon fat. Add white vinegar, sugar, mustard, and pepper. Bring to boil while stirring and pour while warm over the spinach. Toss and serve.

MENU TWO

Caesar Salad

Sunny Fondue

Stuffed Zucchini

Hot French Bread

Pale Moon Lemon Pie

Among other characteristics, Leo has a sense of fun. Here is a menu designed to provide the setting for great food sport—a sort of a do-it-yourself dinner party that brings everybody into the act.

Doubtless, there are many versions of the famous Caesar salad. Here is my way of making it. Leo can be a real showperson if he or she gathers the ingredients together on a tray and makes the salad at the table. Make the French dressing ahead of time so the flavors have a chance to mingle.

Caesar Salad
(serves 6–8)

1 clove garlic
½ cup olive oil or salad oil
2 large heads romaine, washed, torn, chilled
Salt and fresh cracked pepper to taste
2 coddled eggs (simmered in water to cover 1 minute)
Juice of 1 large lemon
8 anchovy fillets, chopped
½ teaspoon Worcestershire
½ teaspoon dry mustard
½ cup grated Parmesan cheese
½ cup *French dressing* (see page 131)
2 cups *croutons* (see page 131)

Crush the garlic in a small bowl and pour the oil over it and let stand 2 or 3 hours. Place the chilled romaine in a large salad bowl, sprinkle with salt and fresh cracked pepper. Pour the garlic oil over all and toss until every leaf is glossy. Break the eggs over the salad, squeeze over the lemon juice, add all the other ingredients, the croutons last, and toss well.

continued

French Dressing

1	teaspoon dijon mustard	1½	teaspoons crushed black
1½	teaspoons seasoned salt		pepper
1	teaspoon Worcestershire	¼	cup wine vinegar
1	teaspoon paprika	¼	cup tomato juice
2	teaspoons onion powder	½	cup olive oil
2	teaspoons parsley	1	cup vegetable oil
1½	teaspoons sugar		

Combine all ingredients in jar. Cover and shake well.

Croutons

Sourdough French bread, cut into cubes	Mashed garlic
	Butter

To make the croutons, rub sourdough French bread cubes with fresh, mashed garlic and sauté in bubbling butter until they are brown and crisp.

This exciting dish is prepared by cooking raw beef cubes in hot oil, then dipping the meat in specially prepared sauces. It's a fun type of meal to serve as guests gather about the fondue pot and prepare their own portion, spicing with the sauces of their choice.

Sunny Fondue

(serves 6)

2 pounds beef tenderloin,
   cut in ¾-inch cubes

2 cups good vegetable or
   peanut oil

The meat should be nicely arranged on a platter with lettuce, lemon wedges, and so forth for garnish. The oil should be preheated at the range to 400°. The oil or fondue pot can then be transferred to the chafing dish burner and the heat maintained.

To Serve: Provide each guest with a salad plate, fondue fork, and regular fork. Place platter of beef cubes, salt shaker, pepper mill, sauces, and accompaniments on table near fondue pan.

To Cook and Eat: Each guest helps themself to sauces and so on, which is put on a salad plate. The guest then spears a cube of beef with the fondue fork and dips it into the hot oil, cooking it to his or her liking. Since the fondue fork will be very hot, the guest transfers the meat to the regular fork and dips it into a sauce and eats it.

Some Suggestions: Boneless strips of chicken breast or shelled and deveined shrimp may be used. Also fresh vegetables may be added.

Suggested Accompaniments:

hot and mild mustards
mixed pickles
chutney

pickled onions
olives

Some Sauces: Blue Cheese, Whipped Cream Horseradish, Western Herb, Curry, Blender Hollandaise, and Blender Béarnaise. (Recipes on pages 133 to 134.)

continued

Blue Cheese Sauce

1 cup mayonnaise
¼ cup crumbled blue cheese

1 teaspoon lemon juice
1 tablespoon chopped parsley

Combine ingredients and chill.

Whipped Cream Horseradish Sauce

From the Fourth House menu, see page 107.

Western Herb Sauce

2 tablespoons finely
    chopped onion
¼ cup olive oil
¼ cup melted butter

¼ cup steak sauce
¼ cup chopped parsley
2 tablespoons chopped chives
    Salt and pepper to taste

Sauté the onion in the oil and butter until lightly browned. Add remaining ingredients and heat. Serve warm.

Curry Sauce

1 cup sour cream
½ cup mayonnaise
1 tablespoon chopped parsley
2 teaspoons curry powder

1 teaspoon lemon juice
½ teaspoon Worcestershire
¼ teaspoon salt

Combine ingredients and chill.

continued

Blender Hollandaise Sauce

½ cup butter or margarine
3 egg yolks
2 tablespoons lemon juice

¼ teaspoon salt
½ teaspoon prepared mustard
Dash white pepper

Heat butter in small saucepan until bubbly but not browned. Put egg yolks, lemon juice, salt, mustard, and white pepper in blender container; cover and run on low speed about 5 seconds. While continuing to run on same speed, add butter in a slow, steady stream until blades are covered; turn to high speed and add remaining butter slowly. Makes about 1 cup. This can also be served on cooked vegetables, fish, or eggs Benedict.

Blender Béarnaise Sauce

2 tablespoons white wine
1 tablespoon tarragon vinegar
2 teaspoons dried tarragon
2 teaspoons chopped shallots
   or onion

¼ teaspoon freshly ground
   pepper
¼ teaspoon sugar
¾ cup *blender hollandaise
   sauce* (see above)

Put all ingredients except hollandaise sauce in small saucepan. Cook rapidly over high heat until most of the liquid is gone. Pour mixture into hollandaise sauce in blender container; cover and run on high speed for 6 seconds. Makes about 1 cup. This sauce is very good with steak.

Since this menu provides a make-it-yourself entrée, you'll want a bit of substance to go along with it. This vegetable dish is almost a casserole in itself.

Stuffed Zucchini
(serves 6)

3	large zucchini	½	teaspoon salt
¼	pound ground beef	¼	teaspoon pepper
1	tablespoon olive oil	⅛	teaspoon thyme
½	onion, chopped	⅛	teaspoon oregano
½	cup soft bread crumbs	1	tablespoon dry white wine
2	tablespoons Parmesan cheese		or lemon juice

Slice the zucchini lengthwise and scoop out the core, leaving about a ⅛-inch rim of meat in the skin. Set the zucchini boats in a shallow pan in ¼ inch of water and bake in a 350° oven about 15 minutes.

In a pan, sauté the meat and drain off any fat. Add the olive oil, the onion, the scooped-out zucchini, which has been diced, and cook until the onions and zucchini are soft. Add the balance of the ingredients (from bread crumbs to white wine). Now stuff the zucchini boats with the mixture, top with additional Parmesan cheese, and bake in a 350° oven for 25 minutes. This recipe also works beautifully with eggplant.

Something cool and refreshing should follow to bring your Leo dinner party to a smooth conclusion. This dessert is light and soothing.

Pale Moon Lemon Pie

Crust

3 cups flour
1 teaspoon salt
1 teaspoon sugar
1 cup shortening

1 teaspoon vinegar
1 egg
5 tablespoons water

Mix dry ingredients together, and cut in shortening. Add vinegar and egg to water, mix thoroughly, and gradually add to the ingredients. Roll out and place on pie pan. Bake at 325° until done, about 15 minutes. Makes two pie crusts.

Lemon Filling

1 cup sugar
1¼ cups water
1 tablespoon butter
¼ cup cornstarch
3 tablespoons cold water

3 egg yolks
2 tablespoons milk
6 tablespoons lemon juice
1 teaspoon grated lemon peel

Combine sugar, water, and butter; heat until sugar dissolves. Add cornstarch blended with cold water. Cook slowly until clear, about 8 minutes. Slowly add egg yolks, beaten with milk and bring to boiling. Gradually add lemon juice and peel. Pour into cool, baked shell.

continued

Meringue

3 egg whites   6 tablespoons sugar
1 teaspoon lemon juice

Beat egg whites stiff but not dry. Add sugar gradually. Add lemon juice.
Spread over filling, sealing to edges of pastry. Brown in slow oven 325°
for 15–20 minutes.

MENU THREE

Bean Sprout Salad

Moon Tide Cioppino

Hot Sourdough French Bread

Sour Cream Raisin Pie

By this time you must know for sure that this Fifth House is an entertaining house, conducive to parties and people. Here is another menu that gives Leo a chance to give everyone a good time.

☆ ⭐ ☆

I'm particularly proud and fond of the salad on this menu. Proud because I created it, fond because it has a uniquely different flavor. It comes under a category (strictly personal) that I have come to call "Now how in hell did I think of that?"

Bean Sprout Salad
(serves 8–10)

1 pound bean sprouts
3 tablespoons soy sauce
3 tablespoons sherry wine
3 tablespoons lime juice
⅔ cup salad oil
3 tablespoons minced
   green onions

1 teaspoon grated fresh ginger
1 teaspoon Ac'cent
½ teaspoon curry powder
½ cup toasted slivered
   almonds

Make dressing from all ingredients (except bean sprouts and almonds) and pour over raw bean sprouts. Mix well. Top with almonds. Allow to stand a few hours before serving.

☆ ⭐ ☆

I'd like to have that zodiac bowl Omarr used for his Neptune's Delight. It would make a wonderful vessel in which to serve my favorite seafood stew. I'd have it piping hot surrounded by great slabs of hot sourdough French bread dripping with butter—so I could dunk the bread in the zesty sauce. I don't care what your zodiac sign is. You've got to love this dish as much as Leo will enjoy serving it to you.

Moon Tide Cioppino
(serves 10–12)

2 medium onions, chopped
1 tablespoon chopped garlic
1 tablespoon chopped parsley
1 tablespoon chopped celery
1 tablespoon chopped green pepper
½ cup olive oil
2 cups solid pack tomatoes
1 cup tomato sauce
2 tablespoons salt
⅛ teaspoon pepper
1 small sprig fresh basil or
1 teaspoon dried basil

1 tablespoon paprika
½ cup sherry *or* dry white wine
4 cups water
2 large fresh crabs, cracked
1½ pounds raw shrimp, in shells
2 pounds fresh clams, washed thoroughly and in shells
2 pounds rock cod, sea bass, *or* swordfish, cut into bite-size pieces

Sauté onions, garlic, parsley, celery, and green pepper in oil until golden brown. Add tomatoes and tomato sauce, salt, pepper, basil, paprika, and wine. Cook 15 minutes over low heat. Add water; bring to a boil. Add cracked crabs and shrimp and clams in their shells. Cook slowly for 1 hour, adding a little more water or wine, if necessary. Add raw fish; cook 20 minutes longer and serve.

Something tart and sweet and just a bit warm to top off this Leo menu.

Sour Cream Raisin Pie

Pastry for 1-crust pie	½ teaspoon nutmeg
2 eggs	¼ teaspoon cloves
¾ cup sugar	1 cup sour cream
¼ teaspoon salt	1 cup seeded raisins
1 teaspoon cinnamon	

Prepare pastry and line an 8-inch pie pan. Refrigerate it while you make the filling. Beat the eggs lightly, then stir in sugar, salt, cinnamon, nutmeg, and cloves. Stir in sour cream and raisins and pour into chilled pastry shell. Bake in a preheated 450° oven for 10 minutes, then reduce heat to 350°, and bake 30 minutes longer or until a knife inserted in center comes out dry. Serve warm.

 # Virgo Menu One

pages 153–158

Mercury Waldorf Mold
Veal Piccata
Starlight Broccoli
Virgo Bran Muffins
Texas Pie

 # Virgo Menu Two

pages 159–164

Cobb Salad
Sixth House Lobster
Half Moon Turnips
Potato Fritters
Pancakes Mercury

 # Virgo Menu Three

pages 165–169

Scallops au Parmesan
Fruit-Stuffed Roast Turkey
Heavenly Cream-Top Salad
Oat Cakes
Moon Mousse

Sixth House
August 23–September 22

VIRGO

Sydney Omarr on Virgo

The Sixth House is Virgo, with Mercury. This is an Earth sign, and it is practical. Born under Virgo, you are health conscious; you take delight, for example, in preparing decaffeinated coffee so well that guests don't know the difference. Cooking, for you, is associated with health, well-being. You want food to nourish as well as provide pleasure. You are not particularly fond of substitutes, but you won't hesitate if the aim is better health.

Now, listen: You are not a stick in the mud, but you have the realization that there is a tomorrow. With food, as in other areas, you tend to stick to rules and regulations. You are meticulous—cleanliness is important and so is order. You plan; you are considerate. You give us joy at the table, and, whether we like it or not, you also strive to protect our health. You are aware of vitamins, mineral content, and because of this you take pains to make food attractive. You avoid excess; your concept of fine food goes hand in hand with nourishment and energy. That's basically the way it is with you in the kitchen.

Your concept of fine food goes hand in hand with nourishment and energy

You are fastidious; you measure with care, in precise amounts. You can be a perfectionist. Carried to extremes, this trait can rob food of pleasure, but, if balanced and the ingredient of common sense is not lacking, it can be constructive. You believe in maintaining patterns: times to eat, play, and sleep. Your menus can be exciting, as Mike Roy will prove in his Sixth House contribution.

Because you strive to make what you serve interesting, your meals are versatile. True, you maintain patterns, but you are ingenious, inventive. You are analytical. You desire reasons; this adds up to intellectual curiosity and helps make you an excellent chef. The arrangement of plates, napkins, flowers is important to you. Your efforts are especially appreciated by Cancers; they make wonderful dinner companions for Virgo. You are practical about food, but not in the sense that Taurus is; you are not meat and potatoes. You are practical in the sense that you feel food is energy, that it can serve to provide strength necessary to finish a task, accomplish a goal.

Cancers make wonderful dinner companions

Your preparation of salads can be the talk of the town. Vegetables are never more attractive than when you prepare them. With Mike Roy's hints, you will be unbeatable. Virgo is crisp, and so is the lettuce you serve. If a beverage is to be cold, it will be with you in charge. If a dish is to be hot, there will be plenty of heat. Nothing lukewarm; your tastes are definite.

Food, for you, is expansive—you are not afraid to experiment, especially with foreign specialties. That's why you delight in exchanging recipes with a Sagittarius. A Virgo and Sagittarius may not agree in other areas, but where food is concerned the two signs add up to compatibility. Discussions of menus and health between a Sagittarian and a

Virgo can be stimulating. The Sagittarian provides you with a sense of security, especially when dining at home. For Sagittarius, you represent a goal. You can inspire these people to attain the heights. This is often done while talking or planning a good meal.

Obviously, you like some health foods. You can probably give us a dissertation on carrots and eyesight, salads and roughage, and so on.

Your harmonious companions are Cancer, Scorpio, Taurus, and Capricorns. With another Virgo, disagreements could arise about whether coffee is harmful, whether the soft drinks contain too much of this or that—another Virgo, unless you are very tactful, adds up to spirited argument, which is not pleasant when consuming food.

Harmonious companions are Cancer, Scorpio, Taurus, and Capricorns

You have a lot in common with Gemini, both signs boasting active, quick Mercury as a planetary significator. But where Gemini is impatient, you can be methodical. Indeed, there is almost always a method to your madness. You know what you're doing, especially in the culinary area. Being served by you is a delight to the eye; Libra appreciates this aspect. But where a Libra may prefer the more exotic dishes, you prefer the more traditional.

Very few can top you when it comes to shining dinnerware, lovely designs, a blending of color combinations. Capricorn guests delight in this, building your ego with compliments. Where romance and dining are concerned, Capricorn and Virgo make a fine combination. A Capricorn affects the romance section of your chart. Both Virgo and Capricorn subjects appreciate small, neat portions of food, but Capricorn inspires you to larger portions where romantic meanderings are concerned. To Capricorn, you represent an ideal. For you, the earthiness of Capricorn can stimulate your appetite in more ways than one.

Where romance and dining are concerned, you make a fine combination with Capricorn

The Saturn of Capricorn and your Mercury ruler combine to form a mutual admiration society in the kitchen. From there, much else can develop. With a Libra, you usually discuss finances over dinner. A Libra inspires you to vary your routine. You are more likely to be adventurous in dining habits when breaking bread with Libra.

You enjoy baking your own bread. You also gain great pleasure in helping others plan for special occasions: you outline menus, suggest special desserts, a unique salad—and you usually cannot overcome the temptation to toss in a health hint or two.

You are more conscious of what you eat than most persons. You study the effects of food and drink. Aquarians express a desire to know more in this area; they make a wonderful audience for you. Thus, you gain pleasure in preparing food for an Aquarius. Natives of this sign pry for your secrets and you are only too anxious to reveal them. Of all the signs you are the one most likely to maintain a diet, and, perhaps, where weight enters the picture, the least likely to need one. You are active enough to maintain a trim figure; you burn up energy and fat is not likely to accumulate.

You are conscious of what you eat

A Scorpio stimulates you to discuss ideas and matters such as relatives and neighborhoods. The Pluto of Scorpio combines with your Mercury causing a broadening of horizons. There is, with Scorpio, usually a community of interests for you. Ideas are exchanged. Over dinner you agree to discard outmoded methods, but the inspiration can be short-lived. The two signs, Virgo and Scorpio, are harmonious, but when dining together, the two of you tend to eat quickly. There is impatience to finish and begin making notes. Check Scorpio's Eighth House menus; you will be amused and inspired to "take a chance" on some dishes that, to you, may appear to be completely devoid of your beloved practicality. Scorpio, you see, desires oysters (for one example) not necessarily for their nutritional value, but for their fabled aphrodisiac powers.

Check Scorpio's Eighth House menus

When I talked to Sid Caesar about astrology, he displayed typical Virgo qualities by relating the importance of exercise and diet for the purpose of shedding excess pounds. Virgo is conscious of food, but, again, always in a practical way: for weight gain or loss, for nutrition, for energy, for vitamins and diet in the main. Ben Gazzara, it seems to me, also typifies Virgo: slim appearance, but plenty of energy. Donald O'Connor is another born under your sign.

You are a discriminating shopper. The vegetables must be fresh, the foods natural—you may haunt health food stores, and raw milk and honey could be on your permanent must-purchase list. You are an inveterate note taker. It is not unlikely that you keep track of the food you eat and serve. That's part of your pattern; you love order, patterns, organization.

You enjoy snacks; Gemini likes this kind of appetizer. You both prefer something a bit substantial between meals. You would rather have many small portions than one big, heavy meal. Food is a health requirement for you. Nibbling a raw carrot, drinking a glass of milk, consuming slices of cheese—these are almost necessities because you are always working, planning, expending energy. For the Virgo with a weight problem, nibbling becomes a fascinating challenge. A Virgo needs snacks, but these must be worked in to fit with the diet. Obviously, Virgo, food occupies much of your time: the thinking and organizing as opposed to the actual cooking, which would be exemplified by Cancer.

Virgos are prominent in the food industry, but mainly in supervisory capacities. Many years ago an astrological organization researched categories related to food. Virgos were included in those who "moved" food off shelves, sold food, enticed people to purchase and consume. But the Chefs de Cuisine Association of California, in lining up chefs and their astrological signs, found that the Virgo group contained fewer than the others. Food serves a practical purpose for you—you may sell it and advertise it, but you are not exactly wild about being confined to the kitchen. The other Mercury sign, Gemini, tends to be impatient, walking into the living room, chatting, and you, too, are apt to become impatient where actual cooking is concerned. That's another reason you're so strong on salads.

With Pisces, dining becomes a challenge because your tastes are apt to run along opposite lines. A Piscean dreams while you analyze. Conversation with Pisces, over dinner, could turn to marriage, partnership, legal papers. Aries may inspire you to consider the handling of huge sums of money. You may get ideas on how to invest. A dinner, featuring Virgo, Pisces, and Aries people, could conclude with the drawing up of a contract calling for you to direct a special campaign—with Pisces and Aries probably putting up the cash.

You would rather have many small portions than one big, heavy meal

Atmosphere is important to you; order and quiet, as opposed to the raucous and busy—that's your speed. Reservations, when dining out, are a contract to you. You expect to be seated "on time." Otherwise, what occurs afterwards, whatever the menu, could produce an unsettled feeling. You want to please, to serve, to instruct. You almost automatically expect that others are that way, too, and when people are late, in seating you or arriving as your guests, you tend to be more upset than members of the other zodiacal groups.

You are a fine food critic. You could excel in that area of journalism, being a restaurant critic. You scrutinize menus. Mike Roy has his job cut out for him in creating the Virgo dishes. Yet, your basic desire is to please. For you, food provides not only nourishment, but brings you together with persons of like persuasions. Intellectual companionship is part of the meal—without it, taste goes flat. Taurus and Scorpio individuals are mainstays in this area. Sagittarius may be the base, the security, and Leo, the mystery, often causing your eyes to pop with displays of extravagance, talk of social reforms, and consumption of huge amounts of food and drink.

People like to impress you. In turn, you desire to be of service. You can generate enthusiasm in others, and this spills over to the area of cuisine. You encourage others to plan intelligently, to avoid waste, to be aware of nutritional values. Your ideas sparkle; you can take the ordinary and dress it up, make it appealing. You may not be the greatest cook in the world, but you could be one of the most appealing.

You get great fun out of perplexed, surprised expressions on the faces of guests. You could cover main dishes in a manner to make them appear to be something else; you are an expert at camouflaging. Now you see it, now you don't; what seems to be this, turns out to be that— and usually it's good for you, too! Leo inspires you in this area. A Leo feels you have a secret that can be commercialized. You feel a Leo is a romantic who, if he or she would shake off the shackles, would dazzle the world. Obviously, Virgo and Leo make unusual dining companions:

Reservations, when dining out, are a contract to you: you expect to be seated "on time"

You can take the ordinary and dress it up, make it appealing

each feels the other knows something along special, secret lines. Often, adding to the atmosphere of mystery, the meetings are clandestine.

You affect a Libra much in the manner that a Leo affects you. Natives of Libra seem to think that you are holding back, that you really have more to say and serve. Cancer people delight you; they give you the feeling that your hopes and wishes can come true. And they appreciate your culinary efforts. You learn from Cancer about food preparation and special menus. Cancer is a great ally when you're planning a dinner party. A Cancer puts your friends at ease, gets them ready to enjoy your chef's delights.

Gemini gets you going on career, ambitions. Dining with a Gemini turns into a talk fest. The talk centers on what can be done to capitalize on your talent, assets, or how to improve your income. A Gemini may discuss your culinary efforts with relatives or neighbors, and could enhance your standing in the community. Pleasing a Gemini at the table could result in a promotion for you. Your prestige rises when Gemini leaves the table satisfied.

You are a good listener and possess a sense of humor. These are valuable assets in the dining room as well as elsewhere. You serve beautifully and you make people feel comfortable. Even if some of your dishes lack the showmanship of Leo, they are substantial, pretty to look at—and tasty. You ask intriguing, intelligent questions; this is flattering to guests, allowing them to display their expertise. Dining with you can be a joy, even if the dishes are not as "solid" as they might be with Taurus wearing the chef's hat.

Dining with a Virgo means one may leave the table wanting more, but also realizing that what was served was wholesome and out of the ordinary. Weight watchers appreciate you, and others are intrigued. And who could ask for too much more?

Cancer is a great ally when you're planning a dinner party

Mike Roy on Virgo

Of all the houses, Virgo's is said to be the most meticulous. If Omarr doesn't mind and with your permission, I'll refer to Virgo as "she." I have the best reason in the universe for this: I'm an authority on Virgo. You see, I have been living with a Virgo in the honorable state of matrimony for over twenty years. Yet sometimes I think I don't know a damn thing about her.

Omarr has her pegged all right. She certainly is most orderly in her thought, her cleanliness, and her attention to health. I suppose Omarr would think it entirely appropriate that she is a nurse. He also says that Virgo is most aware of what she puts in her mouth. And when she feeds you, you might get a lecture on food and health as an accompaniment to the meal.

Of all the houses, Virgo's is said to be the most meticulous

I must say one thing for my author-colleague, Sydney Omarr: his descriptions of people under their respective signs are exactingly accurate. The heavens, the stars, and the planets have been ethereally elusive to me in the past. To be completely honest, I suppose I had some doubt earlier as to the authenticity of the subject. But I know my sign and I've watched for it in Omarr's column. Before I undertook this cooperative effort with my friend Omarr, I did a small survey. (I have long used surveys as means of finding out what my television watchers and radio listeners think about the products I advertise.) I have never knowingly taken a sponsor I didn't have full faith in.

The more I researched the field of astrology, the more convinced I became of its authenticity. The fact that I knew Omarr helped because, if ever there was a creatively searching mind, it is his. I was completely aware of his utter honesty and integrity. In short, I knew he was incapable of speaking anything but the truth. Of the 200 people I talked with about astrology, 120 were avid followers, and 190 knew their zodiacal sign and read a daily astrology column. Some 160 expressed the thought that there was a good deal of legitimacy to it.

I got my first real understanding from one of Omarr's books, *My World of Astrology* (Fleet Publishing Corporation, New York, 1965). These facts and many conferences with Omarr convinced me. I am now a student and I intend to follow through the rest of my life.

Omarr's comments on Virgo exactly describe my wife, Alison. She is a continuous note and memo maker. She shops most carefully. She dreams up wonderful parties, not only for us, but for our friends.

My Virgo wife loves salads—molded gelatins or leafy greens. This taste fits her sign. (I like salads, too. But before I came to California, I thought that lettuce was only something you fed to rabbits.) A word of caution on salads: Be careful with the garlic. Sometimes, I think, we use too much of it—in fact, so much so that we've become a nation of "lymphogarliacs."

Virgo loves salads and baking bread

Virgo likes to bake bread, too. Once upon a cookbook-writing many years ago, I waxed nostalgic over bread. My personal association with this most basic of foods is very close. I can remember coming home from school through the blustery wind-driven snow to the warmth of our North Dakota kitchen. I wore glasses, even as a boy, and when I first opened the door, the warm air from the kitchen's woodburning stove would hit the lenses; the glasses would steam over and my world would be lost in the moisture. But suddenly from out of the depths of that great iron monster of a stove would come an aroma—an aroma that to this day defies description and even now seems to come from the innards of my typewriter as I set these words on paper. I'm speaking of the wonderful, salty, buttery, pungent, yeasty aroma of freshly baking bread.

When the bread was done, my mother would pile the steaming loaves on the table and cover them oh so gently with a clean dish towel. Once in a while, she would let me slice a thick heel from one of the loaves, which I would douse with sweet fresh butter our farmer friend brought each week. And I would pile it high with homemade chokecherry jam. I don't ever expect to taste anything like that again.

Nowadays only a few hobbyists bake true homemade bread. We do make the so-called quick breads. I think we've lost something.

All of which brings us to menu-making for Virgo. The items will have to include gelatins, salads, and breads, which makes them fairly consistent with a balanced diet. But the items will also have to be tasty and appealing.

MENU ONE

Mercury Waldorf Mold

Veal Piccata

Starlight Broccoli

Virgo Bran Muffins

Texas Pie

Salad-lover Virgo should enjoy this fruit and vegetable gelatin dish. As a matter of fact, I've served it as a ladies' luncheon entrée.

Mercury Waldorf Mold
(serves 6 as a side salad or 4 as an entrée)

1 (3-ounce) package gelatin: lemon, mixed fruit, or orange-pineapple	2 teaspoons vinegar
	¾ cup finely diced celery*
	1 cup diced red apples
½ teaspoon salt	¼ cup chopped walnuts
1 cup boiling water	¼ cup mayonnaise (optional)
¾ cup cold water	*Cheese balls*

Dissolve gelatin and salt in boiling water. Add cold water and vinegar. Chill until very thick but not set. Fold in celery, apples, walnuts, and mayonnaise. Spoon into individual molds or a 1-quart mold. Chill until firm. Unmold and serve with cheese balls if desired.

*Or use ¾-cup halved seeded red grapes.

Cheese Balls

1 (3-ounce) package cream cheese   Chopped nuts

To make cheese balls, shape cream cheese into 12 small balls. Roll in chopped nuts.

⚹ 🕊 ⚹

A classic Italian entrée provides a piquant dish to excite the palate of Virgo. By the way, if you can't obtain the prosciutto Italian ham, boiled ham will do nicely.

Veal Piccata

(serves 4)

1 pound veal cutlet, cut very thin (Italian style) into 3-inch pieces

¼ cup butter

2 tablespoons flour

½ teaspoon salt

½ teaspoon pepper

⅛ pound prosciutto ham, sliced and slivered

2 tablespoons stock

1 tablespoon butter

1 teaspoon chopped parsley

2 teaspoons lemon juice

Heat butter in frying pan. Dredge meat in flour, salt, and pepper; place in frying pan and cook over high flame, 2 minutes on each side. Remove meat. Place prosciutto in frying pan, cook 3 minutes, remove from pan and place over veal. Add stock, butter, and parsley to pan gravy; scrape pan well. Cook 2 minutes and add lemon juice. Pour sauce over meat and serve immediately.

Here's another of my favorite recipes for my Virgo wife. It's a great vegetable, but it does nicely as a supper menu entrée, too.

Starlight Broccoli
(serves 4)

1½ pounds broccoli	1 tablespoon capers
1 (3-ounce) package smoked sliced turkey	1 tablespoon sherry wine (optional)
1 (11-ounce) can Cheddar cheese soup	⅓ cup sour cream
1½ cups milk	Bits of Macadamia nuts or almonds
1 teaspoon Worcestershire	

Prepare sauce first: remove two slices of turkey and cut into small pieces. Combine soup, milk, Worcestershire, capers, and chopped turkey. Bring just to a boil and simmer 10 minutes. Add sour cream and wine. Hold in double boiler if serving soon or reheat in double boiler.

Prepare broccoli by washing, trimming stalk end, and slitting lengthwise into flowerets. Put in boiling salted water and cook 8–10 minutes until just tender. Drain. Wrap each stalk with slice of turkey. Put on platter or vegetable dish and pour hot sauce over the broccoli. Garnish with nuts.

In keeping with Virgo's love of bread making, these most healthful bran muffins will soothe her (or his) appetite. She'll also be able to tell her guests to eat several because "they're good for you."

Virgo Bran Muffins
(makes about 22 muffins, 2-inches each)

2 cups all-purpose or whole-grain flour	2 cups buttermilk
1½ cups bran	1 beaten egg
2 tablespoons sugar	½ cup molasses
¼ teaspoon salt	2–4 tablespoons melted butter
1¼ teaspoons soda	1 cup nut meats
1–2 tablespoons grated orange rind (optional)	½ cup mashed bananas (optional)

Combine flour, bran, sugar, salt, soda, and orange rind; stir well. Beat together buttermilk, egg, molasses, and melted butter. Combine the dry and the liquid ingredients with a few swift strokes. Fold in the nut meats before the dry ingredients are entirely moist (½ cup mashed bananas may be added at this time, if desired). Bake at 350° for about 25 minutes.

This is one of those "crazy" pies. There are several of them that have been around since the early settlers' times. It was a great winter pie when there wasn't much fresh fruit. It's sometimes called a sugar cream pie.

Texas Pie

1 unbaked pie shell	1½ cups half-and-half *or* whole milk
½ cup flour	
¾ cup sugar	1 teaspoon vanilla
Dash of salt	Cinnamon to taste

Put all ingredients directly into the unbaked pie shell. Use fingers to blend well gently; dot with butter, and sprinkle on a little nutmeg. Bake at 375° until set like custard. It will have a slightly brown crust on top.

MENU TWO

Cobb Salad

Sixth House Lobster

Half Moon Turnips

Potato Fritters

Pancakes Mercury

A Virgo will probably call this a rich menu, loaded with calories. And then he or she—or you—will rationalize and say that everyone should let go once in a while.

Our salad is brimming with all the healthy vegetables so important to your ideas about food, if you're a Virgo. This is a rather famous salad, featured on the menu of the famed Brown Derby in Hollywood. Many a star has eaten it as an entrée. It was created by Derby owner Bob Cobb.

Cobb Salad
(serves 4)

½ head romaine, minced fine	2 peeled tomatoes, chopped fine
½ head lettuce, minced fine	2 avocados, finely chopped
4 strips crisp bacon, finely chopped	1 pound Swiss cheese, finely chopped
½ pound Roquefort cheese, crumbled	¼ cup parsley
	French dressing (see page 131)

All greens must be finely chopped and arranged in the bottom of a salad bowl. The other ingredients should be arranged in rows across the top of the greens, so that when the salad is brought to the table the viewer is greeted with the multi-colored rows of bacon, cheese, and so on. At the table add French dressing as needed and toss all together.

The French would call this distinctly different lobster entrée "magnifique."
Virgo would feature it as a centerpiece for a happy dinner party.

Sixth House Lobster
(serves 4)

4 lobster tails	1 cup milk
½ cup sliced fresh mushrooms	¼ cup sherry
2 tablespoons diced green pepper	1 teaspoon paprika
3 tablespoons butter	2 tablespoons diced pimiento
2 tablespoons flour	Grated cheese
	Fresh bread crumbs

Boil lobsters in salted water until red and tender, about 12 minutes. Remove and let cool. Hold lobster tails, top side up, and using kitchen shears, cut an oval opening in top of shell. Remove all meat and cube. Cook mushrooms and green pepper in butter until tender. Blend in flour. Add milk. Cook and stir until mixture thickens and boils. Add sherry, paprika, and salt to taste. Add lobster and pimiento. Pile filling into shells. Top with cheese and crumbs. Bake at 375° for 15 minutes.

Of all the vegetables, the ill-considered turnip gets the least attention. Don't discount the turnip. Properly prepared, it's good.

Half Moon Turnips
(serves 4)

1 pound turnips	½ teaspoon dried sweet basil
1 cup boiling water	leaves, crushed
1 slice of onion	Dash of pepper and salt
¼ teaspoon salt	Dash of sugar
2 tablespoons butter or	1 teaspoon lemon juice
margarine	Parsley and paprika

Peel turnips and cut in half. Add turnips and onion slice to salted boiling water. Cook with cover off until tender, about 15 minutes. Melt butter and add seasonings. Pour over drained turnips. Garnish with chopped parsley and paprika.

Here is one of my favorite potato recipes to go handsomely with the lobster.

Potato Fritters
(serves 4)

8 small Idaho potatoes, peeled   2 egg yolks
   and cut in pieces   2 egg whites, beaten stiff
3 tablespoons heavy cream   Salt and pepper to taste

Boil potatoes until tender and drain very dry. Pass them through a food mill or strainer. Beat in the cream and egg yolks. Season with salt and plenty of pepper. Fold in the beaten egg whites. Form the mixture into little balls and drop in deep fat (385°), frying until golden brown. Drain on paper and serve very hot.

I have emphasized several times Virgo's need of, and love for, bread. The dessert is probably an unusual place to find it. But pancakes are considered a type of quick bread. This is probably one of the most exotic pancake recipes you'll ever find.

Pancakes Mercury
(serves 4)

1 cup enriched flour, sifted	Melted butter
3 teaspoons baking powder	Brown sugar
1 teaspoon sugar	1 *marshmallow mix*
¼ teaspoon salt	1 pint fresh strawberries,
1 cup milk	halved or quartered, and
¼ cup light cream	sweetened *or* 1½ ounce
2 tablespoons melted butter	package frozen
1 slightly beaten egg	

Sift together dry ingredients. Add milk, cream, and butter to egg and mix well; add dry ingredients and beat until smooth. Bake 6-inch cakes on lightly greased, hot griddle. Brush melted butter on serving plate; sprinkle with brown sugar. Then spread each cake with melted butter and sprinkle with brown sugar. Stack 6 or more cakes. Cover with marshmallow mix; broil till golden on top. Heat strawberries to boiling point. Cut stack of pancakes in wedges and serve with hot strawberries.

Marshmallow Mix

½ cup sugar	2 tablespoons water
2 stiffly beaten egg whites	1 teaspoon soft butter

Combine sugar and water in small saucepan; cook until sugar dissolves. Pour over egg whites, beating constantly. Beat to stiff peaks. Cool slightly. Beat in butter.

MENU THREE

Scallops au Parmesan

Fruit-Stuffed Roast Turkey

Heavenly Cream-Top Salad

Oat Cakes

Moon Mousse

Omarr had thought that I might have trouble finding menus for Virgo here, but I never doubted for a minute my ability to meet this challenge. After all, I've been meeting it for over twenty years and I'm still going strong. My wife Alison likes this menu and she's one helluva Virgo.

A light and deliciously stimulating appetizer starts this menu.

Scallops au Parmesan
(serves 4–6)

1 pound scallops	½ teaspoon garlic salt
¼ cup chablis	¼ cup grated Parmesan cheese
¼ cup butter	

Pour chablis over scallops and marinate for 2 hours. Melt butter in chafing dish or skillet; add scallops and wine. Sprinkle with garlic salt and simmer 10 to 15 minutes. Just before serving, sprinkle cheese over the dish. Serve hot.

The past several years have seen the turkey emerge from its role as a holiday bird to an "anytime is turkey time" status. Virgos should like it because it's a good meat buy. We like to do a half a bird at a time and here's how.

Fruit-Stuffed Roast Turkey
(allow 1 pound per serving)

8–10   pound turkey, cut in half
        lengthwise; reserve other
        half by freezing
        Large piece aluminum foil

Juice of ½ lemon
Salt and pepper
Seasoned salt
Soft butter

Fruit Dressing

1   package prepared corn
    bread stuffing mix
¼   pound butter or margarine
1   large onion, chopped
½   cup chopped celery
¼   cup chopped parsley
½   teaspoon powdered thyme

½   teaspoon sweet basil
2   fresh peaches, peeled, sliced
6   fresh plums, pitted, sliced
¼   cup dry white wine
½   cup chicken stock
    (use more if you like a
    moist stuffing)

Rub the turkey cavity and skin with lemon juice; sprinkle well with seasoned salt, salt, and pepper. Rub more butter into the skin. Butter the aluminum foil well.

Prepare stuffing as follows: sauté the onion and celery until soft and transparent. Add to the stuffing mix along with the other ingredients and toss lightly. Pile the stuffing on the buttered aluminum foil. Place the turkey on top of the mix, cavity side down. Curl the edges of the foil about an inch up the sides of the turkey. Place foil-turkey in large open pan. Roast in 325° oven about three hours.

Let's face it, the turkey is sometimes rather rich and heavy. Right here we need a refreshingly different taste. This salad should give it to us.

Heavenly Cream-Top Salad
(serves 4–6)

1 (3-ounce) package gelatin:
    lemon or orange-pineapple
¼ teaspoon salt
1 cup boiling water
1 tablespoon lemon juice

¼ cup sour cream
½ cup cold water
½ cup shredded carrots
1 can (8¾ ounces) pineapple
    tidbits

Dissolve gelatin and salt in boiling water. Add lemon juice. To ½ cup gelatin, add sour cream and ¼ cup cold water. Pour into 1½ quart mold; chill until set, but not firm. Mix remaining gelatin and cold water, carrots, and pineapple. Chill until slightly thickened. Pour into mold. Chill until firm. Unmold.

And here is the bread to appease Virgo's appetite.

Oat Cakes

2½ cups oatmeal
 1 teaspoon salt
 3 tablespoons sugar

¼ cup (½ stick) butter, melted
 1 cup sour cream

Mix together oatmeal, salt, and sugar. Blend in butter and sour cream. Chill until dough is easy to handle, then shape into 1-inch balls. Place on baking sheet and flatten with bottom of glass dipped in melted butter, then oatmeal. Bake 20–25 minutes in 375° oven. Serve with honey, assorted jams.

"Smooth," "rich," and "satisfying" are the words to describe this Virgo dessert.

Moon Mousse
(serves 6–8)

16 marshmallows
⅓ cup heavy cream

⅔ cup heavy cream, whipped
1½ ounces Kahlúa

Heat the marshmallows in ⅓ cup cream until softened, fluffy, and smooth. Stir in Kahlúa liqueur. Whip ⅔ cup of cream and fold into marshmallow mixture. Freeze in refrigerator tray without stirring.

Libra Menu One

pages 180–185

Jupiter Gazpacho
Venus Chicken with Grapes and Almonds
Roquefort Chive French Bread
Hot Fruited Cabbage
Orange Torte

Libra Menu Two

pages 186–190

Cheesy Tomato Pie
Salmon Steaks Neptune with Grapefruit
Spinach Pudding
Foil Bread
Lemon Velvet Pie

Libra Menu Three

pages 191–195

Saturn Tomato Rings
Seventh House Stroganoff
Saucy Carrots
Frozen Orange Margo

Seventh House
September 23–October 22

LIBRA

Sydney Omarr on Libra

The Seventh House features the areas of marriage, partnerships, how the public looks at you, and how you relate to challenges. The Seventh House is Libra, associated with Venus. Born under this sign, you are sensitive to the needs of others, an advocate of justice, a lover of beauty, an individual in the sense that you are not bound by conventions if they restrict freedom or civil rights. Libra is an Air sign: justice, beauty, art, sensitivity—these are some of the key words that apply to your sign.

Your touch is delicate; in foods, you prefer subtle flavor. French restaurants appeal to you. You prefer your meat sliced thin—the veal sautéed quickly, perhaps with dill and lemon juice and white wine. Nothing heavy or clumsy for you, Libra. Flavor for Libra is always subtle as opposed to direct.

Food, for you, is variety. You do not want any one dish to dominate so that your mood for other creations on the menu is dampened. You are an investigator, trying and experimenting. Snails suit you fine, butter sauces appeal, too. Libra is symbolized by the scales, and you seek balance—some of this, a little of that—everything piquant, stimulating to the palate. Pleasant and tart, that's the order of the day where your menu is concerned. Lively and charming, that's the tone of your dinner setting. That's Libra, not pungent, but instead tart, delectable, fine.

Flavor is always subtle and pleasant, dinner is lively, charming

Charm is a key word. A continental setting accented by elegance is your cup of tea. Libra signifies beauty; the setting, with you at the helm, is bound to be symmetrical.

Good taste, to you, involves more than the actual savoring of food. It involves the setting, the portions, the appearance. Food, for you, should be fresh—the frozen variety is apt (no pun intended) to leave you cold. In this way, you can be regal, impractical—fresh food, fresh-cut flowers. That's the way it is with Venus-Libra: a striving for naturalness, beauty, without covering, camouflage, or pretense. Asparagus should be its own true green: squash, yellow; peppers, a bright, flaming red; eggplant, purple—the colors ringing true. And the caviar, black and salty—no pretense. Elegance aplenty, but no falsity: cauliflower, white; corn, yellow—delicacy, sensitivity, an awareness of what is natural and what is synthetic are important.

You would rather leave the table hungry than have oversized portions. In this way, you are quite different from another Venus-dominated sign, Taurus. Natives of Taurus are practical, value-conscious; they like plenty to eat, and the design, the arrangement, can be secondary. Not so with you, Libra. Appearance, setting, high artistic standards—these are of paramount importance with you where food, as well as other areas of life, are considered.

You delight in delicacies

You delight in delicacies: the light, the fluffy, the dishes that require balance and careful preparation. Thus, eggs Benedict and soufflés are but two examples of dishes that would appeal to Libra. You are a connoisseur of wine, art, specialties. Aroma, visual appeal—these blend with taste to make a complete balance for you.

Listen, Libra: You are extremely diplomatic. You are a self-critic. But you are kind when it comes to the culinary efforts of others. You will, in effect, grin and bear it. You would do almost anything to avoid bruised feelings. Thus, you often endure a meal, and the host or hostess seems to sense that you are less than pleased. This being the case, it would be better for you to speak up, to be decisive, to offer constructive criticism. Then, others can learn from your experience and intelligently plan a meal at which you are to be a guest.

Haute cuisine, that's a key for a Libra—delicacy and elegance are parts of your menu. The decor adds to the mood, the balance. Food is not the production for you that it might be with Leo. But food is beauty; you feast with your eyes as well as your stomach. Food, for you, is a work of art. It involves color and rhythm, everything in its place and nothing ostentatious.

Your tastes are refined. You are discriminating where companions and restaurants enter the picture. Leos delight you. These people appreciate your liking for imported delicacies. In turn, you admire the Leo flair for drama. Leo and Libra, when dining, make a captivating picture, exemplifying the "beautiful people." A Leo fires your desire for the good things in life, including fancy foods. You are basically shrewd about food. You will take the time-honored recipe over the synthetic, the innovation. In this way, you could be considered conservative. In this area, tradition (maybe even pomp and ceremony), you prefer the company of Capricorn. Natives of Capricorn enhance your sense of security. Capricorn appreciates your home, decorations, art objects. A Capricorn looks up to you, and this causes you to rise to even greater heights. The two signs, Libra and Capricorn, have that much in common: reverence for tradition, preference for the real over imitation, especially in food and dining. In other fields, the two signs are not considered compatible. A Leo is fun and has hopes and dreams. A Capricorn evaluates the silver service and the quality of the meal. In a final choice, you might surprise yourself by selecting Capricorn.

You are a connoisseur of wine, art, specialties

Leos delight you and you admire their flair for drama

You ask questions about food, menus, recipes. You become knowledgeable and, thus, when you pay a compliment, it is appreciated. If you don't like something, you are apt to say nothing, but when a dish is appreciated, you do speak up.

Dining with another Libra brings joy. Two Libras stimulate each other's sense of humor. Laughter rings when Libra gets together with Libra. This means a great deal to you: the *bon mots*, the conversation, the awareness of what is occurring in faraway places.

Dining with another Libra brings joy, laughter

Aries people attract you, but much in the manner that opposites attract opposites. The Mars of Aries and your Venus significator combine to produce warmth, magnetism. There is a physical awareness of an Aries. Dining with someone of this Mars-ruled sign finds you, very often, transfixed and quiet. You admire the vitality of Aries, if not always the taste in food and setting. Aries is a bit too direct for you. The subtle approach goes by the board with Aries, and you miss it. Aries raises his or her voice and the melody no longer lingers. Yet, you are drawn and dinner becomes an event rather than a mere occurrence when it is shared with an Aries.

With a Taurus, dining becomes more of a practical affair than you desire. The Taurus menu does not particularly appeal to you, but it would be good for a change of pace. Almost invariably the subjects of costs, property, basic values, and even inheritance come up when you break bread with Taurus. Those born under Taurus are apt to regard you as a finicky eater, but they admire you and delight in telling anecdotes about this or that special dish of yours that they enjoyed.

You care about appearance and the way your guests react

You care very much about appearance: the way food looks, the impression your dinner companion conveys. You are Venus-oriented, so public relations and the way people react to your food and manner of dress are of great importance. You enjoy dressing for dinner. There is a shimmer to dinnerware, the napkins contain simple, subtle colors and designs. Graceful dining is what you crave. With an Aquarius, you feel you have found the right companion in this sense. Natives of Aquarius attract you physically, much in the manner that an Aries does. But an Aquarius is more apt to suit your requirements for a subtle approach, noble manners, and courtly bearing. An Aquarius does not respond this way to all signs, but with you, Libra, Aquarians fill the bill and are likely to live up to your expectations. This is a creative combination, this blending of Libra and Aquarius. Together, you make a striking couple when dining out. In preparing food, you are inventive, yet basic—an Aquarius-Libra effort in food is admirable. You would enjoy testing some of the Aquarian Eleventh House menus.

With Pisces, dining could become more routine than to your liking. You make appointments with Pisces to discuss work, mutual interests affecting your job and associates. A Piscean is sensitive while you are delicate. Together, you both make concessions. Your meals are apt to be heartier than usual. You are more conscious of health and vitamin content of food. With a Pisces you discuss diet and weight, work and recreation, and the need for exercise.

You harmonize with Leo, Sagittarius, Gemini, and Aquarius

You harmonize with Leo, Sagittarius, Gemini, and Aquarius people, but Capricorn natives have a special "dining appeal" for you. Taurus intrigues because you envy what, at times, appears to be a voracious appetite on the part of these natives. Gemini inspires you to try different, foreign foods. Your taste for the exotic is enhanced with a Gemini. Discussions often turn to literature, writing, advertising, publishing.

Cancer natives fire your ambitions. Leos delight you and make you laugh. With Leo, you often feel that your dreams can become realities. Where Virgo enters the picture, you find mystery, but also have a tendency to feel confined. Planning menus for a number of persons is a problem; Virgo helps in this area. However, you get the distinct (if erroneous) impression that Virgo's taste is pedestrian. Another Libra makes an ideal, if impractical, dining companion. Scorpio amuses you but the conversation soon turns to possessions, income, money. Scorpio reveals secret recipes. You enjoy this display of confidence. However, you tend to feel that a Scorpio is too intense; you prefer light banter and beauty rather than substance in dining.

Cancer natives fire your ambitions

With Sagittarius, the talk is of relatives, brothers, and sisters. The combination of Libra and Sagittarius is compatible, and you particularly enjoy trying new places to dine, places that require a short journey when with a Sagittarian. Natives of this sign could tire you because their forces appear to be scattered. Very likely, you are more ready to rest than to dine when embarking on a gastronomical adventure with those born under Sagittarius. A good rule of thumb is this: When trying a restaurant that is at a short distance, join forces with a Sagittarius. There are similarities in food tastes here, too. The atmosphere is "light," to your liking, and Sagittarius regards you as an almost perfect companion. Capricorn suits your basic needs. An Aquarius excites you. A Pisces helps you select nutritious foods.

Capricorn suits your basic needs

I recall discussing astrology with Libra actress Marsha Hunt. She provided me with her husband's birth data. He had the Sun in Cancer and I ventured the opinion that he was very food-conscious. With a surprised expression she informed me, "That's right—he's a gourmet!" Marsha Hunt exemplifies the delicacy of Libra, and she appreciated having a husband knowledgeable about food and fine dining.

Other celebrities born under your sign include Truman Capote, Johnny Mathis, Brigitte Bardot, and Yves Montand.

An Aquarius excites you

The distilled essence: that is what you appreciate. The fine points, beauty and elegance, candlelight and manners—all of this and more are part of dining where you are concerned. The labyrinth of preparation is as important as the actual eating: it adds up to style, charisma, and that, too, is an essential ingredient where good food and dining enter your sphere. This is not to imply that you are impossible to please. Graceful manners, a sincere effort on the part of a host or hostess find you quite responsive. The point, however, is that dining is more than mere eating—the feast is as much a mental as a physical act for you.

A Pisces helps you select nutritious foods

Fresh fruits and flowers actually seem to aid your digestion. Beauty in your surroundings sharpens your appetite. Rare cheese and a demitasse are essentials for a fitting climax to your grand repast.

You have a wonderful way of making people feel at home, no matter how elaborate the setting. You are a basically kind, just individual. This shows in your role as host or hostess. Your gracious manner puts people at ease; dining with you, then, is an almost assured success.

It's important, Libra, for you to relax while dining, more so than for members of other zodiacal signs. When you're tense, food becomes something your body rejects. Thus, it is essential that you dine in harmonious surroundings and with people who appeal to you in some manner or the other. Avoid the coarse—in food and people. This is not to indicate that you must dine only with people who share your viewpoint. The opposite, in fact, might be true. You enjoy stimulating talk, but avoid those who lack principle. Your sense of justice is so sharply honed that your entire system is upset by one who runs roughshod over the underdog. Prejudice, racial slurs, so-called jokes about ethnic groups stun your sensitivities—and spoil your enjoyment of food. Your Venusian qualities are accented; some take pleasure in arousing your ire. It is foolish to engage in the intimate act of dining with these people.

You are somewhat an arbiter of good taste and good food

You shine at formal dinner parties; they give you a chance to show how well you wear clothes. You exude such charm on these occasions that the most ordinary fare is elevated to gourmet standards. Leo appreciates this in you, perhaps more so than do the other zodiacal members. Know this and test some of Mike Roy's Leo menus. You appreciate being appreciated and a Leo will take even more delight in you when well fed.

You are somewhat an arbiter of good taste and good food. Others sense this, seek your opinions, observe your reactions. You help make life worth living and prove that eating and cooking belong in the category of fine arts.

You exude charm at formal dinner parties

I applaud you, Libra!

Mike Roy on Libra

A Libra likes light foods, delicately seasoned, and desires to have people around, which makes him or her a delightful host. I have always thought that my own taste sometimes runs to the Seventh House. After all, the only true possession of the chef is his or her own sense of taste.

Many factors govern this taste. Give the same recipe to a dozen people (even chefs) and give them identical ingredients and you will discover—if your sense of taste is acute enough—a dozen different results. Much of it is due to the blending, the way a dish is stirred, molded, and formed. Thus does the personal touch of the cook govern the final result of his culinary efforts.

Libra likes light foods, delicately seasoned

Regardless of method, utensils, and materials, historically one fact stands out: No matter how far back you search, human's social structure has always revolved around food and its presentation. The basis of hospitality, yesterday and today, is the sharing of food and drink with friends.

The noted man about the restaurant world, Trader Vic, has some interesting notes to pass on. I know of no more gracious host than the Trader. His travels, combined with his many food operations, make him an authority. According to him, the pleasure of entertaining is doing something you have created and planned. Some people make cooking a project and take hours to prepare a dish. Says the Trader, "That's goofy! You are too busy these days to make cooking the drudgery it was in the past. Most recipes, excluding those for cakes, breads, and certain classical sauces, need not be followed exactly. They can be altered or varied." Vic says that is all most recipes really are—just guidelines. The most fun in cooking is improvising and experimenting.

In this wonderful country of ours, we are blessed with the greatest array of fresh, frozen, canned, and prepared foods in the world. There are spices, condiments, and imported specialties on your grocer's shelves to let you cook in any language and with imagination.

Food, with its related products, is our largest industry. Millions of dollars are spent annually to influence our eating habits. Almost every kind of magazine has a recipe section. Every newspaper has a life section and/or food section. With all this food information at our disposal, there is no need for any meal to be ordinary. All of which should please you, Libra.

Special serving dishes and table decorations, such as fresh flowers, make a family dinner a treat, much to Libra's delight. Dinner by candlelight with table decorations shouldn't be reserved just for guests. Cooking and entertaining can be a gourmet adventure, a source of great satisfaction, a means of self-expression to say nothing of a confirmation of friendship.

All of us have a different philosophy of food, depending on our personal heritage. I don't remember where I heard it the first time, but it is said that if a strange new species of the botanical, animal, or marine world should be discovered and presented to various nations, they would all find different ways of preparing it.

If it could be prepared in a gourmet fashion, a Libra would enjoy it. Omarr has guided us well so let's consider Libra's menus.

Cooking and entertaining can be a gourmet adventure

MENU ONE

Jupiter Gazpacho

Venus Chicken with Grapes and Almonds

Roquefort Chive French Bread

Hot Fruited Cabbage

Orange Torte

There's a subtle delicacy in this Western favorite from down Mexico way.
Served cold, this appetizer is the type Libra should delight in serving.

Jupiter Gazpacho
(makes 6 cups)

1–2 cloves garlic
1 slice white bread, dry,
  crust removed, cubed
⅓ cup salad oil
6 large tomatoes, peeled
1 cup green pepper, minced
1 cucumber, peeled
1 small onion

1 teaspoon salt
3 tablespoons wine vinegar
1 teaspoon Worcestershire
1 teaspoon sugar
⅓ teaspoon crushed cumin
  seeds
Ice cold water
⅓ cup white wine

Crush garlic cloves and put in oil with bread cubes. Let stand at least 1 hour at room temperature. Remove garlic before adding to mixture. Remove skin and core of tomatoes; core and remove seeds from pepper; remove skin from onion. Chop vegetable ingredients fine. Stir vegetables together; add the seasonings, garlic-seasoned oil, and bread; mix together. This should be refrigerated overnight to mellow flavors. Thin with ice water and wine. Garnish with corn chips, finely chopped green onions, stems of watercress, diced avocado, or dollop sour cream, bits of bacon, or cereal.

To me chicken is the most challenging of our everyday foods. One would think we had discovered everything we could do with this fowl. Yet just the other day I dreamed up this dish, tested it, and decided it belonged here when Omarr described the balance characteristic of Libra.

Venus Chicken with Grapes and Almonds
(serves 6)

6 chicken breasts
½ cup flour
¾ teaspoon salt *or*
    1 teaspoon seasoned salt
½ teaspoon pepper
1 teaspoon paprika
2 tablespoons butter
2 tablespoons oil
2 tablespoons finely chopped
    shallots *or* 3 tablespoons
    finely chopped onion with
    1 clove finely chopped garlic

½ cup sliced mushrooms
    (optional)
¼ cup brandy
¼ cup dry vermouth
½ cup chicken stock
½ cup seedless grapes
    or canned grapes
½ cup almonds or cashews
    or walnuts

Mix together the flour, salt and pepper, and paprika, and lightly flour the chicken breasts. Combine oil and butter in a heavy sauté pan and when bubbly and hot, add the chicken pieces. Add the shallots (or onion and garlic) and the mushrooms. Turn chicken so it browns evenly on both sides. When nice and brown add the brandy. Allow to heat and flame it. When the flame dies down, add the wine, stock, and grapes. Cover and simmer 15 minutes. Add the nuts and serve immediately.

We often think of cabbage as a rather heavy dish, but this recipe makes it light and crispy. The short cooking time gives the vegetable a consistency that's most palatable and quite tasty when joined with the fruit.

Hot Fruited Cabbage
(serves 6)

2 apples, chopped
1 onion, chopped
2 tablespoons butter or margarine
½ medium-sized cabbage, shredded
1 cup water

⅓ cup brown sugar
½ cup vinegar
1 tablespoon butter or margarine
½ teaspoon salt
Pepper to taste

Sauté apple and onion in butter for 10 minutes. Add cabbage and water. Cover and steam for 20 minutes. When tender, add the sugar and vinegar. Just before serving, add butter, salt, and pepper.

This crusty, pungent bread is delightful with the chicken.

Roquefort Chive French Bread
(serves 6)

1 loaf French bread, cut in half lengthwise	1 cube soft butter or margarine
1 tablespoon chopped chives	2 ounces Roquefort cheese
	2 dashes Tabasco

Combine chives, butter and mix well. Blend in cheese and Tabasco. Spread on cut sides of bread. Then slash each half loaf on the bias into 1½- or 2-inch slices, being careful not to cut through bottom crust. Place on baking sheet and heat in oven at 400° for 10 minutes, or until hot and crusty.

And now, just the right dessert to crown a perfect Libra meal.

Orange Torte

1 angel food cake
1 quart vanilla ice cream
½ cup frozen orange juice
    concentrate, thawed
1 large banana, diced

1 cup whipping cream,
    whipped
1 cup toasted coconut
    Orange segments

Line a 1½- or 2-quart bowl with plastic wrap. Break cake into chunks about the size of a walnut and layer in bottom of bowl. Soften ice cream to spreading consistency and spread a layer over the cake. Sprinkle with a tablespoon of the orange juice concentrate; intersperse with banana. Repeat layers until all is used, ending with cake. Cover bowl with wrap or foil and freeze in freezer. To serve, remove wrap and place upside down on serving plate. Remove wrap. Cover with mounds of whipped cream; sprinkle with toasted coconut and garnish with orange segments.

Note: To toast coconut, place in shallow pan in 350° oven; stir or shake frequently until coconut is brown. Be careful it doesn't burn.

MENU TWO

Cheesy Tomato Pie

Salmon Steaks Neptune with Grapefruit

Spinach Pudding

Foil Bread

Lemon Velvet Pie

As an opening course, this is a new version of the old classic French Quiche Lorraine. I like it even better.

Cheesy Tomato Pie
(serves 6)

4 cups day-old bread	2 eggs
½ teaspoon dried basil	1 teaspoon salt
3 medium-ripe tomatoes	Dash hot sauce
½ cup grated Swiss or	½ teaspoon dry mustard
Vermont cheese	1½ cups milk

Heat oven to 375°. Oil a 9-inch pie pan. Remove crust and cut bread into 1-inch cubes. Press into pan. Sprinkle with basil. Remove skin and core of tomatoes; cut into ¼-inch slices. Starting at the outer edge of pan, overlap the tomato slices until top is covered. Sprinkle with grated cheese. (Use the blender for grating.) Combine the rest of the ingredients (eggs through milk). Pour gently at the edge of the pan so the liquid will be absorbed by the bread. Bake 30–40 minutes or until cheese is puffy and brown.

Look to the river, Libra, for an entrée that is gloriously delicate, with just the tang to delight you.

Salmon Steaks Neptune with Grapefruit
(serves 6)

1 small onion, thinly sliced	¼ teaspoon pepper
½ cup butter or margarine	¼ teaspoon allspice
1 cup soft bread crumbs (about 3 slices)	4 salmon steaks
	1 medium grapefruit
½ teaspoon salt	Stuffed olives, sliced

Lightly sauté onion in butter or margarine. Stir in bread crumbs, salt, pepper, and allspice; remove from heat. Arrange salmon steaks in a well-buttered, shallow baking pan. Peel and section grapefruit, removing all white membrane and reserving any juice. Pour grapefruit juice over salmon, then spoon onion crumb mixture evenly over fish. Bake at 450° for 10 minutes. Arrange grapefruit sections on top of salmon and continue baking at 375° for 15 minutes or just until fish flakes easily with fork. Garnish with sliced stuffed olives.

A soft green vegetable adds just the right color touch to the salmon Neptune.

Spinach Pudding
(serves 6)

2 (10-ounce) packages
    chopped frozen spinach,
    cooked and drained
2 cups cottage cheese, drained

1 teaspoon salt
½ cup grated Parmesan cheese
2 eggs
    Parmesan cheese for topping

Mix together spinach, cottage cheese, salt, Parmesan cheese, and eggs until well blended. Pour into buttered 1- to 1½-quart casserole and bake in 350° oven for 30 minutes. Serve with additional Parmesan cheese.

And a piping hot, crunchy bread as a starch course.

Foil Bread
(serves 6)

1 loaf sourdough French bread
¼ pound butter or margarine
    Thin slices of onion
    Thin slices of processed cheese

Parsley, finely chopped
Chives, finely chopped
Celery leaves, finely
    chopped

Slice bread evenly to just within an eighth of an inch of the bottom crust. Combine butter, chives, parsley, and celery leaves and spread on the slices. Place thin slices of onion and cheese on each slice. Wrap loaf in foil and heat in a 400° oven until cheese melts and bread is hot, about 20 minutes.

At the risk of seeming repetitious, I submit another version of a lemon pie as a crowning dessert for this seafood dinner. It's completely different and delightful.

Lemon Velvet Pie

1⅓ cups sugar
6 tablespoons cornstarch
¼ teaspoon salt
1½ cups boiling water
3 eggs, separated
2 tablespoons butter
1 tablespoon grated
   lemon peel
⅓ cup strained fresh
   lemon juice

1 teaspoon vanilla
1 envelope unflavored
   gelatin
¼ cup cold water
1 cup light cream
1 (9-inch) pie shell, baked
1 cup heavy cream, whipped
6–8 walnut halves

In saucepan thoroughly mix sugar, cornstarch, and salt; add boiling water, stirring constantly. Bring to a boil over medium heat. Continue stirring; boil 3 to 4 minutes. Beat yolks slightly; add some of hot mixture to yolks, blending well. Return to saucepan; add butter. Cook 2 minutes longer, stirring constantly. Do not boil.

Remove from heat; stir in lemon peel, juice, and vanilla. Remove generous ½ cup filling; reserve for topping. Soften gelatin in water; add to hot mixture, stirring until thoroughly dissolved. Thoroughly blend in light cream. Chill until slightly thickened, but not set. Beat whites until stiff, but not dry; carefully fold into chilled mixture. Pour into your favorite baked 9-inch pie shell; chill until partially set. Spread reserved filling completely over top of pie. Chill until firm. To serve: top with whipped cream and garnish with walnut halves.

MENU THREE

Saturn Tomato Rings

Seventh House Stroganoff

Saucy Carrots

Frozen Orange Margo

This is the place to point out that a Libra would serve a demitasse at the end of every meal. And, too, a Libra might substitute an exotic cheese and fresh fruit for any dessert. The cheese might be a Brie, a Camembert, a Muenster, a Port du Salut, a Gorgonzola, a Roquefort, or a Stilton.

Another first course that fits the general scheme of the sign.

Saturn Tomato Rings
(serves 6)

1 tablespoon (1 envelope) unflavored gelatin	1 cup cottage cheese
2 cups tomato juice	¼ cup finely chopped, unpeeled cucumber
½ teaspoon salt	2 tablespoons chopped green pepper
¼ teaspoon celery salt	1 tablespoon chopped pimiento
1 bay leaf	1 teaspoon grated onion
Dash of pepper	¼ teaspoon salt
Dash of ground cloves	

Soften gelatin in ½ cup tomato juice. In a 2-quart saucepan combine 1½ cups tomato juice, salt, celery salt, bay leaf, pepper, and cloves. Heat to boiling; simmer 5 minutes. Add softened gelatin and heat over medium heat, stirring constantly, until dissolved. Remove bay leaf. Pour into 6 ½-cup ring molds. Chill until firm. To prepare filling: combine cottage cheese, cucumber, green pepper, pimiento, onion, and salt. Cover and chill. To serve: unmold rings onto salad greens; fill centers with filling.

Stroganoff has become an American favorite. It had its origin in the mysterious Near East, and the delicate blendings of its flavorings make it a perfect Libra dish.

Seventh House Stroganoff
(serves 6)

2 pounds beef fillet	1 cup sour cream
1 teaspoon salt	1 tablespoon chopped shallot
¼ cup flour	*or* 1 tablespoon onion with
½ teaspoon pepper	½ clove garlic, chopped
1 tablespoon olive oil	4 ounces sliced mushrooms
1 tablespoon butter	¼ cup brandy
1 tablespoon paprika	½ cup beef stock, canned or
1 teaspoon lemon juice	cubed

Add salt and pepper to flour. Cut beef in strips ¼ x ½ x 1½ inches, and dust with the seasoned flour. Heat oil and butter in sauté pan and add floured beef, along with shallot and mushrooms. Let brown and sprinkle with paprika. Add the brandy, let heat, and set aflame. When flame dies, add the stock and bring to a boil. Add the lemon juice. Remove pan from heat and let cool about 30 seconds. Blend in sour cream. Serve over noodles.

Note: You may use round steak or stewing beef. If you do, follow the above procedure to the point where you add the sour cream. Then let it simmer for 45 minutes before proceeding as above.

The careful shopper, Libra, will appreciate the economy of this vegetable, to say nothing of its simplicity and flavor.

Saucy Carrots
(serves 6)

6 large carrots
¼ cup butter
 Salt and pepper
¼ cup prepared mustard

½ cup honey
2 tablespoons chives or parsley,
  or both

Wash, pare, and cut carrots diagonally into 1-inch slices (about 3 cups). Cook in boiling water until crisp-tender; drain. In a small saucepan combine butter, seasonings, mustard, honey, and chives. Cook, stirring until well blended (about 3 minutes). Mix sauce gently with carrots. Heat for several minutes and serve.

Here is a showpiece dessert that a Libra can make days in advance and store in the freezer. Listen for the "oohs" and "ahs" when you bring it to the table steaming like a volcano.

Frozen Orange Margo
(1 per serving)

1 large fresh orange	Orange juice
French vanilla ice cream	Shelled nuts
Tangerine sherbet	Maraschino cherries
1 ounce orange curaçao	Food coloring (optional)

Take orange, slice 1 inch from top. Scoop out fruit. Mix French vanilla ice cream with tangerine sherbet. Add orange curaçao to a little orange juice. Fill the orange; add shelled nuts and maraschino cherries. Replace top and put in freezer. When ready to serve, put orange in a supreme glass filled with water colored with green or red food coloring. For a special touch, add a small piece of dried ice. It will look like a smoking torch.

So, Libra, this is your House. Select your companions, and begin your adventure in food, fun, and dining satisfaction.

Scorpio Menu One

pages 207–212

Scorpio Oysters on the Half Shell
Finnan Haddie in White Wine
Asparagus Pluto with Two Cheeses
Potatoes Anna
Chocolate Custard Cloud

Scorpio Menu Two

pages 213–217

Marigold Salad
Boxed Oysters of the Eighth House
Fried Tomatoes
Strawberry Pie

Scorpio Menu Three

pages 218–223

Seven Planet Salad
Linguine with Clam Sauce *or*
    Paella
*French Bread
Applejack Crisp

*recipe not included

Eighth House
October 23–November 21

SCORPIO

Sydney Omarr on Scorpio

♏ The natural eighth zodiacal sign is Scorpio. The Eighth House is unique and not easy to understand. It involves the money of a mate or partner; it is connected with other people's money generally and is related to legacies, inheritances. It also has plenty to do with sex. Scorpio is said to rule the "secrets" and the genitals. It is a sign both revered and feared. Born under Scorpio, you have likes and dislikes that are definite. You are perceptive, able to sense the moods, even the thoughts, of others. Scorpio is a Water sign, and you are passionate, intense. Your food tastes run along unorthodox lines, ranging from sauerkraut to oysters. Limburger cheese could also be a favorite. Your desires are strong, and the food you eat, such as salad heavily laced with garlic, tends to linger, in the sense of aroma or taste.

It might as well be said that you tend to be fascinated with foods associated with aphrodisiac powers. Because of you, Scorpio, Mike Roy has made some special, medical inquiries along this line. His Eighth House section should provide enlightenment as well as amusement.

Scorpios tend to be fascinated with foods associated with aphrodisiac powers

You prefer your steak and cheese well aged. Scorpio involves mystery, and is related to the occult, the hidden. This trait carries over to your favorite foods. For example, you do not find the open sandwich to your liking. You prefer, instead, dishes that are covered. Lobster is transformed in boiling water, a transition from one phase of existence to another—from life, to immobility, to a succulent gourmet treat. Steamed clams also appeal to you. Your soups are thick, and your bread is dark, suggesting age. Scorpio is associated with Pluto; you are willing to tear down in order to rebuild. You will chop onions, scallions, celery—tearing down in order to build luscious dishes.

Dining with you, Scorpio, is a unique experience. The food may be considered foreign because even if domestic, the preparation is such that the final product is "different." Your tableware exhibits designs and your menus tend to have an exotic ring. Actually, you are fond of foreign dishes. In this you're similar to Sagittarius, but you desire the native recipes, the food of the peasant. A Sagittarian, on the other hand, goes in for the fancy variety, the more aristocratic foreign flavor.

Your food has a bite to it: there are spices, herbs, flavorings

You would be especially fond of paella, for example, the native fish and rice staple of Spain. Your coplanetary ruler is Mars and you like your wines red. Your food has a bite to it: there are spices, herbs, flavorings. And that, Scorpio, is what you desire above everything else in food—definite flavor. You want your culinary efforts to reflect the flavor of the country, be it Italy, Spain, Portugal, France, Israel, or Germany.

You are secretive: you enjoy probing, doing detective work, discovering the key to mysteries. You delight in extracting a recipe that a chef assures you is a "secret," not to be revealed. Signs most harmonious to you are Virgo, Capricorn, Cancer, and Pisces. With another Scorpio, the meal is robust. Bird's nest soup could be featured; so, too, could other exotic preparations, which Mike Roy will provide in his Eighth House menus. Aged specialties are featured when you dine with another Scorpio, including wine, fine Stilton cheese, and a curry that sets the tongue ablaze.

You desire old, secret recipes. You have some of your own, and your pride sings when others talk of the way you prepare chicken, spaghetti, even a plate of Portuguese sardines (another Scorpio favorite). Taurus loves to dine with you, especially when, as chef, you bring forth a steak, aged and mellow before hitting the flames—tender, red, and substantial after being removed from the fire.

Former Vice-President Spiro Agnew, a Scorpio, should have had some great Greek recipes. I would be willing to wager on the veracity of that assertion. Other celebrity members of your sign include Burgess Meredith, Katharine Hepburn, Robert Ryan, Walter Cronkite, and Jean Seberg.

Food, for you, represents harmony: a good feeling, satisfaction, relaxation, a bringing together of the clan. Somehow, you get along fine with Aquarians in the food area, if not where other aspects of life are concerned. These people, with their far-out views, suit you. Aquarians are a bit more basic in their tastes, though by no means pedestrian, but you feel you can dig in when dining with an Aquarius. You tend, with members of this zodiacal sign, to feel secure, and security and food go hand in hand in your scheme of events. The Uranus of Aquarius symbolizes surprise, even eccentricity: this you enjoy, especially in dining. To Aquarius, you represent authority. If you say such-and-such is the dish the peasant of Mexico enjoys, so be it, as far as Aquarius is concerned. You like that quality of acceptance; it spurs you on, inspires you, and is reflected in your cooking and food preparation.

Through experience, you have learned the necessity of moderation. It is not a lesson you constantly follow: the rules, for you, are apparently made to be broken. You inspire others to go off their diets, and you accept this as a compliment. Your food is spiced, and so is your dining conversation. You abhor the dull, the tasteless; you delight in those with secrets to tell, especially if connected with intimate practices of friends and celebrities.

Harmonious companions are Virgo, Capricorn, Cancer, and Pisces

You inspire others to go off their diets— and you accept this as a compliment

You like foods that have a "wake up" appeal. That is, food that makes one come alive and take notice, food that brings a sparkle to the eye and a slight burn to the tongue. Ancient remedies, including those for hangovers, are part of your culinary repertoire. Poultry intrigues you; you can do plenty with a chicken. Clams and oysters and eggs are probably high on your list—how you savor a dish that purportedly awakens sexual appetites.

Scorpio, you are intense. By this I mean your likes and dislikes are clearly defined. When you love, it is with all your heart, but once a trust is broken, love becomes a stranger. When love goes, so does your appetite, and so does your desire to create in the kitchen. You desire exciting companions, more so than is usual for the other signs. Excitement stimulates you, makes you hungry for experience as well as food. The Eighth House is one of mystery, procreation; it involves the financial condition of one to whom you are linked, money that is bequeathed to you, your dowry, what is yours through inheritance, through ascension to authority.

Your likes and dislikes are clearly defined

A salad bowl that has been in the family for generations is apt to be a prized possession, as are spoons, knives, forks, dishes, cups, and saucers. And, of course, this is especially applicable to favorite recipes. Mike Roy will provide some new stimulation along this line.

You may find an Aries dining companion too much concerned with what effect certain foods will have: will the spice burn, will the coffee keep one awake? Although an Aries shares your co-ruling Mars, there is a tendency when you are with him or her to be less than daring. This is because Aries accents that section of your solar chart having to do with health. You become conscious of what's good for you when sharing food with natives of this sign.

Taurus shares your taste for the substantial

A hearty treat is usually in store when you wear the chef's hat for Taurus. These people share your taste for the substantial; Scorpio and Taurus are sensuous signs and make a unique combination. You are more likely to try new recipes with Taureans than with those of other signs. Conversation, when dining with a Taurus, turns to partnerships, legal maneuvers, and permanent relationships such as marriage.

With Gemini, you find real satisfaction for that curiosity, that desire you possess for privy information. Gemini provides it. A Gemini, in the course of dinner conversation, lets drop secret tidbits. Members of this sign keep you on the edge of your chair, causing you to peek out of the kitchen to get a better look, to hear what is being said. You are fond of drawing a Gemini aside for the purpose of gaining some additional knowledge that is supposedly private and not for publication. Needless to say, you enjoy cooking for Gemini.

You harmonize with Cancer and get many cooking hints from natives of this sign. You especially enjoy trying foreign food delights with Cancers. Faraway places are apt to be the chief topic of conversation. There is definite attraction here and, with Cancer, your appetite is sharpened. Gemini talks and Cancer eats. You enjoy them both but are better able to relax over dinner when with the Cancer-born. Both you and Cancers share an interest in antiques, in objects that are "used" and comfortable. Thus, food from the "old country" often highlights a menu when you're dining with a Cancer. Check the Fourth House dinner productions; many of the dishes should appeal to you. Vary your menus. A mixture of Scorpio and Cancer fare should be ideal for you.

You don't always agree with Leos, but you respect these natives. You tend to be formal when serving a Leo. You "bone up" on certain subjects and might even research the history of the food you prepare. Leo inspires you to become more of an authority on gastronomical delights. Leo affects that part of your chart having to do with authority and standing in the community. Leo also gives you a sense of power. That's why you especially want to impress this sign when in charge of dinner. A Leo gets a kick out of dining with you. This is because you place the spotlight on this dynamic zodiacal person. You may argue over brandy and brands and food techniques, but the controversy will be stimulating—it aids the digestion where you are concerned.

You have fun with Virgo. Your fondest hopes and wishes seem closer to actualities when a Virgo shares your food. There is good talk—the companionship takes on a warm quality. Virgo finds your taste in food a bit too versatile. The variety is wide, when a Virgo is the judge of your

Gemini lets drop secret tidbits, privy information

You harmonize with Cancer and get many cooking hints from natives of this sign

culinary efforts. But, nevertheless, the two of you enjoy each other's company. Even if you find a Virgo's preoccupation with health tiresome, you still gain pleasure when cooking for natives of this sign.

Sagittarius has much in common with you. The classical Sagittarius is fond of fine foreign foods. Your tastes along the foreign food line are a bit lustier, but there is much to talk about. The conversation has to do with money, say, income, personal possessions, and special collections. With Sagittarius, you tend to prepare food in a romantic atmosphere. You also tend to be forgetful, leaving out essential ingredients. So, Scorpio, keep your mind on the task at hand when cooking for a Sagittarius!

With Aquarius, you get a basic feeling of security. You often dine with persons born under this sign. You find that Virgo individuals provide fun, but an Aquarius fulfills a deep-rooted need. It is a need to feel that you belong, that you are wanted and appreciated.

You have a physical reaction to Pisces

You have a physical reaction to Pisces. There is a sharing of secrets here and your taste in food is similar to that of a Piscean. For romance while dining, choose Pisces. These people inspire you to share confidences, including "confidential menus." Your creative urge is sparked with a Pisces; you do better with members of this sign than with others when it comes to creating dishes. Your menus, with Pisces, tend to be more flamboyant. You have a desire to impress—and you prefer the lights to be low. The creative juices flow with Pisces. You gain pleasure in serving Pisces some of those "sexy" foods you are so fond of. When emotions are taut, tense, then you are in your element. A Pisces brings this out in you. A meal is a feast; no Gemini snacks for you. Your appetites are strong, at the table and elsewhere. You enjoy cooking with wine. You relish your before-dinner cocktail and your after-dinner brandy or liqueur.

A hungry guest is as welcome as cool water in a hot desert; finicky eaters leave you cold. Seafood, as indicated, is a favorite: you like to eat it and talk about it and prepare it. A combination of seafood and chicken finds you absolutely charmed, as in paella.

Virgo and you make good dining companions

You belong to the tribe of hearty eaters. It isn't necessarily the amount of food consumed, it's your enjoyment that counts. Your attitude is "hearty." You develop definite likes and dislikes among restaurants. You like dining out, but nothing can replace the pleasure received when your own culinary efforts gain applause. You also are a taster. Gemini snacks and Virgo's bits and pieces don't lure you, but you taste while you cook. You also are aware of aroma to an extraordinary degree. Your sensuous nature is aroused by the smell of food cooking, simmering, being prepared. Your appetite stands at attention. You taste, building up anticipation for the meal to come. It is difficult for others to stay out of the kitchen with you at the helm. The pungent aroma acts like a magnet, drawing people. You regard this as a compliment, which it is.

You prefer dining on a grand scale—plenty to eat, much to talk about, music to listen to as the food settles and eyes become heavy.

You prefer dining on a grand scale: plenty to eat, much to talk about, music to listen to

One of your unusual favorites is asparagus. That's Mike Roy's department: to provide a menu that includes this green delight. It is not unlikely, Scorpio, that you have heard tales about the powers of asparagus. Well . . . if it makes you feel good . . . .

You're fun to dine with, Scorpio. You experiment, ask questions, extend invitations, come up with bright ideas, innovations, different ways of preparing staples. A Taurus individual thinks you're about the brightest personality available. A Capricorn sits back and gazes in wonder, often permitting your servings to chill. (You don't like that very much. There is apt to be some bickering about food with a Capricorn, though you do, generally, get along well.)

Onions, garlic, thick soups, marvelous wines, and tantalizing aromas—all are part of superior Scorpio cooking with astrology.

Bon appétit!

Mike Roy on Scorpio

This is the House of Secrets. Scorpio lives here. Insofar as food is concerned, I don't share your secretive nature. You don't like to tell your secrets and if you have a delicious recipe of your own creation, you may be reluctant to give it out. I previously discussed the subject of different cooks' ways with the same dish. Too, I have always thought that a great dish should delight the world. I have always made my recipes available to those who appreciate them. There are too few good things in the world. If you have something fine, share it with us.

Aphrodisiacs: pepper, oysters, beans, spices, truffles

Another important fact about Scorpio, which I heartily applaud, is that you fit the grand Water sign design like the shell fits the oyster. (If I may be permitted an aside, if you had been alive in the times when mythology was religion, you would have been a follower of Aphrodite, the goddess of love and beauty.) Scorpio, as Omarr indicated, is interested in aphrodisiacs. Aphrodisiacs have long fascinated us, and many interesting tales have been spread about their ability to increase our prowess in the world of sex. Modern day science has, alas, proved most of these false, perhaps built on wishful thinking.

Pepper has long been associated with sexual power. It fits the fiery nature of Scorpio. Oysters are perhaps the most mentioned of the stimulant foods. Beans have a long history as aphrodisiacs, too. The bean has been a symbol of fertility since ancient times. There was a belief that women need only plant beans if they wanted to conceive. Probably, the idea of the bean's fertility derives from the ability of one bean to produce a whole bean plant, with many pods and countless individual beans. In some archaic social systems, woman was the dominating sex; man definitely played a subordinate role and fatherhood was not honored or even understood. Conception usually was explained as being due to the wind and the eating of beans (or the accidental swallowing of an insect).

Barley, traditionally, has been considered a giver of strength. Asparagus, because of its peculiar shape, easily acquires phallic significance. In a number of countries, it is believed that asparagus increases sexual potency. This is especially accepted in Eastern Europe. Potency is often associated with other fruits, roots, and foods of elongated shape. This is not an invention of Freud but comes from many different societies.

The *Encyclopedia Britannica* points out some interesting facts on the subject of aphrodisiacs. It emphasizes that they may be classified into two principal groups: psychophysiological (visual, tactile, olfactory, aural) and internal (foods, alcohol, drugs, love potions, medical preparations). By far the most important to many is the second group, as the preparation of erotic dishes has played a tremendous role in the sexual history of humans. Accordingly, most of these beliefs are not based on physiological facts.

Fish, vegetables, and spices have been among the most popular aphrodisiacs

Of the various foods to which aphrodisiac powers are traditionally attributed, fish, vegetables, and spices have been among the most popular. With the possible exception of fish, with its high phosphorus content, and asparagus, with its asparaginea chemical constituent that acts as a diuretic, none of these foods contains any chemical agents that could effect a direct physiological reaction on the genitourinary tract. Actually, two of the most famous aphrodisiac foods—oysters and truffles—are singularly lacking in elements that might serve to bring on sexual stimulation. Of the composition of the oyster (nitrogen, phosphorus, carbohydrates, sodium, chloride, iodine, calcium phosphates), only phosphorus could induce erotic desire and only if taken in very large quantities. The truffle has even fewer sexually stimulating elements, being composed of water, carbohydrates, albumin, salt, and fats. We must thus conclude that, scientifically, no food, with the possible exceptions noted, can be said to be an aphrodisiac and that the reputation of various supposedly erotic foods is based not on fact but on folkloric tradition.

I rest the case with one last thought: a properly balanced diet produces a healthy body, and a healthy body needs no special attention to carry out its natural functions. I'm sure that the foregoing will never stop Scorpio in his or her lust for the good life. Scorpio, glass in hand and fork ready, will carry on, and more power to them.

For the sake of Scorpio menu making, let's contend that aphrodisiacs do work, in some mysterious fashion, and build our plans accordingly.

MENU ONE

Scorpio Oysters on the Half Shell

Finnan Haddie in White Wine

Asparagus Pluto with Two Cheeses

Potatoes Anna

Chocolate Custard Cloud

I know a lot of people, not only Scorpios, who might utter a silent prayer that this oyster dish would do the job it is allegedly capable of doing.

Scorpio Oysters on the Half Shell
(serves 4)

24 oysters in shell	1 tablespoon Worcestershire
2 tablespoons finely chopped shallots	1 teaspoon chopped parsley
1 tablespoon butter	½ teaspoon Dijon mustard
2 tablespoons flour	¼ pound mushrooms, chopped fine
½ teaspoon salt	1 egg yolk, beaten
⅛ teaspoon nutmeg	½ cup cracker crumbs
3 drops Tabasco	1½ tablespoons melted butter

Open oysters and set aside ¼ cup of the oyster liquid. Remove oysters from shells and chop fine. Wash shells. Cook shallots in 1 tablespoon of butter until soft and tender. Stir in flour and let brown. Blend in reserved oyster liquid, salt, nutmeg, Tabasco, Worcestershire, parsley, mushrooms, mustard, and oysters. Cook 5 minutes, stirring constantly. Remove from heat and add egg yolk. Spoon mixture onto shells. Combine cracker crumbs with 1½ tablespoons melted butter and sprinkle over oyster mixture. Bake in 350° oven 15 minutes. Serve immediately.

I don't know where, exactly, humankind got the idea that seafood was sexy, but I can live with it and so can Scorpio. Here's a delightful smoked haddock entrée for the Eighth House.

Finnan Haddie in White Wine
(serves 4)

10 small onions	1 cup dry white wine
¼ pound mushrooms	3 tablespoons butter
2 pounds finnan haddie (smoked haddock)	4 teaspoons fine bread crumbs
¼ teaspoon thyme	1 cup heavy cream
2 bay leaves	Juice of ½ lemon
	Pepper

Peel the onions and parboil them about 15 minutes in salted water. Clean and slice mushrooms quite thin. In a buttered baking casserole, place the haddock, mushrooms, onions, thyme, and bay leaves. Add the white wine and sprinkle with pepper and bread crumbs. Bake 15 to 20 minutes in a 350° oven, basting several times. Heat the cream and add the lemon juice to it. Serve fish on heated platter with cream on the side.

If the oysters and finnan haddie leave us wanting, let's make sure with our vegetable.

Asparagus Pluto with Two Cheeses
(serves 4)

4 pounds asparagus
½ cup butter
½ cup grated Gruyère cheese

½ cup grated Parmesan cheese
Salt and pepper to taste

Cook asparagus until tender right down to the ends of the stalks. Melt half the butter and put it in a heated shallow dish. Mix the cheeses and put them in another dish. Dip the asparagus first in the butter, then in the cheese, and arrange in layers on a heated serving platter. At the same time, brown the remaining butter and pour, very hot, over the asparagus. Season with salt and pepper.

Of all the potato recipes I know, I think this one is my favorite. I have never served it without getting a lot of questions as to how it is prepared. This could become a secret for Scorpio.

Potatoes Anna
(serves 4)

2 pounds potatoes   Salt and pepper
6 tablespoons butter

Peel the potatoes and slice about 1/16 inch thick. Butter a 1-quart ring mold and line the bottom and sides with potato slices. Dot the bottom layer with butter and sprinkle with salt and pepper; cover with another layer of potatoes and more butter, salt, and pepper. Continue until the mold is filled to within 1/4 inch from the top. The potatoes should be tightly packed. Cover with buttered parchment or brown paper and bake about an hour at 450°. The potatoes are done if they feel tender when a knife is inserted. Unmold carefully on a heated plate. There should be a golden crust on the outside and the potatoes should be soft.

To top off this Scorpio aphrodisiac dinner, let's add the mystery of the egg in the form of a custard.

Chocolate Custard Cloud
(serves 6)

½	pound semisweet chocolate bits	¼	cup sugar
2	cups milk	¾	cup heavy cream
		8	egg yolks

Melt the chocolate in the top of a double boiler. Add the milk and bring to a boil over direct beat. Stir the sugar, cream, and egg yolks together until thoroughly mixed. Add the boiling chocolate gradually, stirring constantly with a wooden spoon. Pour the mixture into individual custard cups, and place them in a pan of hot water. The water should come about halfway up the cups. Bake at 325° for 25 minutes. Chill before serving.

MENU TWO

Marigold Salad

Boxed Oysters of the Eighth House

Fried Tomatoes

Strawberry Pie

Don't forget, Scorpio, to set the scene. I'd use a white tablecloth with gleaming silver, sparkling glassware, and "lustrous" china. I'd be sure there was a single red rose. I'd see to it the fireplace flickered longingly, the lights were turned soft and low, and that some strings serenaded gently in the background. Here is the menu I'd serve in this setting.

If you'd like to inspire conversation, Scorpio, be sure you make this salad at the table.

Marigold Salad
(serves 4)

2 marigold blossoms
2 tablespoons lime juice
1 tablespoon dry vermouth
7 tablespoons oil
1 teaspoon Dijon mustard
½ teaspoon salt

½ teaspoon Worcestershire
¼ pound salted cashew nuts
2 hearts of romaine heads, torn in bite-size pieces
1 heart of iceberg lettuce head, torn in bite-size pieces

Place the salt and 1 tablespoon of the oil in the bottom of a salad bowl. Add 10 or 12 petals from the marigold. Using the heel or bottom of a large spoon, muddle the blossoms into the oil. Add all the ingredients except the greens, nuts, and blossom petals, and blend well. Add the greens, a liberal handful of marigold petals, and nuts, and toss. Serve on chilled plates, and garnish with additional blossom petals.

There's a bit of a story you can tell about this entrée as you serve. It comes from down New Orleans way. It seems that when papa tippled too long at the pub and he had that distinct, intuitive feeling that he would face trouble at home, he would order this recipe. The innkeeper would wrap it in newspaper and papa would wend his unsteady way homeward secure in the knowledge mama would forgive him his sins and welcome him with open arms.

Boxed Oysters of the Eighth House
(serves 4)

1 loaf unsliced, round
    sourdough French bread
4 tablespoons melted butter
1 clove finely chopped garlic
4 tablespoons butter
1 pint oysters
½ teaspoon Maggi's seasoning

¼ cup sherry
2 tablespoons grated onion
6 tablespoons chopped
    green pepper
3½ tablespoons flour
½ cup heavy cream

Cut a horizontal slice off the top of the loaf and pull out the center of the bread. Brush the insides of the loaf and the top with a combination of 4 tablespoons melted butter and the chopped garlic. Melt additional 4 tablespoons butter in a 2-quart saucepan. Add oysters and simmer until the edges of the oysters curl. Remove oysters and set aside. To juices in the pan, add seasoning, sherry, grated onion, and green pepper. Simmer until pepper is tender. Add flour and stir until blended. Add cream and cook until thick. Return oysters to pan. Pour into loaf. Fasten top on loaf with toothpicks. Place on a baking sheet and bake in a 450° oven for 20 minutes. To serve: slice with a very sharp knife, spooning extra sauced oysters over top.

You can prepare this most appropriate vegetable at the table too—in the blazer pan of your chafing dish.

Fried Tomatoes
(serves 4)

1 pound firm young tomatoes	Parsley sprigs

Frying Batter

1 cup flour	¼ cup beer
½ teaspoon salt	⅓ cup lukewarm water
1 teaspoon oil	2 egg whites

Put flour in a mixing bowl and make a well in the center. Put salt and oil in well. Stirring all the while, gradually add the beer and the water. Mix just until smooth. Cover and let stand at room temperature for at least an hour. Just before using, fold in stiffly beaten egg whites.

Tomatoes: peel the tomatoes. (Dip in boiling water for a few seconds and slip off skins.) Cut the tomatoes in quarters, removing as many seeds as possible. Wipe the tomatoes dry and sauté in butter, after dipping in batter. When golden brown, sprinkle with salt and serve immediately with parsley fried this same way. This recipe also works using deep hot fat.

An elegant dessert will serve as a fitting climax for this intimate Scorpio dinner.

Strawberry Pie

2 boxes strawberries
2 (3-ounce) packages cream cheese
2 tablespoons honey
Dash of salt
½ teaspoon milk (to moisten cheese)
½ cup honey
⅓ cup water

1 tablespoon unflavored gelatin
1 cup crushed strawberries, undrained
2–3 drops red food coloring
1½ cups whole berries, hulled, half-sliced
1 (9-inch) pastry shell, baked

Cream together cheese, honey, and salt; moisten with milk. Spread over bottom of pastry shell. Combine in a saucepan: ½ cup honey, water, gelatin, crushed strawberries, and food coloring. Cook over medium heat, stirring constantly until slightly thickened and clear, 10–15 minutes. Cool until mixture mounds. Arrange sliced berries over cream cheese; spoon gelatin mixture over berries. Chill 2 to 3 hours.

MENU THREE

Seven Planet Salad

Linguine with Clam Sauce or Paella

Hot French Bread

Applejack Crisp

For intense and passionate Scorpio, here is still another menu. This is more of a party menu for your sign. Perhaps, Scorpio, you'll find a mate among the guests— or at least companionship for the evening.

In India when the affluent serve curry, it is said a separate serving person carries each given condiment to the table. Since there are seven condiments for this salad, and since we are concerned with the zodiac and the planets, this is . . .

Seven Planet Salad

1 cup French dressing
1 cup Roquefort dressing
1 cup Thousand Island dressing
1 large bowl salad greens, tossed
    lightly with olive oil
1 small bowl chopped egg
1 small bowl chopped anchovies

1 small bowl toasted croutons
1 small bowl chopped green
    onions
1 small bowl Parmesan cheese
1 small bowl cherry tomatoes
1 small bowl sliced radishes

The guests have the fun of building their own salads. Arrange the bowl with the greens first, tossed lightly with olive oil to make them glisten. Then place the condiments and the dressings nearby. A guest may take a plateful of greens, add the toppings, and finally dress the salad with the dressing of their choice.

I like to keep a party simple. This entrée takes a total preparation time of 20 minutes. I can still hear the sighs of my guests from the last time I served it.

Linguine with Clam Sauce
(serves 4 or more)

1   (8-ounce) package of linguine   Salted water

Cook linguine in boiling, salted water until just done (al dente), allowing 4 servings per 8-ounce package. Top with following sauce. Add cheese if you wish.

Clam Sauce

2   tablespoons butter
2   tablespoons olive oil
1   clove garlic, chopped fine
2   tablespoons lemon juice
2   tablespoons dry white wine
1½ teaspoons finely chopped
       parsley

½   teaspoon salt
¼   teaspoon oregano
¼   teaspoon pepper
1   (8-ounce) can minced clams,
       do not drain

Sauté garlic lightly in oil and butter (do not brown the garlic). Stir in the lemon juice and wine. Add parsley, salt, oregano, and pepper. Add clams and juice. Serve over linguine and toss well.

Note: You may find that you and your friends will want to dunk pieces of hot French bread in the sauce.

An alternate entrée to the Linguine with Clam Sauce...

Paella

(serves 8)

1 (3-pound) chicken, cut up	Salt and pepper to taste
½ cup butter *or* ¼ cup each butter and olive oil	2 chorizo (Spanish-style sausages), sliced thinly
1 cup diced pimientos	2 lobster tails, cut in pieces
1 clove garlic, crushed	12 steam clams in shell, washed
2 cups rice	18 shrimp, peeled and deveined
4 cups heated chicken stock	½ cup dry white wine
½ teaspoon saffron	Pimiento strips

Sauté chicken pieces in butter along with garlic until golden brown. Remove and set aside. Add rice to juices remaining in pan and sauté to golden brown. Add chicken stock and saffron to pan and bring to a boil. Season with salt and pepper. Butter a Dutch oven well on bottom and sides. Put half the chicken pieces in the bottom of the casserole; cover with one of the sausages sliced thin and ½ cup of the pimiento. Add about 1½ cups of the rice. Top with remaining chicken, the remaining sausage sliced thin, the rest of the pimiento, and the rest of the rice. Pour in about 3 cups of the seasoned stock. Bake uncovered in a 350° oven for 30 minutes, adding the rest of chicken stock from time to time. Add the lobster and cook for 10 minutes longer. Add clams and shrimp and wine and cook another 15 minutes. Garnish with pimiento strips.

Everybody likes apple pie. For a Scorpio dinner, this is a different version, with a crunchy topping.

Applejack Crisp

3 pounds tart apples, cut in eighths	2 teaspoons cinnamon
1¼ cups sugar	2 tablespoons applejack or apple brandy
1 tablespoon lemon juice	*Crisp*
¼ pound melted butter	

Put apples in deep, buttered baking dish. Mix remaining ingredients and toss well with apples. Bake in a 350° oven for 40 minutes. Then top with crisp.

Crisp

1 cup flour	½ cup brown sugar
½ cup butter	2 tablespoons applejack

Mix until crumbly and pat over apples. Return pie to oven for an additional 15 to 20 minutes or until apples are tender. Remove from oven and sprinkle with 2 tablespoons applejack. Serve warm.

So journey on, Scorpio . . . since I've shared with you, share some of the good things of your life with others— no need for so much secrecy. You never know, maybe some of those aphrodisiacs do work.

Sagittarius Menu One

Scampi Jupiter
Veal Cordon Bleu
Rice or Bulgar Pilaf
Flamingo Pie

Sagittarius Menu Two

Cheese and Bacon Salad
Ninth House Cannelloni
Artichoke Bottoms with Mushrooms
Celestial Pumpkin Pie
Crêpes Suzette

Sagittarius Menu Three

Escargots Sagittarius
Individual Lunar Meat Loaves
Macaroni and Cheese Olé
Zodiac Trifle

SAGITTARIUS

Sydney Omarr on Sagittarius

The Ninth House is associated with long journeys, publishing, philosophy, and foreign lands. In the food area, this correlates with recipes that contain the flavor of faraway lands. The open road, the open mind, communications, and the committing of thoughts to paper—these are aspects of this section of the horoscope designated as Sagittarius. Sagittarius is a Fire sign, with Jupiter as its significator. It is expansive; the expression of ideas is a necessity to a Sagittarian. Sagittarius is the "explainer" of the zodiac, and when preparing meals, members of this sign invariably include dishes that require explanation—the foreign, the unusual. A

Sagittarius can be daring in the kitchen—an original touch is essential. Sagittarius will experiment and be the first to try grasshoppers, for one admittedly extreme example. Snails are surely part of the Sagittarius repertoire, so are desserts with exotic names.

Sagittarians will be the first to experiment

Born under this sign, you also are fond of the outdoors; you find pleasure in barbecuing. Sandwiches to take along on a hike, an exploration of museums or ruins, or an archeological expedition also find favor with you. You are expansive; you put great stock in principles, and you tend to attract those who take advantage of you. You want to do things "on your own," and thus, find fulfillment when wearing the chef's hat. You will go out of your way to shop for a certain ingredient. You are attracted to restaurants that have not gained wide popularity. You want to explain the subtle nuances, the methods of the chef, and the unique plates set before you.

You have much in common with Leo, but you are less of a showperson. Your preparations lack the flamboyance of the classical Leo, but you are likely to be more aware of the history of foods; you blend, test, taste, describe, and provide us with culinary education. While a Virgo discusses health virtues, you talk about the people associated with various concoctions. Food for you is a way of building bridges between people. You adore having guests with diversified views. At times, Sagittarius, you take so much time explaining what we are going to eat that we become impatient, even irritable. You must try to avoid appearing pompous.

Food for you is a way of building bridges between people

Many of your creations are fattening, especially the rich desserts, cream sauces, and the like. In common with a Leo, you are attracted to the flambéed dishes, and, like members of your fellow Fire signs Aries and Leo, you enjoy spices. You are a bit more delicate in your taste than Scorpio, but much less so than Libra. With Jupiter as your significator, you are jovial—fun and food represent an essential combination for you.

You are naturally gregarious, inviting people to dinner on the spur of the moment is part of your dining pattern. You are an innovator and can transform ordinary dishes into apparent exotic delights. Your most harmonious companions are Libra, Aquarius, Aries, and Leo people. With another Sagittarian, you tend to mellow, to seek the more orthodox, the conservative, to discuss family affairs and domestic adjustments. Poetry, music, dramatic readings are apt to be part of the conversational fare when you entertain another Sagittarian.

You gain in an almost spiritual sense when dining on Chinese or Japanese dishes; the mingled flavors intrigue you. So do fresh vegetables, fruits, cheeses. Although you appreciate an elaborate banquet, you are just as much at home with a picnic basket. A loaf of bread, a jug of wine . . . this could provide as much satisfaction as Russian caviar and French champagne.

You spread out your servings: something here, there, and everywhere. And you are fond of spreads; cheese could be one of your favorites. Food that "expands" suits your eye and palate, food that, when cooked, doubles in size. I will leave it to Mike Roy to enumerate along these lines. You are fascinated with the effects foods have on the body, not so much a health addict as is Virgo, but certainly knowledgeable in this area.

You are sentimental about food; various menus and recipes "remind" you of individuals, scenes, situations. You enjoy studying recipes and creating your own. You could be a collector of cookbooks. You think nothing of taking a long journey to test a specialty, to match your opinion with that of the local gourmet.

You are partial to large containers: picnic baskets, bottles with wide bottoms. The small cup, the demitasse belongs to Libra. You desire the big cup. You need room to spread out. Because you prefer "expansive food," you cook with plenty of liquid. You tend to intellectualize about food, thus, you are apt to be more analytical than voracious. You can work wonders with a blender. You are a superb mixer of drinks, nonalcoholic and otherwise.

An ideal dining companion for you is a Libra; he or she gives you a chance to talk, demonstrate, explain, and teach. Libra helps you fulfill your hopes and wishes; you enjoy serving the Libra delicacies even though your own preference runs along more mundane lines.

Cooking with a blow torch would exhilarate you. You check temperatures. An oven thermometer is probably one of your indispensable cooking tools.

You are just as much at home with a picnic basket as a bottle of champagne and caviar

Libra is an ideal dining companion for you

You utilize plenty of butter. It melts, spreads—the same as cheese. When you're dining alone, a book usually accompanies your meal.

You can be pontifical about food. Your desire to teach us is overwhelming. Leo brings out this quality in you. Although Leo likes stage center, you can be counted on to take over with explanations and inspirations. Both are Fire signs, and both Leos and Sagittarians enjoy a "display" when it comes to dining. With a Leo, you learn the rules in order to break them. You add your own variations to recipes.

Butter, cheese, sausages and sauces appeal to you

David Susskind and William Buckley are Sagittarius celebrities. Their dining patterns are apt to match your own. Drew Pearson belongs to this group, and so does former light-heavyweight boxing champion Archie Moore. The latter used to discourse regularly on a so-called secret Aboriginal diet. Moore delighted in "making the weight" at the last possible moment during his halcyon days in the prize ring.

Sausages and sauces appeal. Food containing fat that can be cooked "out" is part of your forte, including bacon and ham. A sauce that originated in a foreign land fits your requirements for "education in the kitchen."

Since you like blending and combining ingredients, you enjoy creating an excellent meat loaf. You gain pleasure from it, both for taste and in the spirit of experimenting.

Sweet and sour cream could be considered staples by you; a soup with sour cream topping probably would delight you. A dessert with sweet or whipped cream would provide a fitting climax to a meal.

Capricorns are in awe of you

Dining with Capricorn inspires you to display your possessions, to discuss food values, and the worth of leftovers. Many Capricorns are in awe of you. This suits you fine; it gives you an opportunity to explain, analyze, and dissect. Your "fun" dining companion is a Libra, but Capricorn serves the purpose when you want to display practical knowledge in the kitchen. Invariably, the subject turns to food costs when breaking bread with a Capricorn.

Aries attracts you physically. Personal magnetism flows and you are especially creative when preparing food for an Aries guest. The Mars of Aries and your Saturn combine to bring action, versatility, and humor into play. The Aries taste is similar to your own, although you are more likely to accent foreign foods. An Aries is more direct, much less patient. It is a good combination; your setting is grandiose with an Aries.

Pisces makes you feel secure in the knowledge that you have something unique to offer: your personality, knowledge, recipes, menus. Pisces appreciates your far-reaching view and respects you. In turn, you feel at home with a Pisces, and you experiment, come up with variations on an old theme, if not entirely new creations.

Taurus enjoys your efforts with a roast. You become more conscious of nutrition when dining with a Taurus. The Venus of Taurus combines with your Jupiter to inspire universal dishes: bread, flour products dominate. With Taurus, you are apt to be more basic, concerned with jobs, associates, general health. Taurus is invaluable in helping you to entertain visiting relatives. Taurus pitches in. The culinary results are practical, basic, and nourishing.

You are attracted to Gemini and the relationship can be a permanent one. You delight in fixing special sandwiches for Gemini. There is much talk, much in common, and the discussion, over food, often turns to partnership and marriage. A Gemini likes snacks, appetizers; you are capable of producing magnificent trays that warm the heart of this native. You are not alike, but the opposite qualities act like magnets: there is a drawing together. A Gemini is apt to think of your meat loaf as a culinary delight and sincerely believes you make the best ham sandwich in the world. You enjoy listening to a Gemini. Perhaps more important, Gemini appreciates your philosophy, your basic humanitarianism. Breaking bread with a Gemini could result in an invigorating evening. The food tastes are similar—up to a point. But both signs, Gemini and Sagittarius, are flexible. A compromise is achieved. Enjoyment of eating and conversation is a hard-to-beat combination. The two of you join forces in alleviating suffering; talk turns to medicine, charity, social justice, and civil rights. Typical picnic fare could be the order of the day when you entertain a restless Gemini.

With a Cancer-born, you are concerned with the origin of the food you prepare. Cancer appreciates your efforts. Natives of this sign delight

You are attracted to Aries and Gemini

Pisces makes you feel secure, at home

in the way you serve your dishes. A Cancer gives you a feeling of plenty; you don't worry about costs, amounts. You are inspired to serve a variety when host to a Cancer native. The Moon of Cancer and your Jupiter are compatible. You disagree in many areas, but lean over backwards to please when it comes to kitchen productions. Cancer represents a chance for you to display your fascination with the unknown, the occult. Astrology also could be a topic of conversation when Sagittarius and Cancer dine together.

Astrology and the occult could be topics when you and Cancer dine together

Your penchant for foreign dishes can be shared with Leo. Both Sagittarius and Leo are Fire signs—Leo loves to participate in your barbecue productions. Glazed ham, produced with flair and showmanship, could also serve you well when with Leo. Conversation invariably veers to philosophy, to poets, writers, little-known religions, or cults. Psychic phenomena and spiritualism are favorite topics over after-dinner spirits. The Sun of Leo combines with your Jupiter significator to produce mutual inspiration. That old chestnut about not discussing religion or politics does not apply when you dine with a Leo. Natives of this sign encourage you to break with tradition, especially in the food area. Thus, the foreign dishes, the variations, the innovations, and the breaking of rules go well when you share culinary efforts with Leo. These persons also appreciate your desire to make even a sandwich a production. Leo's flair for the dramatic is contagious and you enjoy and "catch" it.

Leos encourage you to break with tradition

You can successfully transact business deals when sharing food with a Virgo. The trouble is that dining is apt to become secondary; ambitions play the prime role. You are interested in Virgo's health and nutrition theories, but beyond this you are not exactly wild about his or her choice of food. However, you are pleasantly surprised by the Virgo wit and curiosity, and Virgo could come up with ideas that solve dilemmas. Standing in the community, business, stock market reports—this is apt to be the conversational turn you take with a Virgo while the barbecue sizzles over charcoal flames.

The secretive nature of Scorpio fascinates you. You change dining habits when with natives of this powerful sign. You will enjoy testing the Scorpio recipes. Scorpio enjoys listening to your theories, but, in actuality, it is Scorpio who provides the intrigue and makes you the kind of chef who serves secret delights. A Scorpio is invaluable when you are charged with the responsibility of planning huge banquets. While a Scorpio believes good things come in small packages, you prefer largesse, a spread. The two signs—Sagittarius and Scorpio—are not the greatest mixers, but you always have a willing ear for confidential information, which Scorpio seems capable of providing. A Scorpio admires your possessions, cooking utensils, but the relationship is something akin to a rainbow: one can follow and admire it, but the catching or possessing of it is another story. An evening of dining with Scorpio affects you that way. Your food preference, on those occasions, changes, becomes more subtle—not completely fulfilling your desires or those of the Scorpio.

The secretive nature of Scorpio fascinates you

Your sense of adventure in food is enhanced by Aquarius, and natives of that sign also help you find beauty in food, dishes, silverware, fine serving trays, and cocktail sets. Aquarius helps you add to your anecdotes; this is a good combination and, when dining, the relatives of both signs are often included. Ideas about cooking flow. The key, Sagittarius, is to be discriminating, to choose the best. An Aquarius regards you as a fine friend. You often take short trips with natives of this sign. You find out-of-the-way dining places as Aquarius sharpens your food curiosity.

You already cook with fire. Now, with the added ingredient of astrology, you can be a world-beating chef.

We would like to be on your invitation list, Sagittarius!

Your sense of adventure in food is enhanced by Aquarius

Mike Roy on Sagittarius

Now welcome to the kitchen of experimental Sagittarius. As Omarr points out, you love to try new tastes. You also like fattening things, although I don't know that many overweight Sagittarians. One would think you would weigh a ton, judging from the richness of the desserts you like—along with the cream sauces and sour cream and whipped cream. Maybe you keep your figure by walking it all off on those picnics you delight in.

Sagittarians love to try new tastes and fattening things

Was it a Sagittarian who walked along a country lane in the French province of Périgord? The one who spied a pregnant pig rooting in the ground under a stunted oak tree, digging up little objects that looked strangely like walnuts, though somewhat black in color? The one who said to him- or herself: "Ah, these are truffles. They will come to be known as 'black diamonds of cuisine.'" To this day, the bountiful soil of Périgord yields nothing quite so exquisite as the truffle. "Black as the soul of the damned," they call it there, and quite unfairly, according to Samuel Chamberlain (writing in *Bouquet de France*, a Gourmet book, Gourmet Publishing Corporation, 1952, New York), for it brings prosperity and gastronomic felicity to the whole countryside. Oh, truffles are found in many parts of Southern France—in Italy and Africa, too—but the finest, biggest, blackest, most odoriferous ones come from Périgord.

Actually, the truffle is a tuber (a type of root vegetable) and not exactly a thing of beauty to behold. There are those who can't see or taste too much in a truffle, but if a thin slice proves to be a tasteless wafer, it is because the truffle has surrendered its perfume to the food surrounding it. There are few tubers with so persistent or penetrating an aroma.

It is no fiction that pigs are used to detect truffles, which grow a few inches underground, attached to the roots of stunted oak trees. Small, pregnant sows are the most competent sniffers, excelling certain dogs, which also have the gift. The human nostril, even that of the best

Périgourdine gourmet, is powerless to scent the prize. Mr. Chamberlain describes the taking of a truffle:

> With a chain around her neck, the little pig leads her master from one mysterious cache to another. When she scents her truffle and starts to dig, a tap of the cane on her snout sends her away to seek another prize. In the meantime, her master digs up the black treasure. It is a frustrating existence. In order not to ruin her morale, the farmer rewards her with a handful of corn and even a few scraps of the ebony tuber now and then.

I personally love them. Yes, Sagittarius, I think it could have been you who first discovered this gem of the culinary world.

And it must have been a Sagittarius, with a love of exotic dishes, who first saw that field of thistles along the Mediterranean and decided the fruit of the weed looked delicious, and, having arrived at that decision, gave them the glamorous name of artichoke. The gourmet world has delighted in them ever since.

If you have a garden, you may have snails. You may spend long hours trying to eliminate the pests. It was probably a Sagittarius who decided that snails should be doused in flavored butter and become another of the gourmet world's delicacies.

Sagittarians like to picnic

I could go on—from fried grasshoppers to chocolate-covered ants, to rattlesnake steaks and a host of other things botanical, animal, or marine. But I desist. I leave it to Sagittarius.

As Omarr has told us, Sagittarians like to picnic—foods to take along like sandwiches, barbecues delight them; sausages, bacon, and ham tickle their palates to no end. Here are some menus I have created for you, Sagittarius.

MENU ONE

Scampi Jupiter

Veal Cordon Bleu

Rice or Bulgar Pilaf

Flamingo Pie

Scampi, originally, was an Italian dish, but you'll find it on menus across our country now. Although the true Italian Scampi is a unique example of marine life, we all make it with shrimp. Sagittarians like it because it's loaded with one of their favorites: butter, and more butter.

Scampi Jupiter
(serves 4)

20 large shrimp (about 2 pounds)	1 tablespoon onion, chopped
½ cup butter	¼ cup brandy
2 large shallots, chopped *or* 1 clove garlic, chopped	¼ cup dry white wine
	2 tablespoons lemon juice
	Dash salt and pepper

Select large shrimp measuring about 9 or 10 to a pound. Allow about 5 for each serving. Thoroughly wash shrimp, leaving shells on. Butterfly them by slicing down the back, leaving the tail on. Remove the vein and soak in ice water for 30 minutes.

Pat the shrimp dry in paper toweling and sauté in the butter, along with the shallots or garlic and onion in a blazer pan or chafing dish. Add the brandy, allow to heat and flame. When flame dies down, add the other ingredients. When sauce is bubbly, serve immediately with plenty of hot French bread, using the pieces of bread to soak up the sauce.

For cheese-loving Sagittarius, here is a perfect dish. It carries the name of one of France's most famous culinary schools.

Veal Cordon Bleu
(serves 4)

8 veal cutlets, flattened, lightly salted and peppered	2 tablespoons chopped onion *or* 2 chopped shallots
4 slices Swiss cheese	½ cup sliced mushrooms
4 slices ham	¼ cup sherry or dry white wine
Flour	1 tablespoon lemon juice
2 eggs beaten	¼ cup stock
½ cup bread crumbs	¼ cup chopped parsley
2 tablespoons butter	½ cup heavy cream
2 tablespoons olive oil	

Place a slice of cheese and a slice of ham on a veal cutlet and top with another veal cutlet. Dip in flour, then in egg, then in crumbs. Heat oil and butter in skillet and brown cutlets, and allow to cook about 5 minutes. Remove cutlets to a hot platter and keep hot in a 300° oven while the sauce is made.

For the sauce, add onion or shallots and mushrooms to drippings in the pan and sauté until the onion is transparent. Add the wine and cook 1 minute. Add the lemon juice, stock, and parsley and cook 2 minutes more. Add the cream to smooth the sauce. Pour sauce over the cutlets and serve immediately, garnished with lemon slices.

Man has been cooking rice or cracked wheat in a broth for ages. Bulgar, of course, is cracked wheat. Sometimes it's called groats. You'll find the bulgar pilaf in countries all around the Mediterranean, each locale seasoning it a bit differently. Rice, also, is delicious prepared this way. But if you use rice, I would wash it well under running water until the water runs clear. Then I would dry it and proceed with the recipe. Sagittarius likes it partly because it doubles in size, is transformed, with cooking.

Rice or Bulgar Pilaf
(serves 4)

2 tablespoons butter	2 tablespoons chopped parsley
2 tablespoons chopped onion	½ teaspoon powdered oregano
1 clove garlic, minced	4 cups chicken stock *or* light
2 cups rice *or* 2 cups	stock
cracked wheat	¼ cup pine nuts

In a large casserole melt butter, and sauté onion and garlic until transparent. Add the rice (or cracked wheat) and stir well. Add the rest of the ingredients except the stock and pine nuts. Sauté 5 minutes, stirring occasionally. Add the stock. Cover the casserole and place in a 350° oven for 1 hour. Just before serving, sprinkle the pine nuts over all.

Omarr suggests that Sagittarius likes rich, creamy desserts; he'll find this tangy pie to his taste. It has a sour cream topping, too.

Flamingo Pie

1½ cups (16 crackers crushed)   3 tablespoons sugar
    graham cracker crumbs   6 tablespoons melted butter

Combine and press to sides and bottom of a 9-inch pie pan, reserving a few crumbs for topping. Refrigerate 2½ hours or freeze for 10 minutes.

Filling

2 egg yolks   1 teaspoon vanilla or almond
½ cup lemon juice   extract
1 teaspoon grated lemon rind   ¼ teaspoon red food coloring
1 large (15-ounce) can
    sweetened condensed milk

Put egg yolks in large bowl of mixer and beat well. Beat in the lemon juice, lemon rind, and flavoring. Add the condensed milk slowly. Blend in the coloring. Pour into shell and bake in 325° oven 20 minutes. Top with the following:

Topping

½ pint sour cream   1 tablespoon sugar

Blend well and spread on top of pie. Sprinkle remaining crumbs on top. Return to oven for 5 minutes. Chill well and serve.

MENU TWO

Cheese and Bacon Salad

Ninth House Cannelloni

Artichoke Bottoms with Mushrooms

Celestial Pumpkin Pie

Crêpes Suzette

Now Sagittarius, here's a menu for a dinner which should appeal to most of your taste preferences—from the crispy and different salad to the whipped-cream richness of the pie.

Bacon and cheese dominate the making of this very simple but delicious salad. Those two ingredients alone should make it a favorite of Sagittarius.

Cheese and Bacon Salad
(serves 6)

5 slices bacon, diced
2 tablespoons lemon juice
1 head iceberg lettuce, torn in
   bite-size pieces

6 ounces Cheddar cheese
  Salt to taste

Fry bacon until crisp. Add lemon juice to hot bacon and drippings. Toss lettuce and grated cheese together and sprinkle with salt. Top with hot bacon mixture and toss well. Serve immediately.

Here is another entrée from a far-off land. It had its origin in Italy and there are many versions of it, as happens when a recipe is passed from chef to chef. Here I include my recipe for crepes and spaghetti sauce. This recipe is great for entertaining, because you can do it ahead of time and pop it in the oven.

Ninth House Cannelloni
(serves 4–6)

½ pound beef, cut in
    ½-inch cubes
¼ pound veal, cut in
    ½-inch cubes
¼ cup chopped onion
1 clove garlic, minced
½ teaspoon lemon peel
2 tablespoons butter or
    margarine
1 (10-ounce) package frozen
    chopped spinach,
    cooked and drained

Dash thyme
Dash pepper
½ teaspoon salt
2 beaten eggs
16 *crepes* (see page 242)
1½ cups *spaghetti sauce*
    (see page 242)
1 cup sour cream
½ cup Parmesan cheese

Cook beef, veal, onion, garlic, lemon peel, and butter together for 20 minutes. Add spinach and put mixture through the fine blade of a meat grinder. Season with thyme, pepper, and salt. Add eggs; mix well. Put mixture in a pastry bag and fill each crepe. Arrange side by side in a 10 x 6 x 1½-inch baking dish. Cover with spaghetti sauce blended with sour cream. Bake in 350° oven 10 minutes. Sprinkle with cheese and brown under broiler for 2 minutes.

continued

Crepes
(Makes 16)

6 eggs	2 tablespoons cold water
4 tablespoons flour, sifted twice	¼ teaspoon salt

Place in mixing bowl and beat vigorously to consistency of heavy cream. (If still too thick, add more cold water.) Butter a small frying pan with a piece of butter about the size of a small walnut, and when butter begins to bubble, pour in enough batter (about a tablespoon) to cover bottom of pan with thin layer. Rotate the pan quickly to spread the batter as thin as possible. Brown, flip over, and brown other side. Stack the crepes flat until all are baked.

Spaghetti Sauce

1 pound lean, ground beef	1 (20-ounce) can tomato puree
1 pound ground veal	2 cups beef stock or bouillon
1 cup sourdough bread crumbs	½ teaspoon fennel
½ cup olive oil	½ teaspoon oregano
1 large onion, chopped	½ teaspoon sweet basil
2 cloves garlic, chopped	¼ teaspoon nutmeg
¾ pound mushrooms, sliced	¼ teaspoon rosemary
1 cup burgundy	½ bay leaf
1 (20-ounce) can Italian-style tomatoes	1 teaspoon paprika
	Salt and fresh cracked pepper

Moisten bread crumbs with ½ cup wine and work into the meats. Spread flat on a roasting pan and bake in a 350° oven, stirring a few times, until it is browned. Heat olive oil in a Dutch oven, add onion, garlic, and mushrooms. Cook and stir 5 minutes. Add tomatoes, puree, bouillon, and remaining burgundy. Simmer about 10 minutes. Add the meat and all the spices. Simmer 1½ hours, skimming occasionally.

An ideal vegetable to go with the cannelloni would be artichoke bottoms. These are stuffed with mushrooms and garnished with cheese—again a combination of flavors to satisfy Sagittarius.

Artichoke Bottoms with Mushrooms
(serves 6–8)

8 artichokes	¾ cup *béchamel sauce*
3 tablespoons butter	Salt and pepper
½ pound mushrooms	¼ cup grated Grueyère cheese

Cook artichokes in boiling salted water until tender, about 40 minutes. Drain and remove inner leaves and chokes. Sauté them in the butter. Remove to a flat casserole dish. Slice the mushrooms thin and sauté them in the butter. Add the béchamel sauce to the mushrooms and season with salt and pepper. Fill the chokes with the mixture. Sprinkle with cheese, dot with butter, and brown in a 375° oven about 10 minutes.

Béchamel Sauce

2 tablespoons butter	1 tablespoon chopped onion
2 tablespoons flour	2 tablespoons finely minced ham
2 cups scalded milk	¼ teaspoon nutmeg
1 tablespoon butter (additional)	Salt and pepper to taste

With the 1 tablespoon of butter, sauté the onion and ham until the onion is transparent and golden and the ham nicely brown. Add the scalded milk to this and let steep for 30 minutes. Bring the 2 tablespoons butter to the bubbly stage, stir in the flour, and let cook a few minutes. Strain the milk into the flour-butter mixture, stirring constantly until sauce is thick and creamy with a glossy sheen. Adjust seasoning with salt and pepper and add the nutmeg.

The Sagittarius sweet tooth should find this dessert soul-satisfying. It doesn't necessarily follow that pumpkin pie must be served only on Thanksgiving.

Celestial Pumpkin Pie

1 envelope unflavored gelatin	2 egg whites
¾ cup brown sugar, firmly packed	1½ teaspoons vanilla
½ teaspoon salt	⅓ cup sugar
1 teaspoon cinnamon	½ teaspoon grated orange rind
½ teaspoon ginger	½ teaspoon grated lemon rind
1 can (about 1 pound) pumpkin (1½ cups)	½ cup whipping cream, whipped
2 egg yolks	1 cup coarsely chopped pecans
½ cup milk	1 (9-inch) baked pastry shell *or* crumb crust

Use a 9-inch baked pastry shell or crumb crust. Soften gelatin in ¼ cup milk, then combine gelatin mixture with brown sugar, salt, cinnamon, ginger, pumpkin, egg yolks, and remaining ¼ cup milk in saucepan. Cook over medium heat, stirring constantly until mixture comes to a boil. Do not boil. Cool; chill until mixture is thoroughly cold and mounds when spooned. Beat egg whites until soft peaks form; add vanilla; add sugar slowly; continue beating until mixture is stiff and glossy. Fold into pumpkin mixture; fold in orange rind, lemon rind, whipping cream, and pecan meats. Pile into crust; chill several hours, or until set. Garnish with orange sections, additional whipped cream, and pecans, if desired.

There is an extra recipe for crêpes Suzette. Use the batter for the crepes as I just gave it, adding a tablespoon of brandy and a tablespoon of sugar. Then make a . . .

Crêpes Suzette

Crepes (see page 242)   1 tablespoon sugar
1 tablespoon brandy

Make the crepe batter as shown but adding the brandy and sugar.

Suzette Butter

½ cup sweet butter   ¼ cup orange liqueur (curaçao,
½ cup powdered sugar   Cointreau, Grand
    Grated peel and juice   Marnier)
        of 1 orange   ¼ cup brandy
1 teaspoon lemon juice   Sugar

Cream together the butter and sugar; work in the orange peel, juice, lemon juice, and orange liqueur. Spread the mixture on the crepes. Fold them in half, then in quarters. Put them in the blazer pan of a chafing dish which has been well buttered. Sprinkle with sugar and with the brandy. Ignite and serve flaming.

MENU THREE

Escargots Sagittarius

Individual Lunar Meat Loaves

Macaroni and Cheese Olé

Zodiac Trifle

*Our final Sagittarius menu will satisfy you in almost
all of your favorite tastes. The appetizer is daring. The
entrée is of the meat loaf variety. The casserole has a
macaroni base that doubles in bulk and the dessert is
one of the richest and creamiest I know.*

⚹ 🏹 ⚹

*The idea of eating snails is still considered somewhat more than daring to a
lot of people. But Sagittarius will revel in the dish.*

Escargots Sagittarius
(serves 6)

2	cans snails (about 18 per can)	2 cloves garlic, finely chopped
1¼	cups butter	1 tablespoon chopped parsley
1	tablespoon finely minced shallot	1 tablespoon chopped chives
		Salt and pepper to taste

Blend ingredients thoroughly. Into each snail shell place a nugget of the
butter. Insert the snail in the shell. Seal this opening with a thick coat of
the butter. Place shells on a snail rack or you may use a preheated pie tin
filled with rock salt. Bake in a 400° oven about 7 minutes or until snails
are heated through and butter is foamy. Serve with hot sourdough
French bread.

⚹ 🏹 ⚹

Of one thing you can be sure, Sagittarius: you're not alone in favoring meat loaves and such. Ground meat is still one of the most economical meat courses. Recipes for it abound. Here is a richly different one that you'll be proud to serve to company.

Individual Lunar Meat Loaves
(serves 6)

2½ pounds ground chuck
2 tablespoons grated onion juice
   Salt and pepper to taste
2 tablespoons ketchup
2 slices bread, crusts trimmed
¼ cup dry vermouth
1 slightly beaten egg
1 tablespoon cornstarch
2 tablespoons brown sugar

2 or more tablespoons ketchup
2 or more tablespoons dry vermouth
1 cup pineapple juice
2 tablespoons lemon juice
2 teaspoons soy sauce
¼ teaspoon powdered ginger
½ cup chopped almonds

Soak the bread slices in ¼ cup vermouth and wring out; add it to the chuck, onion juice, salt and pepper, ketchup, and egg. Blend well and mold into 6 individual loaves. Place in a shallow casserole in a 350° oven for 30 minutes. Combine the brown sugar and cornstarch, and blend with the pineapple juice in a separate saucepan. Add the remaining ingredients except the nuts and cook over a medium heat until mixture clarifies and thickens. Drain any of the juice in the roasting pan and cover the loaves with the sauce. Bake 30 minutes longer, basting occasionally. During the last 10 minutes top with nuts.

This hearty starch casserole to go with the meat loaves could also serve as an entrée if a Sagittarian wished. For persons of the Ninth House love their pasta, says Omarr. This one has a flavor from south of the border.

Macaroni and Cheese Olé

(serves 6)

2 cups (8 ounces) uncooked elbow macaroni	½ teaspoon salt
Boiling salted water	1 teaspoon chili powder
2 eggs, slightly beaten	¼ teaspoon pepper
2 tablespoons instant minced onion	2½ cups milk
2 tablespoons dried red or green pepper flakes	½ pound diced sharp Cheddar cheese (about 2 cups)
	1 cup sliced ripe olives
	⅓ cup grated Parmesan cheese

Cook macaroni in boiling salted water until barely tender. Drain thoroughly but do not rinse. Meanwhile, beat eggs slightly in a buttered 2½-quart casserole. Add seasonings and gradually add milk, blending thoroughly. Add hot macaroni, cheese cubes, and olives. Bake uncovered in moderate-slow 325° oven for 30 minutes. Stir mixture lightly with a fork and sprinkle with Parmesan cheese. Continue baking 20–30 minutes longer. Allow macaroni to stand 5 minutes before serving.

Merry old England has not made too many contributions to the world of cookery, if you omit roast beef and Yorkshire pudding. But the English make one of the richest, best desserts I know and, wouldn't you know, they call it "a trifle." After you eat it, plan on dieting for the next three days. But Sagittarius should love it.

Zodiac Trifle

(serves 12, but has to be made large)

1 (3¼-ounce) package vanilla pudding/pie filling mix	2 tablespoons red raspberry preserves
2 cups half-and-half	1 (10-inch) round sponge cake layer
2 tablespoons dark Puerto Rican rum	¼ cup brandy
2¼ cups whipping cream	¼ cup dry sherry wine
3 tablespoons sugar	30–38 whole strawberries

Combine pudding mix with half-and-half. Cook on temperature-controlled top burner, using a low flame at 200° for 12–15 minutes or until mixture comes to a boil and partially thickens. Stir well occasionally. Turn off flame and allow to cool slightly. Mix in rum. Chill pudding thoroughly. Whip 1¼ cups cream and 1 tablespoon sugar until stiff. Fold into chilled pudding mixture. Using a brush, coat a deep 10-inch diameter bowl with raspberry preserves to within 1 inch of the top.

To Assemble: Slice sponge cake horizontally into fourths. Place top slice, crust side up, in bottom of preserves-coated bowl, curving outer edge of layer upward. Combine brandy and sherry, and sprinkle ¼ of mixture (approximately 2 tablespoons) over the cake slice. Next, spread ⅓ of chilled pudding mixture over the surface of the cake slice. Repeat procedure two additional times. Finish by arranging 15–18 strawberries on the top of the third layer of pudding and cover with fourth cake layer, crust side down. Sprinkle with remaining brandy-sherry mixture.

continued

Whip remaining 1 cup cream and 2 tablespoons sugar until stiff. Place whipped cream in pastry bag fitted with a fluted tip. Make 12 mounds of whipped cream around the edge of the bowl and 3 mounds across the diameter. Top each mound with a strawberry. Refrigerate at least 2 hours. To serve, spoon onto chilled dessert plates.

So, Sagittarius, loosen your belt, and live it up. Everything here should stimulate you and please you.

Capricorn Menu One

Tenth House Cold Borsch
Ossobuco Saturn
Rutabaga Bake
Golden Potatoes
Zabaglione Pudding with Sauce

# Capricorn Menu Two

Cold Moon Soup
Wined Tongue
Potatoes Peru
Red Cabbage
Hasty Pudding

# Capricorn Menu Three

Vichyssoise à la Capricorn *or*
Salad Omarr
Fried Pig's Knuckles
Scalloped Cabbage
Lyonnaise Potatoes
Zuppa Inglese

CAPRICORN

Sydney Omarr on Capricorn

Earthy, professional, aware of time and destiny—that's a partial description of Capricorn, the natural tenth zodiacal sign. Born under Capricorn, you have learned that you often have to wait for results, that work is not always immediately appreciated. You can be withdrawn, because although giving the appearance of being cold, you seek warmth to the extent that love becomes as essential as food for your well-being. This being so, you do not promiscuously expose your feelings. They are too tender to be trifled with, and thus, you give the impression of being cool. This is a false impression. Born under Capricorn, you have high principles, ideals, and ambitions. The

Tenth House is associated with career, standing in the community, principle, ambition, ultimate success, and authority. Saturn is your solar ruling planet. It seems, at times, that nothing comes easily, and it is usually later in life that your efforts are celebrated.

Your food likes could be described as peculiar by many. You are fond of vinegar, sour pickles, artichokes, baked rutabagas, and cabbage. You are not averse to a well-aged filet mignon, either!

You are somewhat of a pioneer in the food area; you will experiment

Food is basic, a part of life where you are concerned—not in the sense that you eat to live. Rather, you enjoy meals; you gain spiritual as well as other nourishment from what you eat. You are somewhat of a pioneer in the food area. You will experiment, mixing basic ingredients to come up with something different. You are much aware of time. You are patient enough to tackle dishes that require patience to complete. It is also wise for you to eat "on time."

Being earthy, your tastes run to the basics, but not so much as do Taurus'. Because you are highly principled, you are much concerned with ideas and ideals, thus, good talk, rich talk, meaningful conversation are as important to you at meal time as is a fine wine. Literary giant Henry Miller is a Capricorn; I've often dined with this author of *Tropic of Cancer*. His talk is remembered more than the food. He is also an excellent listener. That's a valuable Capricorn secret: you listen, absorb, and file words, ideas, knowledge that at a later date the subconscious brings forth. Miller eats with relish, enthusiasm; a meal becomes an occasion, a repast. He, like most Capricorns, knows the secret of savoring food. His works, from the *Tropic* books to *The Colossus of Marousi*, are filled with references to eating, to great lunches, dinners. In my opinion, Henry Miller could produce a great cookbook!

Meaningful conversation is as important at meal time as a fine wine

Marlene Dietrich is another Capricorn, concerned with food and astrology. Conrad Hilton, much aware of fine dining, is also a Capricorn. So are Xavier Cugat, Betty Furness, Ava Gardner, and gourmet-actor Danny Kaye, whose Chinese food creations are regarded as masterpieces.

You are partial to dark colors such as black bread. Food that comes from the earth also suits you like mushrooms and truffles. A green lettuce salad pleases you. You desire food you can chew; hard objects, such as walnuts, appear to harmonize with your tastes. String beans, tongue with mustard, and horseradish could also be high on your list of favorites.

You appreciate culinary efforts. Your memories are laced with meals enjoyed in the past. You can recall recipes, those especially associated with one of your parents. Capricorns are shrewd, in the kitchen and elsewhere. You know how to bide your time. You are not one to watch water as it heats to a boiling point; you know it's going to "get there." Saturn is restrictive, so, unlike Sagittarius, you do not like your food "spread out." You prefer orderliness, but a different kind of order than one expects from other Earth sign natives like Taurus and Virgo. Your kind of order at the dining table is one in which certain habits are adhered to: white wine with a fish course, red wine with succulent meat.

Your most harmonious dining companions are Scorpio, Pisces, Taurus, and Virgo subjects. An Aries, however, does provide a feeling of security, and you can make yourself at home when breaking bread with an Aries native. I once arranged a dinner meeting for myself with Aries Gloria Swanson and Capricorn Henry Miller. All went well. Capricorn and Aries enjoyed themselves, especially when the brilliant Miss Swanson regaled us with tales of early Hollywood—the color and spectacle, the pomp and ceremony. Capricorns like references to the past. When serving Capricorn, a good ploy is to refer to previous times when this or that particular dish was served. Capricorn is intensely aware of temperature. Thus, Capricorn can appreciate frozen foods as well as natural or fresh foodstuffs. Capricorn Marlene Dietrich, in writing about steak and its preparation, advises that it be removed from the refrigerator long before it is ready for cooking. Many of us might take this for granted. For a Capricorn, it is important enough to write about. Hot and cold—a Capricorn is aware of these, and is not comfortable if the dining room temperature is "off" in either direction.

Listen, Capricorn: Despite denials, you yearn for recognition, and this applies to the area of cooking as well as in what might be your chosen endeavor. You'll prepare dishes that leave an imprint, a memory. That's your hallmark—something to recall, to talk about at a future

Your most harmonious dining companions are Scorpio, Pisces, Taurus, and Virgo

Capricorns like references to the past

rendezvous. For you, this is a way of life, and so is good food, enjoying what you eat, relishing, savoring both the food and talk.

Of all the members of the signs, you are the one most likely to accent cold rather than hot soup. This is unusual, but it is Capricornian. Of course, we do not refer to hot soup that grows cold. We mean a cold soup preparation, such as vichyssoise. That delightful cold dish, with the main ingredient of potato, is especially suited to you, Capricorn.

Taurus persons attract you. Dinner could lead to romance when shared with natives of this sign. Although Taureans have relatively steady diet patterns, you are inspired to try a variety of dishes when dining with these natives. Taurus looks up to you and wants to impress you, thus, when with you, Taurus is enthusiastic and feels daring in the culinary area. The Venus of Taurus combines with your Saturn to inspire conversation, physical attraction, curiosity. A "smoky" atmosphere prevails here; the lights are low, the flavors are subtle, and Venus and Saturn—romance and reality—intermingle in a very strange, compelling manner.

You enjoy taking your time when making selections from a menu, but Gemini could grow impatient. Gemini might attempt to correct your dining habits. The talk could be bogged down with details about assignments, tasks, chores, relations with coworkers, associates. Gemini, for some reason, believes you are "holding back" and makes it a personal project to break down your restrictions, real or otherwise.

With another Capricorn, reality seems to take wings—it flies away. Two Capricorns do not necessarily harmonize. It seems that when dining together, members of this sign pick foods not exactly to their liking. An element of deception is present. When you dine with another Capricorn you seem, invariably, to choose seafood. Check the Pisces menu; it's a good one when entertaining a Piscean or another Capricorn.

As for the Pisces-born, you are stimulated by their conversation, flow of ideas. Discussion turns to objects of art, gifts, flower arrangements, wines, delicate dishes. You delight in having natives of this sign prepare breakfast, lunch, or dinner. Pisces is creatively inspired by your presence. It is a good combination, especially for dining at home, a house warming, talking about current projects having to do with writing,

Of all the signs, Capricorns are the ones most likely to accent cold rather than hot soup

Two Capricorns do not necessarily harmonize

drama. You are more diplomatic with Pisces than you are perhaps with any other sign. When not eating at home with a Pisces, you enjoy—both of you—taking a journey to find a special chef, friend, or cafe. Talk flows, ideas are plentiful, and so is the wine.

You are invigorated by a workout prior to dining. Riding a bicycle (stationary or mobile), running around a track, having a steam bath—these activities "prepare" you and sharpen your appetite. A Capricorn likes to take time, to prepare, to get ready, to anticipate. This attitude applies as much to food as to other departments of life.

Capricorn likes to take time, to prepare, to get ready, to anticipate

Because Saturn is "dry," you seem to have a perpetual thirst. You are fond of liquids, not only the alcoholic variety, but milk and water. A glass of cool water can bring forth your praise, almost as much as a sip of rare wine. You are aware of values, and, at one time in your life, you could have been a health buff. In this way, you're similar to Virgo. During other periods, you are a gourmet. You usually are aware of the value of what you eat, monetarily, nutritionally, or qualitatively, in comparison to a similar dinner.

You often boil eggs, either for a snack or to be stored for future use. There again is the element of time, your awareness of the future. Like a squirrel you will store nuts—or hard-boiled eggs!

You seem to have an instinctive knowledge of what foods are good for you. You are partial to milk, puddings, soups, foods that contain spinach, and eggs.

You seem to have an instinctive knowledge of what foods are good for you

You are fascinated with Cancers, especially in the food area. These people are fine chefs, and you enjoy eating! You are a bit more daring, much less conservative, when dining with Cancer. Melancholia, however, often clouds the occasion when you share food with Cancer. There is attraction, but either you or the Cancer-born begins to worry about how long the relationship will last. Talk turns to partnerships, marriage, contracts, legal obligations. (For light banter, it is Pisces for you.) For discussions having to do with the changing of unfavorable habits, it is a Cancer. There are some sharp disagreements here, and it is not wise to consume too much alcohol. A discussion could be transformed into a rousing battle, "under the influence."

Leo arouses your interest in the hidden, the occult, the secrets of others, including the sexual patterns of celebrities. With a Leo, you dine on international fare: Japanese, Chinese, French, Greek, Italian. Horizons are broadened, and this you appreciate even though you often accuse Leo of being overly dramatic. Leos admire your methods, techniques. Leos strive to bring you out of any emotional shell, and when you dine with a Leo there is often a new acquaintance present. The relationship here is apt to be tenuous; a break seems to loom as a constant threat. The bright Sun of Leo is an excellent antidote to gloomy Saturn; Leo "drags" you out of yourself. Leo is somewhat of a mystery where you are concerned. You want to discern, to perceive, but no matter how you try, the challenge remains.

With a Leo, you dine on international fare

If you have any dietary habits or rules, they are apt to be broken when dining with a Virgo. Exotic and foreign fare dominates here. Virgo touches that part of your chart associated with long journeys, faraway places. Because you feel a Virgo may be attempting to restrict you, you rebel. You try foods that are not generally in your category. Virgo is usually physically attracted to you. The Virgo appetite increases in your presence. In turn, you become the food adventurer. The two signs, Capricorn and Virgo, are harmonious. You enjoy dining with a Virgo. One reason is that he or she understands food values. You appreciate this even though, at times, you do not appear to take heed. With Virgo, you try oysters Rockefeller, clams, boiled or broiled lobster, to say nothing of linguini and ossobuco. You reach out for something new, different, inspired by the Virgo's exclamations and explanations. When you're entertaining guests from another town or country, Virgo proves a great ally.

Dining with a Virgo could be hazardous to your diet

Dining with Libra could be a delightful experience. Your ego is salved, you could burst with pride, because a Libra encourages you to scale the heights. You can be basic, practical, earthy; Libra is delicate, artistic, balanced. The combination, in other areas, could be distracting, but where food is concerned, there is interest, curiosity, fascination. Your tastes are more mundane than those of Libra, but a Libra feels comfortable with you. You share each other's food. Libra tries what you have ordered, and you return the compliment. In the kitchen, Libras inspire you to make the best of everything, to show finesse, to create a special touch, a garnish, a decoration, a unique tantalizing dessert. With you, a Libra prefers the Capricorn dishes, so if you want to impress a Libra, stick to what you know. With a Virgo, try the foreign dishes, but where Libra is concerned, be yourself in food, personality, conversation, and actions.

Scorpio provides pleasure. Many of your friends were born under this zodiacal sign. Scorpios encourage you to fulfill hopes, desires. For strictly social dining, Scorpio is the perfect partner for you. You are less somber, you are even "flighty." What you must avoid when dining with a Scorpio is a tendency to overindulge in food and drink. Scorpio could face the same problem. When the two of you get together, it could be wine, women (or men), and song: but there is a tomorrow (as you are well aware, being a time-conscious Capricorn). The funny part is that you enjoy making resolutions while with Scorpio—and as you make them, you break them.

What you must avoid when dining with a Scorpio is a tendency to overindulge in food and drink

A Sagittarius admires your possessions, but you may feel confined when dining with natives of this sign. You share knowledge with this Fire sign, and the Jupiter of Sagittarius helps cheer your Saturn. But the meal tends to bog down. You try too hard to impress.

An Aquarian brings gifts when invited to your dinner table. You try to create something new. The atmosphere is not exactly a relaxed one. You are made aware of what you own and lack, as well as your culinary capabilities and shortcomings.

But there is with you always a next time. Hope springs eternal! And this is a valuable commodity, an essential ingredient for enjoying meals and the living of life.

Mike Roy on Capricorn

Omarr has set the stage for one of the most interesting of human dramas. A Capricorn, says he, is earthy. His or her diet, preferentially, springs from the Earth. I find this most interesting. The Earth is the beginning and the end for humans.

I wonder how many of us found a true evaluation of the Earth prior to the time our astronauts, orbiting the Moon and looking back at us, talked in terms of "the Good Earth." When you stop to think about it, the Earth is truly "good." Humans have always placed a highly possessive value on it. To own a piece of the Good Earth is still a dream of many, whether it be a humble home or extensive acreage. In the Scriptures, there is a reference to Earth: "Earth (dust) thou art and to Earth (dust) thou returneth." I find it entirely appropriate that, here in the Tenth House, we should discuss human's use of the fruit of the Earth.

Capricorn is earthy

The art of cooking, like astrology, is so ancient that we don't know its exact origin. There are those who tell us, and they are experts in the field of archeology, that the exposure of meat to flame was probably accidental, but having discovered that cooked meat tasted better, the first "chef" began the art. Way back in the dim recesses of caves, humans wrapped meat in leaves—probably to keep it from becoming too burned—and found that the leaves gave new taste to their primitive culinary effort; and thus began the exacting science of seasoning. There must have been a period when humans tried various roots, barks, and leaves for their edible qualities. An ingenious human found a means of heating water in a stone, hollowed out in the form of a basin. The clay pot succeeded this primitive vessel. Some humans, ages ago, discovered how to make a twig or tree branch into a spit. The pot and the spit, however elementary they were in the beginning, allowed humans to undertake all manner of culinary operations.

The areas around the Mediterranean give us some history in the prehistoric discoveries of the origin of cookery: fragments of pottery, bones, traces of hearths.

In ancient Greece, the cooks were actually bakers. Homer, in *The Iliad* and *The Odyssey*, says it was the host himself, however exalted he might be, who, with the help of friends themselves men of rank, prepared and cooked the meals. Later, slaves came into the picture. In the fourth century B.C., Athenian cooks, as depicted in the Greek theater, were slaves. In spite of their low estate, they played an important, often pompous, part in the life of the city. Poets taunted them for their pretensions. A special law permitted the cook who invented a new dish the sole privilege of making it and selling it to the public.

The Romans—no fools themselves—sent a deputation to Athens that brought back the laws of Solon, Greek art, letters, cooks, and gastronomers. It led to a complete reformation of the Roman table and heralded the Roman banquet or "orgy" we read about today.

It's easy to follow the cook's trail from there. The Roman legions took cuisine to the far corners of the Earth as they were then known. I recently ran across some ancient cooking names. Here are four:

Cadmos, who was a cook for the King of Sidon in Phoenicia, according to legend, introduced writing to Greece.

Archestratus traveled the world, not only to describe its customs, but also to record its eating habits.

Maesenas, says Pliny, was the first to serve at his table the meat of an ass' foal.

Fulvius Hirpinius invented a special cage for fattening pigs for the table.

These are but four, but they are typical of the creative humans who lived for the palate's satisfaction and shared their new discoveries with their fellow humans. All of them looked to the "Good Earth" for the material to develop their art and, having found it, passed it on for the future to enjoy. They point up the nature of the chef, the love of the Earth and the fruits that spring from it. Capricorn, you're in good company. Now let's enter your House and examine your special menus.

MENU ONE

Tenth House Cold Borsch

Ossobuco Saturn

Rutabaga Bake

Golden Potatoes

Zabaglione Pudding with Sauce

Cold soups, says Omarr, should make you happy. And in keeping with Capricorn's fondness of the root vegetable, this ancient recipe should start us off with a flourish. Russia is generally conceded to be the point of origin, but the Armenians and a host of others have long served it. (Sometimes they spell it with a "t" on the end. Both versions are correct.)

Tenth House Cold Borsch
(serves 4)

¾ pound lean beef	½ pound cooked beets, diced
4 cups salted water	¼ red cabbage, coarsely
2 sprigs parsley	chopped
1 leek, coarsely chopped	1 potato
1 carrot	1 onion
1 bay leaf	¼ pound mushrooms
1 clove garlic	1 cup sour cream
3 peppercorns	

Dice the lean beef and put it into a saucepan with 2 quarts of salted water. Bring the water slowly to a boil; skim carefully, and add parsley, leek, and carrot. Add bay leaf, garlic, and peppercorns. Simmer, covered, for 1½ hours, skimming from time to time. Remove the meat from the soup; strain soup into a saucepan and add beets, red cabbage, potato, onion, and mushrooms. Bring to a boil, skim, and simmer, uncovered, for 1½ hours. Return meat. Chill and stir in sour cream before serving.

Here is a recipe you should especially enjoy.

Ossobuco Saturn
(serves 4)

4 veal shin bones, 4 inches long, with meat	1 cup water
1 tablespoon butter	1 teaspoon chopped parsley
2 tablespoons flour	½ clove garlic, chopped
½ teaspoon salt	4 strips lemon peel, 1 inch long
½ teaspoon pepper	1 anchovy fillet, chopped
½ cup dry white wine	1 tablespoon stock
	1 tablespoon butter

Butter a deep skillet. Roll bones in flour, place in skillet, add salt and pepper, and cook until well browned, turning bones over occasionally during browning process. Add wine and continue cooking until wine evaporates. Add cup of water; cover skillet, and cook 1 hour, adding more water if necessary. Five minutes before serving add parsley, garlic, lemon peel, and anchovy and cook 2 minutes longer, turning bones over once. Place bones on serving dish. Add 1 tablespoon stock to pan gravy; add butter, mix well, and pour over bones.

They call them rutabagas in some parts of the country; yellow turnips in others. Whatever you call them, they are delicious, and they belong to Capricorn since they, too, are root vegetables. By the way, this is a most unusual recipe for them.

Rutabaga Bake
(serves 4–6)

2 pounds rutabagas	2 tablespoons melted butter
½ cup fine dry bread crumbs	1½ teaspoons salt
½ cup milk	Large pinch of sugar
2 eggs, well beaten	

Peel rutabagas and cut in cubes, then cover with boiling water. Place a lid on the pan, and cook over moderate heat until tender when pierced with a fork. Drain thoroughly. Mash as smooth as possible, or put through a ricer, then beat in all remaining ingredients. Spoon into 1½-quart baking dish or casserole and bake in a preheated 350° oven for 1 hour.

There's just no doubt about it, the potato is the king of the root vegetables. Capricorn, along with the rest of the world, will find this one of the most different in any collection—so good it could "make" any menu as a starch.

Golden Potatoes
(serves 4)

4 medium potatoes
½ medium onion
1 teaspoon seasoned salt
1 (3-ounce) package pimiento
    cream cheese

½ pint sour cream
¼ pound (about) grated sharp
    Cheddar cheese

Boil potatoes in their jackets until tender. Cool, peel, and slice. Place in buttered 2½- to 3-quart shallow baking dish. Grate onion over potatoes. Sprinkle with seasoned salt. Mash cream cheese and blend with sour cream; spoon over potatoes. Top with Cheddar cheese. Bake uncovered, in moderate 350° oven 30 to 35 minutes or until cheese is melted and potatoes are piping hot.

If Capricorn likes root vegetables and cold soup, he or she loves pudding. Here is one of the most elegant on the face of the Earth. It originated in Italy.

Zabaglione Pudding with Sauce
(serves 4)

6 egg yolks	3 tablespoons brandy
1 cup sugar	1 cup heavy cream, whipped
6–8 tablespoons sherry	*Zabaglione sauce*
1 ounce gelatin	Sliced almonds
2 tablespoons cold water	

In the top of a double boiler, combine the egg yolks with sugar and sherry, and whip the mixture over hot, but not boiling, water until it thickens. Stir in gelatin, softened in cold water and dissolved over hot water. Put the pan into a bowl of ice and stir the zabaglione well until it is thick and free of bubbles. When it is almost cold, fold in brandy and whipped cream and pour into individual molds. Chill the zabaglione, unmold it, and serve with zabaglione sauce. Sprinkle with almonds.

Zabaglione Sauce

3 egg yolks	3–4 tablespoons marsala *or*
2–3 tablespoons sugar	sherry
1½ tablespoons brandy	

To make the sauce: repeat the first process as above, stirring egg yolks and sugar over hot water until the sauce is of the desired consistency. Stir in sherry and brandy and serve immediately.

MENU TWO

Cold Moon Soup

Wined Tongue

Potatoes Peru

Red Cabbage

Hasty Pudding

In preparing, testing, and combining the recipes for Capricorn, I believe I found a most varied and interesting combination of flavors and materials. Here's another menu for the Tenth House.

✳ 🕊 ✳

Cold Moon Soup
(serves 6)

2 (10½-ounce) cans chicken,
     turkey, or beef consommé
¼ cup sherry
     Juice of 2 large lemons
2 (4-ounce) cans mushroom
     stems and pieces,
     reserve juice

1 teaspoon savory salt
8 small green onions
6–8 sprigs parsley
     Sour cream

Combine consommé, sherry, lemon juice, juice from mushrooms, and savory salt. Chop onions, parsley, and mushrooms very fine; add to liquid. Cover; chill several hours. Stir before each serving. Top each serving with a spoonful of sour cream.

✳ 🕊 ✳

For Capricorn, Omarr speaks of tongue as a suitable dish. Try this recipe.

Wined Tongue
(serves 6)

1 fresh tongue, calf *or* veal	1 cup tomato sauce
Butter or margarine	Salt and pepper
1 onion, chopped	2 tablespoons chopped pickles
2 carrots, cut in small cubes	*or* relish
2 cup sauterne, chablis, *or*	½ teaspoon chopped oregano
other white dinner wine	1 tablespoon fresh chopped
	parsley

Cover tongue with water; bring to boiling. Reduce beat; simmer 20 minutes. Cool until easy to handle; remove skin. Brown meat in butter to which onion and carrots have been added. When brown, add wine, tomato sauce, salt, and pepper. Simmer, covered, 45 minutes. Skim off excess fat. Remove tongue, keeping warm. Add chopped pickles and herbs to pan liquid. Cut tongue in thin slices, arrange on serving platter, and pour sauce over all.

Another potato dish, to accompany the tongue. It's peppery and different.

Potatoes Peru
(serves 6)

½ cup cottage cheese
4 hard-cooked egg yolks
1 teaspoon finely grated onion
1 tablespoon finely chopped
      mild green chilies, fresh
      or canned (amount depends
      on pepper strength)
½ cup heavy cream

½ cup oil
    Salt and pepper
6 large (12 small) hot, freshly
      boiled potatoes
    Olive slices
    Radish slices
    Sliced hard-cooked eggs

Put cottage cheese through a sieve and into a mixing bowl. Put egg yolks through sieve and add to cheese. Beat with a wire whisk until smooth. Beat in onion and chopped chilies and gradually beat in cream alternately with oil. Season to taste with salt and pepper. Serve over very hot potatoes, garnished with olive, radish, and hard-cooked egg slices.

This is a perfect vegetable to go with tongue. It is also about as different a version of sweet-sour cabbage as I've been able to come up with.

Red Cabbage
(serves 6)

1 head red cabbage, sliced thin	Dash of pepper
2 onions, sliced	¼ pound butter, chicken,
2 apples, cored and sliced	or bacon fat
½ cup red currant jelly	4 medium-size ham knuckles
1 bay leaf	3 ounces vinegar
Salt	

Mix red cabbage with onions, apples, currant jelly, bay leaf, salt, and pepper. Put butter, chicken, or bacon fat in heavy casserole with tight-fitting cover; add red cabbage, ham knuckles, ¼ cup water. Bring to a boil and cook slowly 2½ hours. Add vinegar at the last minute; remove bay leaf.

Once in a while everyone finds oneself in a position to come up with a dessert at the last minute. This is a Capricorn-type pudding you can whip up in a flash.

Hasty Pudding
(serves 6)

1 (3¼-ounce) package
  vanilla pudding mix
1½ cups milk
¼ teaspoon salt
1 teaspoon shredded orange
  rind

¼ cup sherry
½ cup whipping cream
1 pint fresh strawberries
  or 2 large bananas

Make pudding mix as directed on package, but using only 1½ cups milk. Add salt, orange rind. Remove from heat; stir in sherry; cool. Beat cream until stiff; fold into cooled pudding. Wash and hull berries (or peel and slice bananas). Divide fruit into 6 dessert dishes; top each serving with pudding. Garnish with extra whipped cream and fruit if desired.

MENU THREE

Vichyssoise à la Capricorn
or
Salad Omarr

Fried Pig's Knuckles

Scalloped Cabbage

Lyonnaise Potatoes

Zuppa Inglese

Here is still another menu for Capricorn. This one includes a mingling of classic continental fare and farmhouse dinner table dishes.

Of all the cold soups in cookbooks, perhaps none stands out so much as the classic vichyssoise. This makes a large amount, but it keeps well refrigerated.

Vichyssoise à la Capricorn
(serves 6)

4 tablespoons butter	5 potatoes, peeled, quartered
6 onions, sliced	1 quart milk
4 leeks (no green), sliced	1 pint half-and-half
6 cups chicken stock	1 pint heavy cream

Heat butter in large saucepan; add onions and leeks, cover, and simmer until soft. Pour in chicken stock and add potatoes; cover and simmer 45 minutes. Sieve through food mill or strainer. Return to saucepan, add milk and half-and-half; bring to a boil. Strain again; cool and add heavy cream. Refrigerate overnight. Makes 4 quarts.

Every sign—regardless of its propensity for cold soups or what have you—should have at least one salad. Since Omarr has mentioned that Capricorn likes a cool salad, let's name this alternate first dish after our teacher.

Salad Omarr

(serves 4-6)

1 head lettuce or other greens	12 deviled egg halves
3 tomatoes, peeled, halved	6 canned artichoke hearts,
12 stalks cooked broccoli	halved
12 anchovy filets	*Wine-cheese dressing*

To assemble salad, line salad plates with crisp greens. Place tomato half, cut side up, in center of each plate; top tomato with broccoli stalks; lay anchovy filets crisscross over broccoli. Arrange deviled egg halves and artichoke hearts around tomato. Pass wine-cheese dressing.

Wine-Cheese Dressing

1 cup salad oil	½ teaspoon salt
½ cup sauterne *or* other white table wine	½ teaspoon garlic salt
¼ cup California wine vinegar	½ teaspoon coarsely ground black pepper
½ cup grated Parmesan cheese	½ teaspoon paprika
2 eggs	¼ teaspoon Worcestershire
1 teaspoon salt	

Combine all of the above and beat until well blended. If dressing is not to be used immediately, store in covered container in refrigerator and beat well just before serving. Yield: about 2 cups.

This recipe is really delicious and quite different.

Fried Pig's Knuckles
(serves 6)

6 pig knuckles	Flour
1 large onion, chopped	Bread crumbs
1 clove garlic, minced	1 egg, beaten
3 whole cloves	Seasoned salt
1 tablespoon chopped parsley	Pepper
¼ teaspoon thyme	Paprika
Salt and pepper to taste	½ cup olive oil

Wash knuckles well and place in a Dutch oven with onion, garlic, cloves, parsley, thyme, and salt and pepper. Cover with boiling water and simmer gently for 2 hours. Remove knuckles and pat dry with a paper towel. Beat egg; add seasoned salt, pepper, and paprika. Dip the knuckles in flour, then in egg mixture, then in crumbs. Heat olive oil in a large skillet, and fry the knuckles until they are golden brown on all sides. Serve garnished with lemon wedges.

Here's another way with cabbage for Capricorn to consider.

Scalloped Cabbage
(serves 4–6)

1 head cabbage	Salt and freshly ground black
½ cup butter	pepper
1¼ cups rich cream sauce	½ cup freshly grated Parmesan
	cheese

Shred cabbage and soak in salted cold water for ½ hour. Drain well. Melt butter; add shredded cabbage and simmer, covered, until cabbage is just tender, but not browned. Line a large casserole with ½ simmered cabbage. Add ½ of cream sauce; sprinkle with freshly ground black pepper and ½ of grated Parmesan. Add remaining cabbage; pour remaining sauce over the top and add more pepper and remainder of Parmesan. Place in a 350° oven and cook until the casserole bubbles and the top is golden brown, about 30 minutes.

In looking back over what we've done, I am delighted by the numerous varieties of potatoes we've come up with. Here's still another.

Lyonnaise Potatoes
(serves 6)

2 beef bouillon cubes	4 cups cubed cooked potatoes
½ cup boiling water	½ teaspoon salt
¼ cup (½ stick) butter	¼ teaspoon pepper
½ cup finely chopped onion	¼ cup finely chopped parsley

Dissolve bouillon cubes in boiling water; set aside. In a large covered skillet melt butter; sauté onion for 5 minutes. Add potatoes; sprinkle with salt and pepper. Pour bouillon over potatoes. Cover and simmer about 15 minutes or until potatoes are heated through, stirring occasionally. Sprinkle with parsley and serve immediately.

Another recipe from a classic continental menu is this pudding-like dessert. Again, the Italians created it, but it translates literally as "English soup." It probably gets its name from the thin sauce.

Zuppa Inglese
(serves 8–10)

6 egg yolks	½ teaspoon lemon extract
6 tablespoons sugar	½ cup cream sherry
1 tablespoon orange juice	1 angel food cake (day old)
1 teaspoon vanilla	

Beat egg yolks and sugar until thick and lemon-colored. Add orange juice, vanilla, and lemon extract; slowly beat in sherry. (Sauce will be thin.) Cut the cake into three layers. Place one layer on a serving platter deep enough to hold sauce; pour over ⅓ of sauce. Repeat with second and third layers. Refrigerate overnight. To serve, cut into slices.

I've liked this stay here in the Tenth House. It was fun. I think Capricorn will find it fun, too. There's ample proof here that this is, indeed, the "Good Earth."

Aquarius Menu One

pages 293–298

Cucumbers in Yogurt
Lemon Salmon Casserole à la Eleventh House
Eggplant Sandwich
Fleecy Cloud Dessert

Aquarius Menu Two

pages 299–304

Aquarius Salad
Shrimp Salad Rolls *or*
  Tomato Crabmeat Stacks *or*
  Slaw Fishwiches
Uranian Lemon Crunch Bars

Aquarius Menu Three

pages 305–309

Guacamole Puffs
Planetary Ham with Champagne Sauce
Flaming Yams
Greek-style Green Beans
Cherry Angel

Eleventh House

January 20–February 18

AQUARIUS

Sydney Omarr on Aquarius

 The Eleventh House is that section of the horoscope that concerns the quality of friends, hopes, and wishes. It is related to social reforms, humanitarianism, to prescience, even prophecy. It is that part of the chart that enables an astrologer to measure degrees of popularity and fame. Aquarius is the natural Eleventh House. It is a sign connected with the planet Uranus, and it is associated with astrology, aviation, the space age, invention, and innovation. If you were born under the sign, many regard your interests as being "far out," since they include extrasensory perception, astrology, aviation, and electronics. Aquarius belongs to the Air trinity; there are more famous people born under Aquarius than under any other sign. Incidentally, more people are born during this time period than any other. You are the one most likely to be fascinated by the idea of cooking with astrology. However, Aquarius, you are not overly fond of spending time in food preparation, although you could be a food faddist.

Light and airy—that's the way you like your food. Angel food cake would be one of your favorite desserts. Although not as addicted to health foods as a Virgo conceivably could be, you tend to take up special diets. Heavy food depresses you, because to you, it slows the thinking.

More people are born during this time period than any other

You often prefer to start light, finishing a meal with a substantial imaginative dessert. Just as Leo is apt to have children around at meal time, you are fond enough of pets to prepare special treats for them. Your eating pattern is apt to be as unorthodox as are your ideas. Your reactions are quick, sudden, and your meal planning can be that way, too. Thus, it's important that you develop recipes which, while being prepared, allow you time for thinking, talking, and demonstrating salient points.

You are more of a vegetable eater than a consumer of meat. Foods peculiar to Aquarius include cucumber, yogurt, eggplant. You also have a fondness for potato salad. You are intrigued with space travel, curious about the diets, the foods consumed by astronauts. Fruits and cold cuts are high on your food list, and you can make a meal of a salad, especially Caesar salad.

You are fascinated with eating while traveling

In the food area, you have much in common with Gemini: you can eat while on the go. Where a Sagittarius will delight in picnic fare, you are fascinated with eating while traveling: in a car, on a ship, train, or while flying.

Your desire is for foods with a reputation for providing energy. Scorpio wants food that makes one sexy. You prefer action food; that is, you want to consume food that doesn't slow you down. It might be best for you to enjoy light meals more often rather than great quantities at one sitting.

Your ruling planet is Uranus, symbolizing the sudden and eccentric. You do not follow the crowd; your tastes in food, as in other areas, are avant-garde. Conversation and friends are essential ingredients with your meals. For you, dining bridges the gap between ideas, cuts away pretense, enables you to exercise intellectual curiosity: to discuss, ask, test, strive, to know yourself better through, say, the divining arts and sciences. You adore being surrounded by astrologers, writers, and artists, those who help answer basic philosophical questions. You are concerned with the future and, thus, would be fascinated by condensed foods, those that are compressed for mobility, easy travel. Like a Capricorn, you have an awareness of time, but not the patience of that taciturn sign.

Harmonious dining companions are Sagittarius, Aries, Gemini, and Libra

Harmonious dining companions for you include Sagittarius, Aries, Gemini, and Libra. With another Aquarius, you could get bogged down on a fine point; a discussion on a subtle, but minor matter conceivably could dominate, causing loss of interest in dining. On the other hand, with Sagittarius you glow, basking in the light of warm conversation. There is an exchange of vital ideas. Before the meal is finished, you and Sagittarius could come up with plans to change the world. You learn from each other, and you could profit by exchanging recipes with a Sagittarius.

You are intuitive, a natural teacher, because you inspire and spread enthusiasm. In the kitchen you learn by doing. You are the true individualist, willing to experiment in order to please a special guest. The following recipes and menus will find a mark where your cooking is concerned.

Lemons and avocados especially delight you

You like to utilize lemons in your culinary creations. Eggs Benedict could be one of your productions. You enjoy making hollandaise sauce, although you must curb a tendency to use too much lemon juice. The tart taste of lemon appeals to your Uranian nature: quick and clean. A lemon meringue pie would suit you fine as a dessert. Other favorites in this area would include lemon pudding and lemon soufflé.

Avocado is another Aquarian delight; you could become an expert at whipping up a tangy guacamole. People born under the other Air signs, Libra and Gemini, would especially appreciate this treat when served.

You are talented at selecting food gifts for others: wines, cheeses, fruits, and the like. Champagne is a favorite Uranian beverage. The bubbles and the "effect" are typically Aquarian.

Actress Kim Novak, when I dined with her, proved to be a typical Aquarian: more interested in talking astrology than in the consumption of food. This can be a charming trait, but a bit distracting if one attempts to concentrate on food. Other celebrities born under your sign include Mia Farrow, Gore Vidal, Eartha Kitt, Paul Newman, Tom Smothers, and Joey Bishop.

Your ideal companion is Sagittarius

When dining with Taurus, you feel comfortable, but your tastes in food are not alike. This bothers Taurus more than it does you. With a Taurus, there is a secure feeling. You get the impression that nothing will change. You also find Taurus immovable where opinions are concerned. Nevertheless, a Taurus fascinates you in the food area. You admire the Taurus appetite for basic foods. In turn, a Taurus looks up to you and tries to emulate you. Disagreements arise, but the steadiness of Taurus make you comfortably drowsy, and what starts out as an argument ends as an amiable agreement to disagree.

Your ideal companion is Sagittarius; these people affect that part of your chart associated with wish-fulfillment. A Sagittarian is able to keep up with your flights of imagination, and can get you interested in a more dedicated approach to food. Many of your tastes are similar. For example, that picnic basket of Sagittarius represents "dining out" in a literal sense. It also symbolizes eating on the move or while traveling. This appeals to you. The conversation, the ideals espoused, can be as tantalizing as any dish when Aquarius gets together with Sagittarius. There can be physical as well as mental attraction here, and a good way to get a serious relationship started is over a fine repast—a combination of Sagittarius and Aquarius foods, a mixture of menus. Try it and see!

Cheese, oranges, and tomatoes appeal to the Aquarian palate

Cheese, oranges, and tomatoes appeal to the Aquarian palate. You are artistic and, while painting or writing or studying lines, you are apt to be found nibbling on cheese, peeling an orange, or eating a tomato. If sculpting, which Aquarius is capable of, you like nothing better than a sip of champagne, a helping of cheese and avocado. Food is energy for you, and finding an outlet for creative energy is as important to you as a meat-and-potatoes meal might be for others. Friends who provide "food for thought" are more valuable to you than a loaf of bread.

You are Aquarius, the harbinger of things to come; you perceive the future, and your designs, in words or colors, often provide us with a glimpse of tomorrow.

Aquarians are the harbinger of things to come

You are physically attracted to Gemini, but find it hard to pin these natives down to an opinion, a definite stand. This applies also to the food area. With a Gemini guest, provide lots of snacks and appetizers. Check Mike Roy's Third House section for some valuable hints along these lines. Romance is often the subject when you're sharing food with a Gemini. It is an enjoyable experience. Your creative energy flows, and ideas fly back and forth. Conviviality is essential for you when dining, and a Gemini provides that ingredient.

With Leo, you are inspired to be versatile in the kitchen. You admire the showmanship of this native, as well as the sense of drama. Your food tastes are not flamboyant enough to impress a Leo, but your conversation and ideas make up for that shortcoming. Discussion often includes astrology, food, and even marriage. Dining with Leo could become a regular occurrence.

You are physically attracted to Gemini

You enjoy taking short trips with Aries, especially to out-of-the-way eating places. The Mars of Aries combines with your Uranus significator to produce action, quick decisions, impulsive desires. Thus, with an Aries, you might decide to dine at an odd hour or you could choose something entirely outside of the Aquarian taste. Arians are exciting, but you burn up a tremendous amount of energy with these people, and you are apt to do more moving about than eating. Together, Aries and Aquarius symbolize impatience. The dishes you serve will probably be easy to prepare, but you could be hungry less than an hour after you've eaten! An Aries finds you a delightful companion, but if a third party is present, the odds are that he or she could leave the table famished, albeit stimulated.

With a Cancer-born, you become more conscious of food values, and your tendency to be a food faddist could come to the fore. A new diet finds you wanting to share knowledge with Cancer. This isn't good for sumptuous dining, but Cancer sympathizes with your latest food kick. To a Cancer, you are somewhat mysterious. These natives enjoy hearing about your latest "discoveries." The two of you, Aquarius and Cancer, could lose weight together!

Cancer and Pisces find you mysterious

Another who finds you mysterious is Pisces. These sensitive souls have a kinship with your intuitive faculties. Pisces helps you select utensils, points you in the direction of excellent buys, and gives you a feeling that what you create in the kitchen is worthwhile. The Neptune of Pisces combines with your Uranus to produce an atmosphere that can be described as "mediumistic." This means that as you dine with Pisces, you sense potential; you peer through the veil that hides secrets, subtleties. Intriguing. And you develop a taste for the rare, for delicacies. A Piscean helps you discern the difference between dining and merely eating.

Capricorn is a great help when you are preparing dinner for groups, clubs, or special organizations. The practicality of the Capricorn Saturn serves as an excellent balance for your erratic Uranus. Capricorn is more restricted than you are, more conventional. A Capricorn will see to it that you have some bread on the table, some potatoes that are hot. You try new foods when with Capricorn, something a bit more basic than is your habit. Capricorn expresses the view that you may not be getting your money's worth. They also help you to stock up on essentials. To you, Capricorn represents the clandestine, the underground. You are intrigued, but not entirely comfortable.

You try new foods when with Capricorn, something a bit more basic

Virgo, in the food area, affects you in a manner that whets your appetite for foreign foods. The Mercury of Virgo and your Uranus make for bright, even brilliant ideas. You write to a Virgo, correspond, telephone. You could also take a lengthy journey with Virgo, even to test the skills of a noted chef. With a Virgo, you seem to be inspired to prepare exotic dishes. Your unique tastes intrigue natives of this sign; they encourage you to experiment with foods that provide a supply of added energy. A Virgo thinks your food fads make sense; the two of you could enjoy dining together, but not seven days a week. When together, Virgo and Aquarius tend to go to extremes (exotic to health-and-fad foods).

If it were up to you, Aquarius, dining habits would be revolutionized. You would streamline utensils and find ways of gaining necessary nutrition without necessarily preparing a meal. Anything, including food, that distracts you from an exposition on social justice or the philosophical worth of a Spinoza or a Nostradamus is apt to be regarded as an imposition. (Taurus might find this hard to understand!)

With a Libra, you enjoy foods associated with other lands. The Venus of Libra and your Uranus make a romantic combination. Among other things, you find romance in dining with a Libra. Members of this sign tend to build your confidence and your ego. This is because they find you stimulating, physically attractive. It is not unlikely that you could become involved with Libra. (It could start while exchanging recipes.) A Libra is more delicate about food than are you. You learn—especially something about the use of sauces. You particularly enjoy the dining company of a Libra while traveling. Natives of this sign affect that part of your chart having to do with philosophy, publishing, and long journeys. You'll probably read about food at the instigation of Libra. Incidentally, a Libra would share your liking for avocado and eggs Benedict. (You also like food that contains air: puffs, light crusts, fluff, and flakes.)

Romance can be found when dining with a Libra

With Scorpio, you are more apt to settle down to the business of eating. That's because you often discuss business with natives of this sign. Scorpio fires your ambitions. You may disagree in other areas, but both you and a Scorpio are in harmony with the idea that you can accomplish important things in this life. Scorpio is concerned with your goals. In the kitchen, a Scorpio encourages you to use intuition. You change ingredients, experiment; you come up with new names for old dishes, and new ways of preparing traditional fare. With Scorpio, you are never satisfied with the ordinary. Food preparation becomes more of a production

Scorpio is concerned with your goals

when you are with a Scorpio, and you both agree the extra effort was worth it.

It would not be at all surprising, Aquarius, if you married an excellent cook. While you provide inspiration, your mate would, very likely, be happy rattling those pots and pans!

Mike Roy on Aquarius

As we enter the Eleventh House, again I follow Omarr's leads concerning the residents who dwell here. Light and airy must be the nature of the food in the Eleventh House kitchen, with a distinct emphasis on lemon. Although chefs may not, in particular, reside here, they certainly like to visit. For if there is one distinctive ingredient to "refresh" a given dish, it is lemon. This golden citrus fruit supplies a juice that cuts through fats, keeping foods like avocados, peaches, potatoes, and many others from oxidizing or turning black. It is almost a must with fish and poultry, and, certainly, it adds zest to many recipes. So you'll find a liberal use of lemon in the Aquarius menus.

Light and airy with lots of lemon suits Aquarius

Again, I notice that what I have really emphasized here is that elusive, almost impossible to define object of all cooks—taste. I am not alone. Emperors, kings, and presidents, not to mention others, have sought the "one true taste." Mythology gave us words like "ambrosia" and "nectar." Many have written about their experiences with "taste."

Born in 1755, Jean Anthelme Brillat-Savarin, from the little French town of Belley, is generally considered to be the greatest gastronome of all. In 1789 he was a deputy; in 1793, mayor of Belley. To escape proscription, he fled to the United States, where he taught French and played the violin in New York. He writes of a hunting party in Connecticut where he tried a dish of gray squirrels cooked in Madeira. He found wild turkey superior to the domestic breed.

Brillat-Savarin's work *Physiologie du Goût* (translated as *Physiology of Taste*, published in 1925) is considered by the cooking world as the epitome of culinary writings. He would go to any length to experience a new "taste," and many famous recipes bear his name. On his return to France, after the fall of Robespierre, he became a noted judge. He worked at this time on his now-classic book. His only companion, besides his manuscript, was a dog who answered to the name of Ida. She followed him everywhere and sat on the bench next to him in court. During the hunting season, the judge's presence was sometimes pungent, due to his habit of shooting small game birds and then carrying them around for days in the pockets of his coat to give them proper aging.

It's interesting to pursue this quest for taste. I could set forth many other examples. One can be found in the southern corner of Burgundy (La Bresse) where *Poularde de Bresse* is a contribution to the gastronomic world. Poularde is a young hen that has been submitted to an ovariotomy so that she can be fattened more easily. Samuel Chamberlain, in *Bouquet de France*, writes:

> Thus relieved of myriad worrisome details, these placid hens avoid domestic cares completely. Indifferent to the chatter of the young, the rivalry of other females, and the philandering inconstancy of the male, she may devote her entire time to the pleasant business of fattening herself on the best corn. More than one critic has reflected upon this skilled alteration which results in such subtle refinements of taste. Capons have suffered similar indignities with resultant plumpness and freedom from vagrant thoughts. Regardless of the ethical points involved, these are the most famous fattened pullets in the world....

And there are those among us who will tell you that we have only begun the search for "taste." The road ahead will have many turnings. Who knows? Just around the next curve in the road may be a delight that will excite the world anew.

So, Aquarius, we take ourselves to your kitchen, following Omarr every step, in quest of the menus to excite you, with your special tastes.

MENU ONE

Cucumbers in Yogurt

*Lemon Salmon Casserole
à la Eleventh House*

Eggplant Sandwich

Fleecy Cloud Dessert

Our Aquarius menu opens with a food to satisfy fully. Cucumber and yogurt are among your favorites, says Omarr. And here is a recipe item to fill that need. (I'd serve a brown bread with it.)

Cucumbers in Yogurt
(serves 4)

½ cup vinegar
½ cup water
 1 teaspoon dill weed
 1 teaspoon salt
 5 whole black peppercorns

1 large cucumber, thinly sliced
1 medium onion, thinly sliced
1 cup plain yogurt
   Tomato wedges for garnish

Combine vinegar, water, dill weed, salt, and pepper; add cucumber slices, and chill in refrigerator at least 2 hours. Add the onions to the cucumber mixture; then add the yogurt. Serve in individual bowls with tomato wedges for garnish.

The use of lemon, in the form of juice and as a main ingredient of hollandaise sauce, makes this casserole an ideal dish for Aquarius. You can use canned hollandaise for convenience, but I've included the recipe in case you want to make it yourself.

Lemon Salmon Casserole à la Eleventh House
(serves 4)

1 can (1 pound) salmon	⅓ cup chopped green pepper
12 ounces *hollandaise sauce* (page 296)	2 tablespoons finely chopped onion
1 teaspoon grated lemon peel	½ teaspoon salt
2 tablespoons freshly squeezed lemon juice	⅛ teaspoon pepper
⅓ cup chopped celery	2 cups biscuit mix
	⅔ cup milk

Drain salmon; remove skin and bones and flake with a fork. Blend together 6 ounces hollandaise sauce, lemon peel, and juice. Add salmon, celery, green pepper, onion, salt, and pepper. Place in well-buttered 1½-quart casserole. Combine biscuit mix and milk with a fork to form a soft dough; drop by tablespoonfuls over salmon mixture. Bake at 400° for 25–30 minutes or until biscuit topping is richly browned. Serve casserole topped with remaining warm hollandaise and sprinkled with freshly snipped parsley, if desired.

continued

Hollandaise Sauce

¼	pound butter	2 tablespoons warm water
3	egg yolks	Few grains cayenne pepper
1½	tablespoons lemon juice	

Be sure ingredients are at room temperature. (I like to measure the ingredients into the top of a double boiler and let stand at room temperature for an hour.) About 10 minutes before serving, place over boiling water (being sure the top pan does not touch the water in the bottom pan) and stir with a whip, gradually adding the water as the mixture thickens. (I have success placing all the ingredients at room temperature in a blender and letting it run 10 seconds. Then I cook in a double boiler as above.)

Other Serving Suggestions: You'll be interested (if you're not already aware) that this sauce is magnificent with broccoli, asparagus, and other vegetables. Added in equal proportions to a good béchamel or cream sauce, it makes an elegant "supreme" sauce over leftover turkey or with poached fish. Aquarius might like to use it, too, for eggs Benedict. This is a simple dish. For each serving: make the sauce. Fry two slices of Canadian bacon. Poach two eggs. Split an English muffin and toast it. Place the toasted muffin halves side by side on a hot plate. Add to each half a slice of the bacon, then the poached eggs. Top with hollandaise. A thin slice of truffle should be added for a garnish. If you can't afford the truffle, use half a black olive.

The vegetable course takes us to another Eleventh House favorite: the eggplant. This is another unique way with it.

Eggplant Sandwich

(serves 4)

2 medium (or 1 large) eggplant
  Flour
1 cup olive oil
2 egg yolks
½ pound Mozzarella cheese,
    diced fine

2 tablespoons Parmesan cheese
1 egg, beaten
  Bread crumbs

Peel and slice eggplant ½ inch thick. Dip in flour and sauté in olive oil until golden and tender. Combine egg yolks and cheeses. Spread about a tablespoon of the mixture on ½ of eggplant slices. Cover with remaining slices, like a sandwich. Dip the sandwiches in flour, then in beaten egg, then in bread crumbs. Brown them well in oil remaining in pan.

A light and airy dessert tops off this meal. Delight in it, Aquarius. It's designed just for you.

Fleecy Cloud Dessert
(serves 8-10)

2 cups canned unsweetened pineapple juice	½ cup cold water
2 tablespoons Grand Marnier	6 egg yolks, well beaten
1½ cups sugar	6 egg whites, stiffly beaten
1 teaspoon salt	1 cup heavy cream, whipped
2 tablespoons unflavored gelatin	3 dozen ladyfingers
	Crushed pineapple (optional)

Combine pineapple juice, Grand Marnier, sugar, and salt in a saucepan. Heat, stirring occasionally, until sugar is dissolved. Remove from heat. Soften gelatin in cold water, and dissolve into hot mixture. Gradually stir into the egg yolks. Chill until partially set. Fold in egg whites and whipped cream. Line bottom and sides of a well-oiled 9-inch springform pan with ladyfingers. Pour in the filling and chill until firm. Garnish with additional whipped cream and well-drained crushed pineapple if desired.

MENU TWO

Aquarius Salad

Shrimp Salad Rolls or
Tomato Crabmeat Stacks or
Slaw Fishwiches

Uranian Lemon Crunch Bars

Now, Aquarius, about that appetite of yours and its appreciation of a salad as an entrée: here's a salad that makes a lovely entrée, or you can serve it as an accompaniment dish.

Aquarius Salad
(serves 1 as an entrée or 4 as an accompaniment)

2 slices bacon
1 heart romaine lettuce, chopped
¼ head iceberg lettuce, chopped
2 tablespoons shredded red cabbage
1 radish, sliced
½ cup diced cooked turkey

½ cup diced cooked ham
2 hard-cooked eggs, chopped
½ cup chopped tomato, seeds pressed out
2 lengthwise slices avocado
Parsley
1 colossal black olive, unpitted
Dressing

Fry bacon until crisp. Drain. Place mixture of romaine, iceberg lettuce, cabbage, and radish slices on chilled serving plate. Arrange one layer each of turkey, ham, chopped egg, and tomato in a spoke-like design on top of salad. Crumble bacon in center and arrange avocado slices to one side of bacon. Garnish with parsley and olive. Serve with dressing.

Dressing

⅔ cup red wine vinegar
⅓ cup olive oil
2 tablespoons ketchup
¾ teaspoon salt
1¼ teaspoons leaf oregano, crushed
¼ teaspoon sweet basil

¼ teaspoon rosemary
1 clove garlic, crushed
1 teaspoon black pepper
¼ teaspoon Ac'cent
½ teaspoon paprika
1 tablespoon fresh lemon juice

continued

Combine all ingredients. Flavor is enhanced if dressing is allowed to stand overnight. Serve at room temperature over chilled salad. Yield: 1⅓ cups.

As I promised, here are three sandwich entrées. They are satisfyingly different, and, again, they include the ingredients to appeal to Aquarius—the lemon, tomato, and salad composition.

Shrimp Salad Rolls
(serves 4)

½ pound shrimp, fresh or frozen	¾ teaspoon salt
2 cups shredded lettuce	Pepper to taste
½ cup chopped celery	1 tablespoon lemon juice
2 tablespoons chopped onion	¼ cup sliced ripe olives
¼ cup mayonnaise	4 hot dog rolls

Clean shrimp; cook and cut into small pieces. Toss shrimp with remaining ingredients except rolls. Split rolls and hollow out slightly. Butter, toast, and fill the rolls with shrimp mixture.

Tomato Crabmeat Stacks
(makes 4 triple-decker sandwiches)

1 (7½-ounce) can crabmeat, drained, flaked
½ cup diced celery
2 teaspoons chopped pimiento
2 tablespoons chopped green pepper
½ cup sour cream

8 slices bread
¼ cup melted butter or margarine
4 large (or 6 medium) tomato slices
1 cup grated sharp Cheddar cheese

Combine crabmeat, celery, pimiento, green pepper, and sour cream; mix lightly. Trim crusts from sliced bread and brush with butter. Spread 4 slices of bread with crab filling, top with 4 more slices of bread and cover each slice with a large tomato slice or 1½ medium slices. Top with cheese. Place on cookie sheet and bake at 400° for 10–12 minutes or until cheese melts.

Slaw Fishwiches
(serves 4)

1 package (9 ounces) frozen breaded fish sticks	½ teaspoon grated lemon peel
1 package (1 pound) frozen French fried potatoes (optional)	2 tablespoons freshly squeezed lemon juice
6 large French rolls	1 teaspoon sugar
3 cups shredded cabbage	¼ teaspoon salt
	⅛ teaspoon pepper

Place fish sticks and potatoes in shallow pan; heat in oven following package directions. Meanwhile, split rolls lengthwise about ⅓ from the top; partially hollow out bottoms of rolls. Place in oven to heat a few minutes before fish sticks are done. Combine cabbage with remaining ingredients; place a generous spoonful of slaw in hollow of each warmed roll. Add 2 fish sticks and sprinkle with additional salt, if desired. Cover with remaining slaw and tops of rolls. Serve with French fries, and if desired, fresh lemon wedges, pickles, and ketchup.

For a light take-along dessert, here is a sweet that should appeal.

Uranian Lemon Crunch Bars

1 (15-ounce) can sweetened condensed milk
½ cup lemon juice
1 teaspoon grated lemon rind
1½ cups flour

1 teaspoon baking powder
½ teaspoon salt
⅔ cup butter
1 cup brown sugar
1 cup uncooked oatmeal

Blend milk, lemon juice, and rind and set aside. Sift flour, baking powder, and salt together. Cream butter and sugar; blend in oatmeal and flour mixture. Crumble. Spread half of crumbled mixture in an 8x12x2-inch pan. Cover with lemon mixture. Top with balance of crumbled mixture. Bake at 350° until brown around the edges, about 15–20 minutes. Cut into bars or squares.

MENU THREE

Guacamole Puffs

Planetary Ham with Champagne Sauce

Flaming Yams

Greek-style Green Beans

Cherry Angel

Most of us are aware of cream puffs as a dessert or those delicious eclairs that satisfy our sweet tooth but broaden our waistline. We also are familiar with those dainty little pastry puffs filled with cheese, meat, or fish mixtures that we use as appetizers. They all spring from the same recipe and I've been sure to include it here for a rather unusual use of the famous puff.

Guacamole Puffs

Guacamole

2 medium tomatoes, peeled and chopped

2 tablespoons grated onion

1 teaspoon chopped green chilies

2 tablespoons lemon juice

1 teaspoon salt

2 avocados, mashed

Combine all ingredients and use to fill puffs. Serve the puffs on a chilled plate on a leaf of lettuce, garnished with a lemon slice.

Puffs (Pâté à Choux)

1 cup water

¼ teaspoon salt

½ cup butter

1 cup sifted flour

4 eggs

In a saucepan combine water, butter, and salt; bring to a rolling boil until the butter is completely melted. Remove from heat and add the flour all at once. Beat thoroughly (I like to use a wooden spoon) until the mixture leaves the sides of the pan and forms a ball. Let stand 3 minutes. Beat the eggs in one at a time, beating each egg until a smooth batter is obtained. Drop from a tablespoon onto an ungreased cookie sheet, leaving a 2-inch space between each drop. Bake at 400° for 15 minutes. Reduce heat and bake at least 10 minutes more or until puffs are golden and dry. Let cool. If you are making desserts, the puffs may be filled

continued

with sweetened whipped cream or a custard. If you wish to make those little appetizer puffs, drop from a teaspoon rather than the tablespoon.

Planetary Ham with Champagne Sauce

1 whole ham or ½ ham or
    thick ham slice
Prepared mustard
Cloves

Brown sugar
Pineapple bits or cherries
Champagne sauce

Trim skin and excess fat from ham. Spread with mustard; stud with cloves and rub lightly with brown sugar. If you wish, you may secure fruit to the ham with toothpicks. Bake in a 325° oven to heat through. Serve with the sauce.

Champagne Sauce

½ cup orange juice
½ cup pineapple juice
⅓ cup grape jelly
½ cup brown sugar

1 cup champagne
2 tablespoons lemon juice
1 tablespoon cornstarch in
    ¼ cup water

Melt brown sugar in a heavy skillet. Add remaining ingredients except starch and water and bring to a boil. Add starch and water, and stir into sauce to thicken slightly. It should be a bit on the thin side.

Yams are a traditional accompaniment for ham. This recipe is spectacular when you bring it to the table flaming.

Flaming Yams
(serves 6)

Grated rind of 2 oranges	1 teaspoon cinnamon
¾ cup brown sugar	½ teaspoon cloves
¼ cup dark rum	¼ teaspoon ginger
6 cooked yams, sliced	2 tablespoons butter

Butter a 1½-quart casserole well. Sprinkle with half the orange rind, ¼ cup of the sugar and 2 tablespoons of rum. Layer half the sliced yams; sprinkle with ¼ cup brown sugar, ½ teaspoon of the cinnamon, ¼ teaspoon of the cloves, and ⅛ teaspoon of the ginger. Add rest of yams and sprinkle with remaining ingredients except rum and butter. Dot casserole with the butter and bake in a 350° oven for 45 minutes. Heat remaining rum; set aflame, and pour over casserole.

A new way that's really an old way is always welcome. This recipe should be appreciated by Aquarius, because the piquant and herb-and-tomato-based sauce goes hand in hand with this House.

Greek-style Green Beans
(serves 6)

1½ pounds green beans	1 medium onion, sliced
¼ cup olive oil	½ teaspoon sugar
2–3 large tomatoes, peeled and chopped *or* 1 (16-ounce) can of tomatoes	½ teaspoon salt
	¼ teaspoon oregano
	Dash of pepper

continued

Beans that are past their prime and becoming just a bit tough are fine for this dish. Break in lengths and place in a heavy pot with remaining ingredients. Simmer, tightly covered, until beans are tender, about an hour.

Residents of the Eleventh House, as we have said before, like airy things— angel food cake among them. Here's a dessert that will measure up to the definition.

Cherry Angel

1 angel food cake, cut into
    1-inch cubes
1 can cherry pie filling
1 package instant vanilla pudding

1½ cups milk
1 cup sour cream

Place half the cake cubes in a 9 x 9 x 2-inch pan. Save about ⅓ cup of the cherry pie filling for garnish. Spread the rest over the cake in pan. Cover with the rest of the cake. Combine the pudding mix with milk and sour cream and beat until smooth. Spread over cake. Refrigerate six hours. Garnish with rest of cherry filling.

So, Aquarius, off to the kitchen and, as we say when we serve at our house, "Enjoy!"

Pisces Menu One

pages 321–326

Clam Chowder Neptune
Escalloped Veal Flambé
Braised Celery
Rice Madrilène
Astrologer's Chocolate Cheese Pie

Pisces Menu Two

pages 327–332

Celery Pisces
Twelfth House Sole
Braised Lettuce
Casserole Potatoes
Brown Betty

Pisces Menu Three

pages 333–338

Lobster Bisque Neptune
Olived Chicken
Stuffed Mushrooms
Cheese Puffs
Starlit Pineapple Dip

Twelfth House
February 19–March 20

PISCES

Sydney Omarr on Pisces

As we enter the Twelfth House, we are struck by a touch of tender loving care: by beauty, by sensitivity, by an exotic quality that is both overwhelming and delicate. That's part of this sector of the horoscope, which is Pisces, associated with Neptune, the planet of illusion. Obviously, if you were born under this sign, your tastes in food and other areas run to the subtle. There is an evanescent quality that prevails. Pisces belongs to the Water element. Waves come and go; there are ripples and the smooth-as-glass appearance can be deceiving.

You are intrigued with what goes on behind the scenes. Often, the world of dreams is more real to you than is so-called actuality. The Twelfth House is associated with motion pictures, television, theater, with clandestine meetings and meanings, with secret adversaries, with vapor-like effects, with vanishing acts—now you see it, now you don't.

You enjoy meal planning. It's not as much of a production as with a Leo, but it is a tour de force.

The writings of Piscean Anais Nin best illustrate your intrinsic qualities. Her words float as if being written on water. Miss Nin, whose *Diary* is destined to make literary history, claims that my knowledge of Pisces is "miraculous." She is kind.

The Twelfth House is associated with motion pictures, television, theater

Actress Jennifer Jones, another Pisces friend, has a screen image that reflects many of your qualities. And those include an almost psychic awareness, an ability to suffer and exult with us, that indefinable "human" trait that enables you to identify with us, to become involved.

It is not surprising that your tastes in food reflect your character: subtle, delicate, exotic, unique, selective. Seafood would be a favorite; fillet of sole in all its variations should intrigue you. Soups, especially of the fish variety, stand high on the list, with bouillabaisse a special treat.

Seafood, veal, and soups rate high in your book

Shellfish, too, rate high in your book. You are fond of celery, the taste and the color suit you. In the meat department, your choice is likely to be veal or veal kidneys, although you could also enjoy lamb kidneys. In this, you have something to share with Libras, also fond of kidneys.

Just as Aquarius likes "food that contains air," you are inordinately attracted to food that is something of an illusion, appearing to be something other than it is. Some of your favorite dishes have transparency; you like to see through them. Food cooked and wrapped in paper fulfills your poetic requirements, too: fish and chicken are good this way.

As a classical Piscean, you are a fan of the ballet, you appreciate fine writing, you probe mysteries of the mind. Where Virgo is analytical, you are intuitive. Where an Aries is direct, you are subtle. Where Taurus is blunt, you are delicate. And you are attracted to delicacies in food. Harmonious dining companions for you include Capricorn, Taurus, Cancer, and Scorpio. With another Pisces, there is stimulation, exchange of thoughts and opinions, but, oddly enough, you tend to eat too quickly when dining with a member of your own sign. An almost Gemini- or Aquarian-like quality takes over. You do feel comfortable and at home with Gemini. You enjoy watching these natives relish snacks, and you gain pleasure preparing hors d'oeuvres for Geminis.

Food, for you, provides mental stimulation. Good humor, laughter is an essential ingredient at your table. You are especially fond of being and dining with writers, those of an artistic temperament, people who have style and charisma. You are "mediumistic" enough to perceive what makes others tick, and what their food preferences might be.

Harmonious dining companions include Capricorn, Taurus, Cancer, and Scorpio

Nothing pleases you more than learning the modus operandi: how one applies a special touch, an herb, an ingredient, why a dish is a success for one chef and only ordinary in the charge of another. You perceive—you want to know why and how. In this area, a Cancer makes an excellent dining companion. There is attraction; beyond that, Cancer knows food and offers valuable hints, which you deeply appreciate. For creative dining, choose the Cancer-born. These people affect that part of your solar horoscope having to do with personal magnetism, the creative process. There is harmony as well as attraction: the Cancer Moon is "sympathetic" to your Neptune significator. Both are Water signs; both kinds of people are perceptive and sensitive and understand the ups and downs of moods. Plainly, you have much in common with Cancer. Invite a special Cancer friend to dinner. It will be a memorable occasion. And, by all means, check the Fourth House for Cancer menus and combine some of the recipes with your own. Then you'll be cooking with astrology!

You are especially fond of people with an artistic temperament

Capricorn helps you fulfill some of your hopes, wishes. The Saturn of Capricorn lends a "base" to your Neptune; there is greater solidity. You enjoy breaking bread with Capricorn. Domestic issues are discussed, and so is romance. Although quite different, the two signs are in harmonious aspect: an evening with a Capricorn provides you with joy and results in a feeling of elation. You understand Capricorn. Many people of the other signs cannot say the same.

You have a way of bringing forth latent talents, in culinary and other areas, that Scorpio might possess. With a Scorpio you discuss philosophical trends, publishing, the politics of foreign nations—and with Scorpio you are most apt to enjoy foreign food. Scorpio brings out in you that talent for utilizing extrasensory perception; a Scorpio intrigues you with tales of the supernatural. You are awed and inspired. In this mood, your own intuitive powers come to the fore. You enjoy traveling with Scorpio, perhaps to test a food specialty; you will go out of your way to sample a delicacy that only a certain chef can create. A Scorpio is physically attracted to you; there is an air of intensity when natives of this sign are your dining companions. But you enjoy it!

Scorpio brings out in you that talent for utilizing extrasensory perception

Aries individuals make you aware of what you lack in the way of staples and utensils. You have a desire to aim toward perfection with an Aries. This is not the ideal combination, but there are enough differences to make it interesting. Aries is convinced you carry some secret formula up your sleeve. This amuses you. In turn, you regard an Aries as one who can give you the secret of increasing income potential. Your tastes in food are not exactly opposite, but one could not say they are similar. A combination of First and Twelfth House menus would be in order. That way, you could both experiment. Ultimately, the talk is likely to turn to money, bargains, possessions. Aries is headstrong, direct. You are fascinated by the quality, just as Aries is by your delicate touch, your whimsical smile, your almost fey manner.

You enjoy cooking with steam: the evaporation of water is interesting to the nature of Pisces. When Mike Roy guides you through the Twelfth House, there will be much on this particular aspect of Pisces cooking.

You enjoy cooking with steam: the evaporation of water is interesting to the nature of Pisces

Aquarius touches that part of your chart that is very Pisces-like. It is associated with secrets, undercover activities, actions requiring utmost discretion. Thus, you enjoy dining with natives of Aquarius: the Uranus of that sign complements your Neptune. Universal subjects come up for discussion. Plans are transformed into action. You discover, in concert with each other, ways to dissolve evil, eradicate hunger, promote spirituality, and make the world a better place in which to live. With such topics, it behooves you both to fortify yourselves with good food.

Fortunately, you appreciate the Aquarian "airy" morsels and Aquarius has a "taste" for your special, subtle, delicate preparations.

With Taurus, dinner is a time for fun. Robust Taureans appreciate your poetic approach. As for you, Taurus represents the fulfillment of curiosity. You get your questions answered through a Taurus. The Taurus Venus blends with your Neptune; a sense of luxury prevails. Thick soups dominate, and perhaps, a combination of lobster and steak, if you're really going all out in entertaining Taurus.

You get your questions answered through a Taurus

As stated previously, the "airy" quality of Gemini strikes a responsive chord. Furthermore, with a Gemini, you are able to talk about home, parents, property, and how to improve living conditions. Gemini can be counted on to come up with ideas.

Dramatic Leo bolsters your confidence and feeds your ego. You are more aware of vitamins and minerals when preparing food for Leo. Natives of this sign affect that part of your chart having to do with health, employment, special services, and pets. With a Leo a pet could be present at dinner, to say nothing of children, and the occasion takes on a festive air. It's very good to have Leo as a helper when you're planning a reunion, entertaining associates, coworkers. You do not have a Leo's flair for drama with food, but Leo appreciates your own unique touch.

A Leo finds you sexy rather than fragile. When dining with Leo, you are apt to be self-conscious about what is served and the manner in which the food is presented. You want to please but fear that the Leo will miss the flaming dish, the bright sayings, the celebrity anecdotes. Together, Leo and Pisces (Sun and Neptune) tend to consume solid food, more to the liking of the Earth signs, Taurus, Virgo, Capricorn.

Leo finds you sexy rather than fragile

The Fire and Water of Pisces and Leo do not mix; but a compromise between Twelfth and Fifth House selections could solve the dining dilemma. You are more adaptable than Leo, so it will be up to you to make the choices. If you serve with a flair, and mix in the ingredient of flattery, you'll succeed. A Leo may know he or she is skilled, talented, but a Leo also wants to be told. If you do the telling, then Leo will relish your offerings.

You are fond of olives, almost as much as Aquarius is of lemon. Olives, mixed with your salad or combined with other foods, add up to a special treat for you. It's the suggestion of a "secret taste," subtle and sophisticated, that gets to you where olives are concerned. A very dry martini, surrounding an olive or two, would find a customer in you. Generally, however, you prefer beverages with a less direct "kick."

With a Virgo, you enjoy secrets, a kind of undercover alliance. You particularly break diets with Virgo. Eating something you are supposed to avoid gives you a strange feeling of accomplishment with Virgo. This is because with a Virgo a subterranean atmosphere prevails: you share confidences. Sometimes this goes so far that you form a permanent relationship, such as marriage.

You tend to break diets when with Virgo

Your taste in dining is similar to that of Libra. But you could get bogged down with details when entertaining natives of this sign. Perhaps this is because you strive for perfection. It would be better to relax: Libras appreciate your taste for fine food. And, of course, you understand Libra's desire for French cuisine and the like (check Seventh House). Libra arouses your interest in the occult. A before- or after-dinner seance could occur when you're dining with a Libra. You relish a rendezvous with a Libra. It often concludes with tasteful dishes and food for thought, as well. In this case, the thought processes turn to the hidden (typical Pisces fare), to efforts to communicate with discarnate entities. Ordinarily, Libra does not sway this way, toward the mysterious. Yet, when with you, Libra curiosity springs in the direction of the occult. You, of course, are receptive. The key is to find time to eat!

Your taste in dining is similar to that of Libra

Libras and Pisceans learn from each other in the food area. The Libra sense of design and appreciation of floral arrangements draw responses from Pisces. For your part, you intrigue Libra by your attitude of permissiveness. That is to say you are not rigid in your food standards. Certainly you enjoy fish, but you are not averse to many of the Libra Seventh House specialties, either.

Strangely, a Libra brings out in you an apparent ability to foretell future trends, cycles. A good stock market discussion over dessert and demitasse would not be at all remiss. It's wise to have Libra with you when spending an afternoon at the race track, too; the truth of the matter is that Libra thinks you can accomplish almost anything you decide to do. Perhaps this rubs off and sharpens whatever psychic faculties you might possess. Dining with a Libra could add up to fun and profit!

Your food selections are probably more daring when preparing for a Sagittarius than for anyone from any other sign. Your desire is to impress the Sagittarius. Natives of that sign touch your ambitions, make you conscious of standing, prestige, career, possible promotions, and general advancement. Thus, you want to impress them with "something different." Probably the easiest way to please Sagittarians is to drive out to the countryside with a picnic basket. Another way is to sizzle steaks. Or get charcoals glowing and barbecue a chicken, a roast, chops. When all is said and done, the fact remains (see Ninth House) that Sagittarius feels comfortable with you. There is no need to take special pains. However, it is likely that you will: so, remember that a Sagittarius is fond of foreign food, likes foods that spread out and take up room.

Your food selections are more daring when preparing for a Sagittarius

The effect on you is to focus conversation on achievement, profession, one of your parents; you tend, in other words, to be businesslike with a Sagittarius. When in charge of dining with a Sagittarian, you select numerous Capricorn dishes (check Tenth House). This is because Sagittarius accents your tenth Solar sector, causing you to display (when with Sagittarius) many characteristics in common with Capricorn.

You are an excellent dinner companion for almost anyone. Piscean Pamela Mason, who seems to enjoy discussing astrology with me, often turns up at restaurants I frequent. Her companions are happy as she chatters in a vibrant fashion, lending a festive air to the occasion.

You are an excellent dinner companion for almost anyone

That's the way it is with you, Pisces. When you bring forth your inner resources, life becomes more pleasant for us all. Your Neptunian touch, ever so subtle, contains a secret—and when you tell it, we feel it is for our ears only.

Mike Roy on Pisces

And so our journey through the signs of the zodiac nears its termination. Cooking and astrology have been ever present through the ages; they will continue to affect humankind as we wind our way through all the tomorrows into eternity.

Here in the Twelfth House, we find residents who love the theater. The delicate nature of their preferences brings out subtleties in cuisine. An evanescent aura, a gossamer web of fantasy and illusion takes you into a world of tissue-thin softness and light. There are lovely recipes of just such a nature.

But I would tarry for a moment to tell you of a precious gift I once received, and, in turn, I would pass it on to you. The setting and the nature of the event could well have been staged by Pisces.

One evening many years ago, my Virgo wife Alison and my Libra daughter Robin (then four years old) were driving with me through the byways of the San Fernando Valley in California. One of us glimpsed a sign that said "Sasha's Palate—Fine Food." We elected to try it.

When we entered, the first thing that captured our attention were the walls, lined with paintings and etchings. Shelves and room dividers held sculpture of rare, warm beauty. As we settled into our chairs, we noticed the coloring of the walls and ceiling. They were "brave" beyond description—a mingling of reds, greens, purples in a combination that only a daring artist would use. The effect was restful and relaxing, surprising as it might sound.

The menu carried myriad items described almost in prose-poetry. We ordered drinks, with a soft drink for Robin. (We had recently moved into a house that we liked very much and always toasted it with: "Here's to a happy house.") Robin raised her glass in the toast, saying: "This is a happy house."

The owner of Sasha's Palate, standing nearby, overheard her and came to the table to introduce himself. And so my family and I met Atanas Katchamakoff. We were friends ever after. But at the table, on

The delicate nature of Pisces' preferences brings out subtleties in cuisine

that evening, he became not only a friend but a teacher. He introduced me to culinary methods and tastes I had never encountered before.

Atanas was, indeed, a sculptor and artist. It was his wife who bore the name Sasha. And she was a talented artist in her own right, working in ceramics. I have not the words to describe their work. It is something one has to experience for oneself.

Atanas took me through his restaurant. When we arrived in the kitchen, I noticed a small gold shelf in the brick work that held the glowing coals of charcoal over which he roasted his famous shish kabob. Occasionally, a cook would reach for the shelf, pick up an imaginary bottle, and sprinkle its illusory contents over food cooking on the coals. I asked my host about it.

"That," he said, "is a bottle of love. You cannot cook without it." And then he pointed out a sign above the broiler that stated "Cooking is love. Love is cooking."

As we finished our delicious dinner and said goodbye to our new-found friends, Atanas Katchamakoff handed me an imaginary bottle of his "love," saying: "Here is your own bottle of love. Always remember that cooking is love. Love is cooking."

One Christmas we received from Atanas and Sasha a beautiful book, which tells his story and carries prints of all his art works. The forepanel of the book carries what he calls, simply, "a statement." His thoughts apply to art, but to me they apply to cooking, too:

> . . . I believe that art emerges inevitably from the heart of one man and finds its reality in the hearts of others. The substance in which a work of art is realized may become the property of a museum or a private collector, but the essence of the work, that in which it is timeless and, to some degree perfect, belongs to all.

Man's longing for grace, beauty, and precision is instinctive and every work of art, again to some degree, is a fulfillment of this longing. The artist, feeling within himself the nobility of this hunger, is impelled to produce, out of the truth within him and out of his chosen materials, an object of poise and finality—which shall be a law unto itself—a small universe of meaning, a moment of swift wholeness. This object, because of its truth and beauty, when seen by others will cause their hearts to experience a sense of wholeness. The primary function of a work of art is to increase the joy of living and, in the moment of recognition, to bring to others the grace and dignity of Godliness in that most divine of attributes—creation.

The true joy of cooking is for the enjoyment of those who eat what you prepare

Atanas Katchamakoff is speaking of art. I know he would say the same for cooking. He gives words to thoughts I have been trying to express for many years. The true joy of cooking is for the enjoyment of those who eat what you prepare.

And one thing more: I, in turn, pass on to you a bottle of love. Use it wisely and well and it will never empty. For its contents will be returned to you a hundredfold by those who sup at your table and enjoy the dishes you prepare with love. Here are some of them, especially for Pisces.

MENU ONE

Clam Chowder Neptune

Escalloped Veal Flambé

Braised Celery

Rice Madrilène

Astrologer's Chocolate Cheese Pie

Residents of the Twelfth House fancy seafoods and chowders, among other light and dainty dishes. Here is a chowder for them.

Clam Chowder Neptune
(serves 8)

¼ pound diced salt pork
2 medium onions, sliced
2 tablespoons flour
½ teaspoon seasoned salt
¼ teaspoon pepper
¼ teaspoon Ac'cent
1½ teaspoons salt
¼ teaspoon savory
¼ teaspoon thyme

4 medium potatoes cut in
   ½-inch cubes
1½ cups milk
1½ cups light cream
2 cans (15 ounces) minced
   clams, drained, but
   reserve liquid
1 tablespoon butter
   Chopped parsley

In a large kettle (Dutch oven) simmer salt pork in a little butter until golden. Add onions and cook until transparent. Stir in flour, seasoned salt, pepper, Ac'cent, 1½ teaspoons salt, savory, thyme, reserved clam liquid, and potatoes. If liquid does not cover ingredients, add water to cover. Cover and simmer until potatoes are tender. Meanwhile, in a separate saucepan, heat the milk and cream until just simmering, and stir it into the potato mixture. Add clams, butter, and parsley. Taste for salt content, and add more if needed.

*Of all our entrée meats, none, probably, is more delicate than veal.
Consequently, it belongs to Pisces especially.*

Escalloped Veal Flambé
(serves 8)

2 pounds veal, sliced very thin
   Salt and pepper
4 tablespoons butter
2 tablespoons chopped shallots
   or combine onion and
   garlic

1½ cups sliced mushrooms
½ cup cognac
1 cup whipping cream
2 tablespoons chopped
   parsley

Place veal between two sheets of wax paper, and flatten with mallet or
flat side of cleaver to about ⅛ inch thick. Cut into pieces about 3 inches or so square. Salt and pepper the pieces. Melt butter in heavy skillet,
and brown the meat quickly on both sides. Remove the meat to a hot
platter. Cook the shallots and mushrooms in the skillet just until tender.
Return the meat to the skillet, add the cognac, and set aflame. Return
meat, mushrooms, and shallots to the hot platter. Add the cream and
parsley to the skillet and heat it, stirring frequently. Pour the sauce over
the veal.

We've become so accustomed to eating our celery crisp and raw that we've forgotten how delicious it can be as a cooked, hot vegetable. I think, Pisces, you'll like this recipe.

Braised Celery
(serves 8)

2 bunches celery	1½ cups consommé *or* beef stock
4 teaspoons chopped tarragon	Soft bread crumbs
4 tablespoons chopped parsley	½ cup butter
1½ cups dry white wine	Salt and butter

Wash and trim the celery and cut lengthwise into quarters, then crosswise into 3-inch pieces. Boil in salted water for about 20 minutes. Meanwhile, simmer, uncovered, the herbs in white wine until reduced by a fourth, about 20 minutes. Add salt and pepper and stock. Drain the celery and put it in a buttered shallow casserole. Pour the herb-wine mixture over it. Sprinkle with bread crumbs and dot with butter. Bake 30 minutes in a 350° oven.

The use of rice in our menus has increased by leaps and bounds. For the Twelfth House, here is a dainty recipe that's light and filmy.

Rice Madrilène
(serves 8)

2 cups long-grain rice	6 drops Tabasco
2 cans consommé madrilène	4 tablespoons butter
½ cup water	2 tablespoons lemon juice

Wash the rice well in a sieve under running water until water runs clear. Shake out as much water as possible. Sauté the rice in butter, stirring well so that each grain of rice is coated. Add the rest of the ingredients, and bring to a boil. Cover tightly, and place in a 350° oven for an hour. The rice should be a delicate pink.

Light, frothy, and airy are words to describe this most unusual cheese pie—or, if you will, cheese cake.

Astrologer's Chocolate Cheese Pie

1½ cups crushed vanilla or
    chocolate wafers *or* cookies
½ cup melted butter
1 (8-ounce) package cream
    cheese
½ cup sugar
1 teaspoon vanilla

2 eggs, separated, slightly beaten
1 (6-ounce) package chocolate
    chips, melted
1 cup whipping cream
¾ cup pecans, almonds, *or*
    walnuts, chopped

Make a crumb crust by adding melted butter to cookie crumbs and blending well. Press onto bottom and sides of a 9-inch pie pan, and bake for 10 minutes at 350°. Cool. Blend cream cheese (at room temperature) with ¼ cup of the sugar, vanilla, egg yolks, and melted chocolate. Beat the egg whites, gradually beating in the other ¼ cup sugar. Fold into the chocolate mixture. Whip the cream and fold in. Add the nuts and fill the pie crust. Refrigerate 6 hours.

MENU TWO

Celery Pisces

Twelfth House Sole

Braised Lettuce

Casserole Potatoes

Brown Betty

The following menu for Pisces approaches true gourmet levels. The sole may take a bit of time, but it's well worth it. We have become so salad conscious that we forget the French gave us a wonderful way of braising lettuce years ago. So, Pisces, take up the challenge and try these dishes:

You just may find a theatrical reaction from your guests when you serve this very different first course.

Celery Pisces
(serves 8)

2 celery hearts	*Vinaigrette sauce*
2 cups chicken stock *or* consommé	Watercress
	Parsley
1 teaspoon pickling spice	Anchovy strips
Juice of half a lemon	Pimiento
Salt to taste	
1 cup *French dressing* (see page 131)	

Cut celery hearts in eighths lengthwise and arrange in a shallow pan. Cover with stock, spice, lemon juice, and salt. Simmer about 15 minutes, or until celery is tender. Drain. Arrange on a platter. Cover with French dressing, and chill at least 4 hours, turning occasionally. Drain off the dressing, and use it with the ingredients for the following vinaigrette sauce.

Vinaigrette Sauce

Dressing (left over from recipe above)	2 tablespoons finely minced onion
¼ cup pickle relish	2 tablespoons chopped capers
	1 tablespoon black caviar

continued

Combine all the ingredients. Garnish the platter with watercress and parsley. Dress the salad with the vinaigrette and lay a strip of pimiento and an anchovy crosswise on each piece of celery.

Of all the recipes for fillet of sole I know, this is truly one of the most elegant. The final taste makes it well worthwhile. Try it and taste it. You'll love it.

Twelfth House Sole

(serves 8)

8 fillets of sole
1 (8-ounce) lobster tail
1¼ cups all-purpose cream
¼ teaspoon cayenne pepper
¾ teaspoon salt
⅓ cup finely chopped onion
2½ tablespoons clarified
    sweet butter
¾ cup white champagne
3 tablespoons flour

⅓ cup *hollandaise sauce*
    (see page 296)
⅓ cup all-purpose cream,
    whipped
¼ pound fresh mushrooms,
    stems removed
1 lemon
⅓ cup canned baby shrimp,
    drained
Parsley

Trim ends from fillets of sole. With a knife, chop together trimmings from sole and meat from lobster tail to resemble a puree. Mix seafood puree with ¼ cup cream, cayenne pepper, and ¼ teaspoon salt. Pour in buttered 10-ounce custard dish. Place custard dish in pan containing 1 inch hot water and cover pan. Steam over a simmer flame for about 10 minutes or until mixture is set. Turn mousse out onto a plate and cool. Divide into 8 portions. Place 1 portion on shiny side of each fillet. Gently roll up.

continued

Bring to a simmer over a medium flame, onion, 1 tablespoon butter, champagne, and ½ teaspoon salt. Add rolled fillets. Cover with a circle of waxed paper and poach over a medium-low flame for about 3 minutes or until done. Carefully remove cooked fillets to a clean cloth to drain. Fold a portion of the cloth over the fillets to form a loose cover and keep warm in the low-temperature oven. Pour 1 cup of cream into skillet containing champagne stock. Bring to a simmer over a low flame.

Combine flour and remaining 1½ tablespoons butter to make a beurre manié. Add small portions of beurre manié to the champagne cream stock, stirring constantly until thickened. Strain. Fold sauce, hollandaise, and whipping cream together.

Wash mushroom buttons in water and juice from ½ the lemon. Cut each button into thin lengthwise slices. Simmer in water and juice of remaining ½ lemon about 3 minutes or until tender. Drain.

Place fillets on ovenproof platter. Sprinkle with mushrooms and shrimp. Pour champagne sauce over fillets. Broil 4 inches from full flame for 2–3 minutes or until browned. Garnish with sprigs of fresh parsley.

I don't know why this vegetable isn't more popular. It certainly has food value and the taste is delicious. The steaming, and covering with paper, make it Piscean.

Braised Lettuce
(serves 8)

2 heads lettuce	2 cups (approximately) hot
Kitchen string	beef stock
Salt and pepper to taste	Buttered brown or
Juice of 2 lemons	parchment paper

continued

Cut the lettuce heads in quarters and tie with string so they will hold their shape. Arrange them on the bottom of a large pan and sprinkle with salt and pepper and the lemon juice. Add stock to cover. Cover the kettle with buttered paper and place the lid. Bake in 350° oven for 45 minutes.

For a starch we turn to a version of mashed potatoes that are nicely seasoned and will lend a new variety to your recipe collection.

Casserole Potatoes
(serves 8)

4 cups mashed potatoes	Salt and pepper to taste
2 cups cottage cheese	Melted butter
½ cup sour cream	½ cup toasted, chopped
2 tablespoons grated onion	walnuts *or* almonds

In a buttered 2-quart casserole, combine potatoes, cheese, sour cream, onion, and salt and pepper. Brush top well with melted butter. Bake in a 350° oven for 30 minutes. Put under broiler for a few minutes to brown. Sprinkle with nuts.

If you top the dessert with a large dab of whipped cream, your guests will love you. It's a good, old-fashioned American dish.

Brown Betty

1 cup dry bread or graham cracker crumbs

¼ cup melted butter

2½ cups peeled, diced, or sliced: apples, peaches, cherries or cranberries

¾ cup packed brown sugar

1 teaspoon cinnamon

¼ teaspoon nutmeg

¼ teaspoon cloves

½ teaspoon salt

1 teaspoon grated lemon rind

1 teaspoon vanilla

3 tablespoons lemon juice

4 tablespoons water

½ cup raisins

Combine crumbs and melted butter. Line the bottom of a baking dish with ⅓ of crumb mixture. Sift brown sugar, cinnamon, nutmeg, cloves, and salt. Add lemon rind and vanilla. Place ½ of apples in the dish. Cover the layer with ½ of sugar mixture. Sprinkle with 1 tablespoon lemon juice. Add 2 tablespoons water. Cover the apples with ⅓ of crumb mixture and ¼ cup of raisins. Add the remaining apples and sprinkle them as before with the remaining sugar mixture and 2 tablespoons lemon juice, 2 tablespoons water, and the remaining ¼ cup raisins. Place the last ⅓ of crumb mixture on top. Cover the dish and bake for about 40 minutes, in a 350° oven, until the apples are nearly tender. Remove cover, increase heat to 400°, and permit pudding to brown for about 15 minutes. Serve hot.

MENU THREE

Lobster Bisque Neptune

Olived Chicken

Stuffed Mushrooms

Cheese Puffs

Starlit Pineapple Dip

As Omarr has suggested, Pisceans love the theater. A Pisces wants to be on time so he will not disturb his seat neighbors when he arrives and he loves to prepare for after-theater dining ahead of time. This is a lovely after-theater menu, but it will do nicely as a regular dinner.

The combination of the lobster and wine makes this a great soup for a late evening supper. It can be prepared in minutes. It can be made ahead, but then add the sherry after you reheat it.

Lobster Bisque Neptune
(serves 6-8)

2 cans cream of mushroom soup
1 pint half-and-half
  Milk
¼ pound Roquefort cheese, crumbled

1 cup (7½-ounce can) lobster in bite-size pieces
1½ ounces sherry
  Parsley

Empty soup into top of double boiler. Measure half-and-half into empty soup cans, filling remainder of second can with milk. Blend well, and add crumbled cheese. Heat in double boiler until cheese melts. Add the lobster and sherry, and let the lobster heat through. Garnish with chopped parsley.

Pisces has an affinity with olives, Omarr says. Here is still another recipe, unusual and most tasty, that features the olive. It can be prepared ahead of time and then popped in the oven to finish when you want it.

Olived Chicken
(serves 6–8)

2 chickens (fryers), cut up	1 cup sliced stuffed green olives
¼ cup butter	1 cup dry white wine
1 (20-ounce) can solid-pack tomatoes	1 tablespoon Ac'cent
	1 cup cream, warmed
1 onion, minced	Salt to taste
2 tablespoons bell pepper, minced	Chopped parsley
	Chopped chives
½ pound sliced mushrooms	

Sauté the chicken in butter until golden. Add the remaining ingredients with the cream being last, and simmer 30 minutes. (If you want to hold in refrigerator until later, do so at this point.) Bake in 350° oven, uncovered, for 30 minutes.

Here's a light vegetable to accompany the chicken.

Stuffed Mushrooms
(serves 8)

16 large mushrooms	2 tablespoons parsley
4 slices bacon	1 cup soft bread crumbs
1 finely chopped onion	1 teaspoon seasoned salt
2 tablespoons chopped green pepper	

Remove stems from mushrooms and chop them fine. Cook the bacon until crisp. Pour off all but about 2 tablespoons of the fat. Cook the mushroom stems, onion, green pepper, and parsley until transparent and tender. Add the bread crumbs, seasoning, and enough water (if you have chicken stock use it) to moisten. Stuff the mushroom caps with the mixture. Place in a well-buttered shallow casserole and bake in a 350° oven about 20 minutes. (These too can be prepared ahead of time and popped in the oven when ready.)

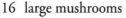

A light and thin starch will provide Pisces with one of those paper-thin dishes he likes so well.

Cheese Puffs
(serves 8)

8 large *puffs* (see page 306)	½ cup tomato sauce
½ pound grated sharp Cheddar cheese	3 chopped green onions
2 eggs	1 clove garlic, minced
3 green roasted chilies, chopped	¼ cup butter, at room temperature
½ cup sliced, stuffed green olives	Salt to taste

Remove tops from puffs. Combine remaining ingredients and fill the puffs. Replace the top. Bake in a 350° oven for 30 minutes. Again, fix them ahead and take to the oven as needed.

We've become a "dipping" nation. Every party we attend will feature one, or more, so-called dips, often of cheese or sour cream and onion soup mix. The method makes a wonderful prepare-ahead dessert. I would wrap the pineapple in plastic wrap to refrigerate.

Starlit Pineapple Dip

1 large fresh pineapple	¼ cup milk
¼ cup powdered sugar	1 package candy red hots
1 package cream cheese	1 ounce white crème de menthe
2 ounces cottage cheese	

Quarter pineapple and remove core. Cut and scoop out inside and slice. Put fruit back in shell and sprinkle with powdered sugar. Chill. Mix cheeses and milk; whip to creamy paste. Put 2 tablespoons red hots in like amount of water and heat until hots are blanched white. Drain and discard candy. Pour candy juice and crème de menthe into paste and mix. Chill well. Serve pineapple with sauce to dip it in.

And so, Pisces, go to the theater, secure in the knowledge that a lovely supper awaits you and your guests a half-hour after your return home.

Substitutions and Measurements

APPENDIX

Substitutions

1 square chocolate	=	2½ tablespoons cocoa and ½ tablespoon shortening
1 cup pastry flour	=	1 cup bread flour less 2 tablespoons
1 teaspoon baking powder	=	¼ teaspoon baking soda and ½ teaspoon cream of tartar
1 cup milk	=	½ cup evaporated milk and ½ cup water or ½ cup condensed milk and ½ cup water (reduce sugar in recipe)

1 cup sour milk	=	1 cup milk and 1 tablespoon lemon juice or vinegar
1 cup butter or margarine	=	⅞ cup salad or vegetable oil (recipe may need added salt)
1 cup sugar	=	¼ cup corn syrup
	=	1 cup maple syrup (reduce liquid in recipe ¼ cup)
	=	1 cup honey (reduce liquid in recipe ¼ cup)
	=	1 cup molasses (add ¼ to ½ teaspoon baking soda)
1 tablespoon fresh herb	=	1 teaspoon dried herb
1 whole egg	=	2 egg yolks plus 1 tablespoon water
1 teaspoon corn starch	=	2 tablespoons water
Lemon juice	=	vinegar
Wine	=	apple juice, cider, beef or chicken broth
Ac'cent seasoning	=	any seasoning salt

Common Measurements

	Pinch or dash	=	less than ⅛ teaspoon
3	teaspoons	=	1 tablespoon
5⅓	tablespoons	=	⅓ cup
16	tablespoons	=	1 cup
2	cups	=	1 pint
4	cups	=	1 quart

4	quarts	=	1 gallon
1	liquid ounce	=	2 tablespoons
8	liquid ounces	=	1 cup
8	quarts	=	1 peck
4	pecks	=	1 bushel

Butter:

½	pound	=	1 cup
¼	pound	=	½ cup or 8 tablespoons
1	stick	=	½ cup
½	stick	=	¼ cup
1	ounce	=	2 tablespoons

Flour:

1	pound	=	3½ cups
1	ounce	=	4 tablespoons

Sugar:

white

1	cup	=	7 ounces
1	pound	=	2¼ cups

brown—firmly packed

1	cup	=	7 ounces
1	pound	=	2¼ cups

confectioners'/powdered

1	cup	=	4 ounces

Meat (chopped):

½	pound	=	1 cup (solidly packed)

Eggs (large):

½	whole egg	=	2 tablespoons
5	whole eggs	=	1 cup
8–9	whites	=	1 cup
12	yolks	=	1 cup
9	eggs	=	1 pound

Milk:

evaporated	1 can	=	1⅔ cup
dry	1 cup	=	2⅓ ounces
skim	1 quart	=	¾ to 1 cup plus 4 cups of water

Miscellaneous:

Macaroni:	1 cup (4 ounces)	=	2¼ cups cooked
Noodles:	1 cup (2⅔ ounces)	=	1½ cups cooked
Oats (rolled):	1 cup	=	3 ounces
Rice:	1 cup (7 ounces)	=	4 cups cooked
Spaghetti:	1 cup (3⅓ ounces)	=	2⅛ cups cooked
Green pepper:	1 cup	=	1 large, chopped
Tomato:	1 cup	=	1 large, diced

Approximate Can Sizes

Can Size	Weight	Contents
6 ounces	6 ounces	¾ cup
8 ounces	8 ounces	1 cup
No. 1	11 ounces	1⅓ cups
12 ounces	12 ounces	1½ cups
No. 303	16 ounces	2 cups
No. 2	20 ounces	2½ cups
2½	28 ounces	3½ cups
No. 3	33 ounces	4 cups
No. 10	106 ounces	13 cups

Oven Temperatures

Very slow	275° F	135° C
Slow	300° F	150° C
Moderately slow	325° F	165° C
Moderate	350° F	175° C
Moderately hot	375° F	190° C
Hot	400° F	200° C
Very hot	450–500° F	230–260° C
Broiling	500° F (or over)	260° C

Deep-Fat Frying Temperatures

Fritters, doughnuts, and uncooked mixtures	370°F	190° C
Croquettes, meatballs, or cooked mixtures	390° F	200° C
French-fried potatoes		
First frying	370° F	190° C
Second frying	390° F	200° C
Breaded chops	360–385° F	180–195° C
Fillets of fish	370° F	190° C
Small fish cooked whole	370° F	190° C

Cooking Meats with Meat Thermometer

To use a meat thermometer, make an incision in the center of the meat through the fat side and insert thermometer to center. Do not allow thermometer to rest on bone.

Rare beef roast	140° F	60° C
Medium beef roast	160° F	70° C
Well-done beef roast	180° F	80° C
Medium or slightly rare lamb	170° F	75° C
Well-done lamb or mutton	180° F	80° C
Well-done veal	165° F	73° C
Well-done pork	185° F	85° C

Cooking Meats Without Meat Thermometer

Cuts of meat	Temperature		Minutes per Pound	
Best cuts of beef				
with bone	300° F	150° C	rare	18–20
(as standing rib roast)			medium	22–25
			well-done	35–40
Tender beef roast				
without bone	300° F	150° C	rare	23–25
(as sirloin tip, rump roast, etc.)			medium	27—30
			well-done	40–45
Less tender cuts				
(chuck, etc.)	300–350° F	150–180° C		45
Lamb, pork, veal	300–325° F	150–160° C		30
Ham	300–325° F	150–160° C		30
Chicken	300–350° F	150–180° C		30
Turkey	300–350° F	150–180° C		18–25
Braised meats	325–350° F.	160–180° C.		18–25

(browned first, then liquid added—use for very tough meats)

Metric Equivalents

1	ounce	=	28.35 grams
1	pound	=	453.59 grams
1	gram	=	.035 ounces
1	kilogram	=	2.2 pounds

1	teaspoon	=	4.9 milliliters
1	tablespoon	=	14.8 milliliters
1	cup	=	236.6 milliliters
1	pint	=	473.2 milliliters
1	quart	=	.95 liter
1	gallon	=	3.8 liters

INDEX

REACH FOR THE MOON

Llewellyn publishes hundreds of books on your favorite subjects! To get these exciting books, including the ones on the following pages, check your local bookstore or order them directly from Llewellyn.

ORDER BY PHONE

- Call toll-free within the U.S. and Canada, 1-800-THE MOON
- In Minnesota, call (612) 291-1970
- We accept VISA, MasterCard, and American Express

ORDER BY MAIL

- Send the full price of your order (MN residents add 7% sales tax) in U.S. funds, plus postage & handling to:

  Llewellyn Worldwide
  P.O. Box 64383, Dept. K506-1
  St. Paul, MN 55164–0383, U.S.A.

POSTAGE & HANDLING

(For the U.S., Canada, and Mexico)

- $4.00 for orders $15.00 and under
- $5.00 for orders over $15.00
- No charge for orders over $100.00

We ship UPS in the continental United States. We ship standard mail to P.O. boxes. Orders shipped to Alaska, Hawaii, The Virgin Islands, and Puerto Rico are sent first-class mail. Orders shipped to Canada and Mexico are sent surface mail.

International orders: Airmail—add freight equal to price of each book to the total price of order, plus $5.00 for each non-book item (audio tapes, etc.).

Surface mail—Add $1.00 per item.

Allow 2 weeks for delivery on all orders.
Postage and handling rates subject to change.

DISCOUNTS

We offer a 20% discount to group leaders or agents. You must order a minimum of 5 copies of the same book to get our special quantity price.

FREE CATALOG

Get a free copy of our color catalog, *New Worlds of Mind and Spirit.* Subscribe for just $10.00 in the United States and Canada ($30.00 overseas, airmail). Many bookstores carry *New Worlds*—ask for it!

Visit our web site at www.llewellyn.com for more information.

Sydney Omarr's Astrological Guide to Love and Romance

Sydney Omarr

How does Aries' great passion for discovery affect his sex life? Why must Pisces be wary of Virgo in matters of the heart? What makes the cerebral side of sex so important to Taurus? Can Gemini successfully manage love relationships with more than one person at a time? What draws Cancer into secret love affairs? Can Scorpio direct and control his very strong sex drive?

The answers to these questions and many others are revealed by Sydney Omarr in this re-release of his classic guide to love and romance. Men and women complain equally that artistry and technique is too often lacking in lovemaking. While this book may not make you a great lover, it will help you to become more aware, sensitive, creative, dynamic—and will lead you to develop the kind of lovemaking technique that will cause you to be sought after by those who appreciate "an artist at work."

ISBN: 1-56718-505-3, 5³/₁₆ x 8, 368 pp.   **$12.95**

Your Pet's Horoscope

Diana Nilsen

If you're a bold Sagittarian who enjoys hiking in the Sierras, you may be frustrated with a Cancer dog who just wants to cuddle up at home. On the other hand, you would find an Aries to be an adventurous companion. The sign of the zodiac under which your pet was born explains why he behaves the way he does, and helps you learn how to best deal with his personality. It also explains the relationship dynamics between the two of you.

Now you can learn about your pet's idiosyncrasies, along with specific health-related issues; physical, psychological and emotional tendencies; and possible pitfalls. Whether you already feel an incomprehensible bond between the two of you—or you curse the day you brought him home—understanding of what makes your pet tick will help you see him in a better light. Don't know your pet's birthdate? It's easy to figure out your pet's sign with the handy questionnaires provided. Don't have a pet? This book can guide you to finding your animal soul mate.

ISBN: 1-56718-488-X, 5 x 6, 192 pp., 100 illus., softbound   **$7.95**

Llewellyn's Personal Service Reports

Simple Natal Chart
If you want a detailed birth chart and prefer to do your own interpretations, this is the service for you. It is loaded with information, including a chart wheel, aspects, midpoints, major asteroids, and a glossary of symbols, plus a free booklet! (Tropical zodiac/Placidus houses, unless specified.)

❑ **Simple Natal Chart APS03-119** **$5.00**

Personality Profile Horoscope
Jargon-free and loaded with insight, this is our most popular reading! Based on the interpretation of your birth chart, this ten-part reading offers a complete look at how the planets help shape who you are and what you do. Learn about your inner self and your outer image. Discover your career strengths and emotional needs. Very reasonable price, too!

❑ **Personality Profile Horoscope APS03-503** **$20.00**

Personal Relationship Reading
Have your love relationships been . . . less than fulfilling? Want to know what kind of person is right for you? Then this report is the one for you! The Personal Relationship Reading reveals your real needs in a relationship, what kind of people to look for, and what kind of people to avoid in your search for the perfect mate.

❑ **Personal Relationship Reading APS03-506** **$20.00**

Compatibility Profile
Find out if you are really compatible with your lover, spouse, friend, or business partner! This is a great way of getting an in-depth look at your relationship with another person. Find out each person's approach to the relationship. Do you have the same goals and values? How well do you deal with arguments? This service includes planetary placements for both people, so send birth data for both and specify the type of relationship (i.e., friends, lovers, etc.). Order today!

❑ **Compatibility Profile APS03-504** **$30.00**

How To Order:
1. Indicated name and number of service report desired.
2. Your full name, address, and daytime phone number.
3. Your **exact** birthdate, birth time, and birth place (including city, county, state, and country). *Use birth certificate for the most accurate information.*
4. Make check or money order payable to Llewellyn Worldwide, or send credit card type (MC, Visa, etc.) and number, plus expiration date and your signature.
5. Mail to: Llewellyn Personal Services, P.O. Box 64383, Dept. K506-1, St. Paul, MN 55164-0383 Or fax to: 651-291-1908.

Allow 4-6 weeks for delivery • No phone orders please • All reports are computer-generated